The Virtual Banking Revolution

The Customer, the Bank and the Future

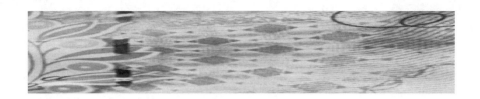

The Virtual Banking Revolution

The Customer, the Bank and the Future

James Essinger

INTERNATIONAL THOMSON BUSINESS PRESS
I(T)P® **An International Thomson Publishing Company**

London • Bonn • Johannesburg • Madrid • Melbourne • Mexico City • New York • Paris
Singapore • Tokyo • Toronto • Albany, NY • Belmont, CA • Cincinnati, OH • Detroit, MI

This book is dedicated, in respect and admiration, to Rob Farbrother, one of the leading, and most creatively minded, revolutionaries.

The Virtual Banking Revolution

Copyright © 1999 International Thomson Business Press

First published by International Thomson Business Press

 A division of International Thomson Publishing Inc.
The ITP logo is a trademark under licence

British Library Cataloguing-in-Publication Data
A catalogue record for this book is available from the British Library

First edition 1999

Typeset by LaserScript Limited, Mitcham, Surrey
Printed in the UK by TJ International, Padstow, Cornwall

ISBN 1–86152–343–2

International Thomson Business Press
Berkshire House
168–173 High Holborn
London WC1V 7AA
UK

http://www.itbp.com

Contents

Figures

Tables

Preface

This book examines what must be regarded as the most important single trend in the banking industry today: the momentum for banks to seek to deliver routine and commoditized services via mechanisms that incorporate communications technology, with this trend being at the expense of encouraging customers to visit physical branches.

What is true of the banking sector is also true of the retail financial services sector generally: delivery mechanisms are becoming increasingly non-physical. Indeed, it is already the case that for many people the location of their own bank branch is irrelevant to them, or close to being so. All that matters is that they have access to cash when they need it and to other payment facilities.

The result is that, today, there is an increasing tendency for people to receive banking services in a comparable fashion to how they receive utilities such as water, gas or electricity. For most of us the precise physical location of our water, gas or electricity supplier is irrelevant to the benefits we receive from these utilities. Very likely we don't know where the utility company is located, and even if we did, it wouldn't matter to us.

This development carries enormous repercussions for all types of retail financial institutions and for consumers in all walks of life. It could be argued that the development is very much more than simply an interesting phenomenon in the financial services sector; that it affects us in many aspects of our lives. It is certainly perfectly just to call it a revolution, as it is effecting a huge transformation in our ability to gain access to cash and payment facilities.

Many people are still unaware just how wide-ranging the revolution is. On a recent visit to Santa Barbara in California, I was able to withdraw funds via an automated teller machine (ATM) from my Midland Bank account in the United Kingdom even though I was more than 6,000 miles away from my home town of Canterbury, where my branch is located. Knowing that I would be able to withdraw funds abroad when on holiday meant that I had purchased fewer traveller's cheques prior to my departure than I would otherwise have done, and also that I did not have to incur the risk of carrying dollars around before setting off for any shopping expedition. It was, in fact, exactly as if I were withdrawing funds via an automated teller machine in Canterbury: the only difference was that the currencies were not the same.

Yet the enormously useful facility of international ATM withdrawal is only one aspect of the revolution. Most of us are already able to gain access to information about our bank accounts via the telephone, whether we access this from home or (strictly speaking illegally) from work. We can also use the telephone to transfer funds between accounts and to effect payments to third parties. In addition, we can purchase goods from most retail outlets simply by presenting one of a variety of plastic cards, including ones which connect the check-out directly to our bank account.

Some of us living in the United States or France are able to make use of special bank cards containing a tiny microchip which allows us to carry details of many of our bank accounts around with us in one card and to use a special key-ring for reading our respective balances in those accounts.

Some of us are able to use these special bank cards to pay for goods by pre-loading the cards with invisible cash and spending it at shops which have compatible terminals. Increasingly, some of us are even able to incorporate details of air tickets onto these special cards and to present them at the airport for instant check-in. The days when bank cards are used only to gain access to banking services are already numbered, and within ten years or so the notion that a bank card can only access banking services will probably seem as outdated as the idea that in order to obtain cash from your bank you have to visit your branch and cash a cheque.

The point is that the revolution is a revolution in the widest of senses. It makes our lives easier, it gives us more control and knowledge about our bank account, it provides us with remote cash access facilities wherever in the world we might be, it reduces security risks stemming from a need to carry cash, it allows us the opportunity to benefit from new technologies that integrate banking services with other important services. Generally, it removes the problems which, until the past few decades or so, people have always had in obtaining access to cash when, and where, they need it. By solving this problem, it increases the mobility of labour and makes leisure opportunities more accessible, thereby giving us opportunities to live richer and fuller lives than has been the case in the past.

This revolution is the virtual banking revolution.

'Virtual banking' may seem like a gratuitously jargonistic terms, but it is a logical use of a word which precisely defines the matter under discussion here.

The *Shorter Oxford English Dictionary* lists as one of the definitions of the word 'virtual' the following:

That [which] is so in essence or effect although not formally or actually; admitting of being called by the name so far as the effect or result is concerned.

This is not a new definition; it dates from 1654. A familiar use of the word virtual in this context is to describe the image which we see in a mirror. This is known as a virtual image. It is an image in every sense, except that we can't enter a virtual image and we can't manipulate things we see in it.

Another, more recent, use of the word virtual in this context is the increasingly familiar notion of 'virtual reality'. This is a reality which we can certainly enter in a visual sense and, to some extent, in a tactile sense. In a virtual reality system, however, what we see and what we feel is by no means real. Virtual reality describes the effect produced by a type of computer system which allows the user to experience an approximation of a 'real' sensory experience, with the elements of sense-data that produced the overall effect of reality simulation being organized by a computer program.

Virtual reality is impossible without computers, because an immensely powerful device is required to control the experience and the only technology we currently have available to handle this is computer technology.

Virtual banking is also impossible without computers because the delivery processes and methods require extensive local memory and processing power, which interface with remote communications devices.

Generally, a useful definition of virtual banking is:

Any banking service delivered to the customer by means of a computer-controlled system that does not directly involve the inside of the bank's bricks-and-mortar branch.

The purpose of this book is to assist professionals in the banking or retail financial services industry to make the most of their financial institution's potential by exploiting to the full opportunities to deploy virtual banking services. The purpose of this deployment is to win more customers and to develop the institution's strategic progress around the continued delivery of virtual services.

The purpose of the book is therefore fundamentally practical. I have written it not merely to tell the story of the virtual banking revolution – although this is certainly one of my overall objectives – but also to assist readers with identifying trends they can apply within their own institution and thereby help their institution to obtain higher levels of revenue and greater profits. I pay particular attention to likely future developments in virtual banking, because any banker who wishes to make the most of the revolution has got to have an intelligent awareness of how the revolution is going to be developing in times to come.

I have been writing about electronic banking services since 1986, when I had the good fortune to work for a public relations consultancy which was acting for one of Britain's first shared ATM networks. At first, I had little idea what a shared automated teller machine actually was, and even less idea that my work on this account would be a springboard for an interest which has persisted for more than a decade and which has itself been a springboard to a wider range of interests connected with the relationship between people and technology. This wider interest has resulted in many other books, including the popular science book *The Cogwheel Brain*, which I am currently co-authoring with Doron Swade and which tells the fascinating story of Charles Babbage's attempts to build a digital computer out of cogwheels during the nineteenth century.

I mention this because the story of *The Cogwheel Brain* seems to me to lie at the start of a process which, at least for the time being, has culminated in the virtual banking revolution. Charles Babbage always foresaw that his ingenious cogwheel machines should be brought into being for very practical reasons: in the case of the first machine – the Difference Engine – to calculate mathematical tables which were frequently erroneous when calculated manually; in the case of his much more sophisticated and truly computer-like machine – the Analytical Engine – to carry out a much wider range of mathematical and algebraic calculations, all of which were designed to make life easier for his Victorian contemporaries. Sadly, a lack of funding, his difficulties with manufacturing a sufficient number of precision parts in the requisite short time-frames, and – to some extent – his own failings in understanding the political climate of his day, conspired to prevent him from completing his work successfully. He never, however, saw his engines as ends in themselves but rather as tools to gain a control over quantity which would otherwise not be available. His machines were never completed in his lifetime (although his life's work was vindicated in 1991 when Doron Swade and his team at London's Science Museum successfully completed a fully operational version of one of Babbage's Difference Engines) and so the nineteenth century had no information technology revolution. Nineteenth-century banks continued to be stuffy, pompous and arrogant organizations which expected customers to feel privileged that the bank was prepared to deal with them at all. If the reader concludes from this that I believe technology to have played an essential role not only in transforming banks into the highly competitive, customer-friendly entities they are today but also, generally, in creating the relatively egalitarian, sane and pleasant societies those of us in the developed world are fortunate enough to live in, he or she would be right.

Had Babbage completed his engines by the middle of the nineteenth century, we might have had a virtual banking revolution by the 1890s, and an austere and black-coated Harrods customer, shopping for turbot and kidneys in the last decade of the nineteenth century, may have paid for his goods by presenting a small pasteboard card featuring holes punched in a pattern unique to his own card. As things turned out, this didn't happen, and it was to be another hundred years before the virtual banking revolution got underway in earnest.

But now it is underway, and it is having a huge impact.

Acknowledgements

I would like to thank all of the following, who greatly assisted me with the preparation of this book:

Roger Alexander (Barclays Bank), Rob Baldock (Andersen Consulting), Terry Bourne (Total Systems), Peter Brackstone (Switch Card Services), Richard Chadwick (Sainsburys Bank), Tony Collins (Customer Contact Centre), Richard Duvall (Prudential Banking), Rob Farbrother (PayPoint), Molly Faust (Amex), Paul Feldman (Nationwide Building Society), Kevin Flanagan (Bristol & West), Allen Gilstrap (Amex), Julian Goldsmith (Sector Public Relations), Anne Goodwyn (AIT), Rowan Gormley (Virgin Direct), John Hardy (LINK), Richard Hicks (AIT), Louis Hill (Visa Cash), Sam Hinton (Fiserv), Suzanne Holcombe (PSI Global), Isabelle Hubert (Carrefour), Catherine Kirk (Connect), Mike Meltzer (NCR), Kevin Russell (Prudential Banking), Bernard Simpson (Nationwide Building Society), Philip Springuel (Organisation and Technology Research), Richard Tyson-Davies (APACS), Glenn Weiner (Amex), Geraldine Welham (Switch Card Services), Tony Wood (Virgin Direct).

My sincere thanks also to Kay Larkin, my commissioning editor, and to my colleague Helen Wylie.

The virtual banking revolution: the customer angle and your own agenda

Introduction

The purpose of this book being not merely to examine the virtual banking revolution as an interesting phenomenon, but also to provide specific pointers to how you can take advantage of the revolution in order to maximize your own financial institution's success in the future, it makes sense to start our analysis by focusing on your own commercial objectives.

During more than a decade of writing business books, I have moved from producing works which adopt a relatively magisterial, even dispassionate, attitude towards the material under discussion to those which make the readers' needs paramount from the beginning. This progression is in many respects a response to how the market for business books has developed. Back in the 1980s, the appetite for books which chronicled the often alarmingly rapid process of change within the business world – and especially within the banking and finance arenas which have always been my own areas of specialization – was so great that the urgent need was to set down what was happening, rather than be explicit about how the reader could benefit from this material. It was not so much that writers deliberately set out to leave the reader to sink or swim, but rather that they saw as their top priority the requirement to ensure that their readers had access to the requisite volume of material without delay.

Besides, it was probably still too early to make any definitive statement about the impact of the changes which were coming to the banking and finance arenas. It was rather like playing a tough game of poker, you don't count your winnings until the game is over. Technology was causing so many modifications to the way the banking and finance arenas were developing that it was too soon to make any grand conclusions.

But that was then, and this is now. Today, intense competition among publishers of business books, coupled with the recognition that readers are nowadays generally much more knowledgeable and also want real value for money from their expenditure on business publications, means that it is essential to consider the readers' precise needs when writing a book such as this.

That said, in my view many business books go too far in this direction, and devote so much space to interactive material that the book becomes more like a teaching aid rather than a provocative and stimulating account of the subject under discussion. Which is not to say that relating the material under discussion to the readers' needs is anything other than extremely important.

The increase in knowledge among readers deserves particular mention. This increase in knowledge is especially true as far as technological matters are concerned: anyone writing a book such as this must first of all assume that the reader has a very considerable knowledge of fundamental technological points, whereas at the start of the 1990s these issues would have needed to be laboriously defined and spelt out by the writer.

It is surely in both our interests for me to assume that you have a knowledge of the fundamental principles of banking technology, including the nature of the hardware used within the banking industry and, in broad terms, a knowledge of what software does when running on this hardware. Other, more complex, technological issues will be explained when they arise.

I shall also assume that you are involved in the retail end of the financial services or banking world rather than the wholesale end. In fact, the virtual banking revolution is not solely a development in the retail banking sector; clearly, wholesale banking is also affected by the move towards virtual delivery methods and by the increasing use of remotely delivered services. However, by far the most important impact of these new developments is in the retail banking arena, and it would be misleading to suggest otherwise.

I won't necessarily assume that you are currently working for a retail financial institution, but will certainly presume that you have some vested interest in helping such an institution to maximize its success. We live in an epoch where the advisory professions enjoy a burgeoning importance, and many lawyers, consultants and other advisers, while not engaged full-time with a particular financial institution, make most or all their living from the financial sector. Alternatively, your interest may be technological: you may be involved with hardware, or software for a computer systems organization which seeks to develop its business with retail financial institutions.

And of course you will also be a consumer of retail banking services yourself. This book is not written for consumers; it is intended for professionals who are ultimately involved in the *supply* of financial services to the public. However, we are all consumers of these services as well as banking industry professionals, and our status as consumers often helps with an understanding of what aspects of the retail banking revolution are likely to be helpful to our own institution.

Why? Because no virtual banking initiative can hope to be successful unless it appeals to consumers in the first place. Fortunately, we do not need to resort to abstract analyses if we are to assess the likely appeal of a virtual banking initiative to consumers: we can, to a large extent, simply consider how much it is likely to appeal to *us*.

Above all, I shall assume that one of your fundamental purposes in reading this book is to improve your understanding of what is happening in virtual banking and make use of that improved understanding in your own professional life. Inevitably, maximizing the book's usefulness to you in this respect demands from me a relatively polemical approach to the material under consideration, because it is my job to point out not only *what* is important but also *why* it is important. Furthermore, no one can possibly expect to write an interesting business book unless he or she is profoundly interested in the subject-matter and energized by it. As well as this, I intend to be reasonably polemical because, at least as far as this book is concerned, I am your guide to the virtual banking revolution and I would be failing you if I did not acknowledge that your time available for reading books such as this is limited and you expect a good return on your time.

From here on in this book I use the word 'bank' as a convenient way to denote *any* retail financial institution involved with providing banking services to the general public and to businesses. This means that institutions such as building societies, savings houses, thrift institutions and similar organizations are included under this convenient definition. Note that consequently the word 'bank' does not necessarily mean 'bank' according to the narrow legal definition stipulated in many national jurisdictions. Incidentally, much of the material in this book will also apply to institutions which sell more specialized types of retail financial services, such as insurance and investment products.

Finally, even though women are of course as abundant in the banking industry as men and just as likely to be customers of banks, there is no avoiding the fact that 'he or she', and its various related forms, are extremely tiresome to read. I therefore only use the male pronoun, but solely for ease of writing and reading.

Virtual banking and a bank's overall commercial objectives

Whatever the nature of your own relationship to the retail financial services industry, it is reasonable that you have a professional desire to increase the likelihood that all of the following happen in the future at any bank with which you are involved:

- increase customer bases for all profit centres;

- increase overall breadth and quality of services;

- decrease the proportion of routine transactions carried out in the branch;

- increase proportion of profitable sales transactions (e.g. sales of loans, mortgages, insurance, investments and pensions);

- improve general customer satisfaction;

- increase speed of response to customer requirements;

- reduce overall risk of the institution incurring financial loss;

- increase penetration of under-18 customer market;

- increase quality of the institution's marketing initiatives;

- increase retention rates of staff and perceived staff morale;

- reduce overall operational costs of the institution;

- increase overall revenues in line with the requirements of the institution's business plan.

The importance of the virtual banking revolution is revealed by the simple observation that *all* these crucial objectives can be furthered by a bank moving to a more virtual type of operation.

Later in this chapter I return to these specific points, and discuss how exactly the virtual banking revolution increases the likelihood of the institution being able to meet each of the objectives. However, in order to ensure that my conclusions seem logical and justified, it is first necessary to step back and look at banking from the customer's point of view. Doing this will no doubt be a regular part of your agenda as a professional with an interest in banking; all I am doing here is seeking to formalize that activity.

Banking and the customer

People only use banks because they need to, not because they really want to: banks are a necessary evil. Unless the customer is a pathological miser, he doesn't want what the bank can provide (i.e. money and access to payment facilities) but rather what the money can bring. Only the fact that we live in advanced societies which have evolved money as a common standard for barter makes banks, or their money, of any interest to us at all. On a desert island, with our ship stranded offshore and sinking, only the very foolish would prefer to swim out and return with gold bars rather than salted pork.

This point, that banks only supply what is a means to an end, rather than the end in itself, is a fundamental problem facing the banking industry.

It is useful for us to talk about the problem in terms of the notions of primary and secondary degrees of usefulness. Employing this terminology, we can see – for example – that a car dealership clearly offers the *primary* degree of usefulness because the things it has to sell are examples of things that people can use directly.

On the other hand, a bank which offers loans to buy cars is only providing a *secondary* degree of usefulness.

It is interesting to note that many banks are currently making strenuous efforts to deal with this problem by offering products which provide a primary degree of usefulness rather than only a secondary degree. For example, in the United Kingdom, Barclays Bank has purchased a car dealership and some of its branches now sell car loans. Another way in which banks are trying to be seen as offering a primary degree of usefulness rather than just a secondary degree is in their creation of direct links with estate agencies rather than the simple offer of a mortgage, as is the case with Lloyds Bank and the Black Horse estate agencies. Furthermore, banks around the world use window displays in their branches which show specific tangible things – or symbols of things (e.g. models of houses and shiny new motorcycles) – which the customer will want rather than just the money which facilitates the purchase of these things.

For a bank, there is no obvious solution to the problem that by its nature it will be restricted to offering secondary degrees of satisfaction. Entering into joint ventures with organizations that offer primary degrees of usefulness certainly helps, but the bank can hardly overcome the basic problem that customers don't really want what the bank can provide but rather the things that can be *bought* with what the bank can provide.

The impossibility of avoiding this problem places banks under a particularly heavy obligation to understand how their customers think and what their customers want. Certainly, no examination of the virtual banking revolution can get underway until these issues of customer motivation and customer desire have been addressed.

Still, there is one positive aspect to the problem. The very fact of banks only being able to provide a secondary degree of usefulness means that customers tend to want their interaction with the bank to be as brief as possible, so that they can get their hands on the money or payment facility and go off and start buying the things they really want.

Consequently, there is usually something straightforward and relatively simple about customer motivation and customer behaviour as far as their bank is concerned. It is therefore possible to generalize about this behaviour and motivation and feel that the generalizations are founded on safe ground.

We might very pertinently start by asking why customers use banks at all. I would propose six reasons for this. A listing of these six motivations, in what might reasonably be proposed as a descending order of importance, follows below.

Reasons why people use a bank's services

1   *To keep their funds safe and secure.* There can be little doubt that this is the most fundamental and important reason of all. Cash kept at home will always represent a serious security hazard, and the greater the amount of cash kept there, the greater the hazard.

2   *To obtain interest payments and other return on investment.* In many respects this reason goes hand-in-hand with the first one: people rightly regard interest payments and other returns as the reward for putting their money in a safe place.

3   *To obtain convenient access to cash.* Once the customers' funds are in safe hands and interest is being earned on them, the next most important reason for using a bank's services is to give the customers access to cash.

The need to provide such access has always been a big headache for banks. In the past, the majority of counter transactions undertaken at a bank branch involved the cashing of a cheque or some other kind of cash withdrawal (i.e. involving a passbook). Undoubtedly the prime benefit of the virtual banking revolution to banks is that it provides them with a robust and customer-friendly alternative to having to deploy extensive branch resources to encashments.

4   *To obtain convenient access to payment facilities.* After the need to obtain access to cash, obtaining access to payment facilities is clearly the customer's next big priority. The virtual banking revolution provides customers with a remarkable range of such payment facilities, mainly based around the plastic bank card.

5   *To obtain access to loan facilities.* Most customers – even very wealthy ones – need access at some point in their lives to facilities to borrow money, especially in order to buy expensive items such as a car and a house, apartment, or other type of property.

A specialized type of loan is the overdraft, which allows a customer to withdraw funds from his account or make payments from it even if there are no funds in the account. Overdraft limits will typically be marked in advance and the customer is expected to adhere to them. For example, if a cheque is drawn which exceeds the level of the overdraft, the bank may not pay it. The principal difference between loans and overdrafts is that the loan is regarded as drawn as soon as it is made, with interest being levied on the whole amount of the loan, whereas with the overdraft, interest is only levied on funds withdrawn as part of the overdraft facility.

6   *To obtain status and equality with peer groups.* This is an increasingly important customer motivation for using a bank's services.

Typical examples of products that seek to exploit the status-seeking desire of some customers are gold and platinum credit cards which usually come with certain special privileges, as well as access to a range of virtual banking services.

Products that confer equality with peer groups are mainly important to the young. Most banks have some products designed to be targeted at younger customers, and usually marketed and advertised according to a youthful theme.

Status seeking on the part of well-paid professionals is an increasingly important motive for using and buying banking services, and likely to become even more important in time to come. Banks are, naturally, keen to increase their customer base of hard-working people with high incomes and will take all sorts of steps to win customers over using products that convey status. As well as providing tokens of status such as gold credit cards, banks have recognized that providing a more personal level of service is another way to give customers the sense that they have status. Balancing this desire to offer some level of personal service with the sheer need to minimize the number of administrative staff (most retail banks have about one member of staff for every 100 customers) involves many banks in difficult managerial and administrative juggling acts.

Published research on customer attitudes to banking and technology

There is far less published survey material showing customer attitudes towards banking in general and electronic banking in particular than one might expect. I have looked at many different surveys produced by a variety of banks and retail financial institutions both in the United Kingdom and abroad, and only two of these have a quality of findings which is worth setting down here. I have also unearthed a helpful survey by an international research organization, although (as I explain later) the usefulness of this survey is to a certain extent reduced by the nature of the sample.

Why is good-quality survey material so sparse? There are several reasons.

First, customer surveys conducted by banks are often poorly thought-out, or use samples which cannot possibly be representative of the general population. Another difficulty is that even where these two problems don't apply, too many customer surveys involve questions which are designed so obviously to 'beg' for a particular answer that the response is essentially a foregone conclusion. If, for example, a survey asks customers whether they think they will be making more use of plastic bank cards in 10 years' time than they do nowadays, it's highly unlikely that any respondent is going to answer negatively, as an obvious issue of status is involved, and the question influences the respondent too much anyway.

Instead, it would be more useful to try to obtain from respondents a profile of their attitudes towards electronic banking services now and to try to predict how these attitudes might change in the future. However, banks rarely do this. The reason is that most of them conduct these surveys in order to gain publicity in the *consumer* media, and they are consequently more interested in producing findings which are more or less sensational and which might generate column inches of print rather than material which might reveal interesting *industry-related* points about customer attitudes.

This is not to say that banks never undertake interesting and detailed investigations of customer attitudes. They do, but these really interesting surveys are usually carried out on the banks' behalf by a large market research organization, and the conclusions are – understandably – regarded as so commercially confidential and sensitive that the last thing the bank wants to do is to make them available to any general publication likely to be read by competitors.

The lack of quality customer material dealing with attitudes towards banking generally and electronic banking in particular should not bother us unduly, because our very status as consumers of these services ourselves will allow us to reach important conclusions through mere introspection and self-awareness of our own attitudes towards the banking services we use.

There is another factor, too. While it is generally true that developments in technology take place in response to changing customer demands, a good case could be made out for believing that developments in electronic banking tend to be led by the banks and technology organizations with which the banks work rather than by customer demand. This point may seem obscure or even illogical at first sight, and needs elucidation.

Unquestionably, most new applications of technology are driven by customer demand. To take what might be termed the proto-application of computer technology, Charles Babbage designed his cogwheel calculating machines in order to deal with the problem of inaccurate mathematical tables, which were a great serious source of anxiety to the mathematical and scientific worlds of the early nineteenth century.

Since then, it has generally been the case that technology is deployed in response to customer needs. The *Titanic* was built not because the White Star Line wanted to win newspaper coverage by constructing the biggest ship of all time, but because in the first decade of the twentieth century there was a great surge in the numbers of people who wanted to travel from Europe to North America and back again, and there was consequently a demand for a ship that would take a large number of people (more than 2000) at one time.

Extended laterally, this reasoning holds good for most applications of technology, but when we come to certain high-tech applications it starts to become doubtful whether it is the inventor's drive to complete the invention successfully which is the motive force in bringing the application to the world, or customer demand for it.

For example, there is no particular reason to suppose that people in the 1880s had any greater desire to communicate with other people who lived beyond earshot than, say, people living 50 years earlier, yet it was the 1880s that saw the first use of the telephone. Surely it is incontestable that Bell saw that his device had enormous potential and that if it could be successfully achieved from a technological perspective, it was essential he do so.

Similarly, in the case of many 'niche', incremental applications of computers – as well as the first, basic idea of building a machine for handling calculations and processing information – it is likely that the availability of the new technology, and the fact that someone has decided to create it, is what is determining the application, rather than customer need for it. In effect, after the invention has been put onto the market, the customer demand is created for it.

Naturally, launching new technology in this way is extremely risky for the organization in question, because there is the ever-present danger that the application will be launched because it seems technologically interesting to the organization rather than because there is some proven demand for it. Anybody who has worked in the banking technology field will be aware of many examples of such disasters, especially relating to wholesale banking.

The computer industry in a more general sense is also susceptible to such disaster. An example of a more general type of disaster was the ill-fated attempt in the early 1990s on the part of several large computer companies (including well-established ones and start-ups), to launch a hand-held computer which used as its interface a special electronic pen.

Basically, what these organizations were aiming to do was produce an electronic notebook in which the user could hand-write information, which would be 'read' by the computer, thereby enabling the storage of this information in computer memory.

So much money was lost by venture capitalists on pen computers that it seems unbelievable that no serious attempt was ever made to try to gauge public acceptability of the idea. The only pen computer system which is currently fairly widely available is the Newton computer, sales of which have been disappointing. Pen computing has to be regarded as substantially unsuccessful, probably for the very simple reason that people *like* to use a purely manual note-taking system, are more comfortable with this, and regard the move to transfer this information into computer memory as a more formal process. The technological difficulties of making pen computers reliable certainly contributed to the demise of the idea as a major industry initiative, but the lack of public demand seems to have been the nail in the screen.

Electronic banking initiatives, however, have suffered no such lack of acceptability among their target markets. It would, indeed, be no exaggeration to say that ever since the launch, in the 1970s (strictly speaking the 1960s, but the 1970s saw the move to widespread use) of automated teller machines, every incremental new offering of electronic retail banking has won immense customer approval. This has even been true of applications – such as electronic funds transfer at point of sale (EFTPoS) – the benefits of which to the consumer might not initially have seemed very clear.

When I first started writing about EFTPoS in the mid-1980s, I was pretty much convinced that this would be an unsuccessful application, at least as far as reaching a mass market was concerned. There seemed no real advantage to a customer in using EFTPoS rather than paying with a cheque, because the cheque payments would, at least, give the customer three more days of 'float' before the payment was deducted from the customer's account.

I was wrong. EFTPoS has been a great success, and this has not been affected by the increasing tendency for EFTPoS payment to be made instantly against the customer's account rather than after a three-day clearing period (early EFTPoS transactions tended to feature such a delay, although the intention to switch to instant debit was always there). Under the circumstances, the only reasonable conclusion, then as now, was and is that people *like* using plastic cards to pay for things. Probably this liking is a mixture of a sense that plastic cards confer status. Certainly banks have gone to great lengths to design the plastic cards so that they look attractive, and to incorporate security devices into them – particularly holograms – which obviously confer status benefits in addition to security advantages. The status conferred by plastic cards appears to be in addition to the sheer and simple convenience they provide by enabling payment to be made by simply removing a small piece of plastic from one's wallet. No need to write out a cheque, no need to count out cash. And, best of all, in due course, the customer receives a statement detailing what he has spent.

Again and again, the history of electronic banking has confirmed this liking for plastic cards on the part of customers. In many respects this liking is surely what is going to define the future of electronic banking in the twenty-first century.

It follows from all this, then, that the relative lack of good service of consumer attitudes towards banking and electronic banking need not concern us to a great extent, because there seems little doubt that electronic banking initiatives which have a clear benefit for the public are likely to be popular, and possibly extremely popular. Which is not to say that market research surveys in this arena are completely unavailable, or that we should attach no credence to them at all. In particular, the findings of three surveys in recent years seem very much worth listing here. These are now discussed in turn.

The Girobank survey of 1994

In 1994 the UK retail bank Girobank conducted a survey of 1000 adults selected randomly throughout the United Kingdom and asked them specific, non-loaded questions about their attitudes to their bank. The findings, which are represented graphically by the accompanying figures, include the following:

■ A little more than one-fifth of the people surveyed said they went into their bank branches more than once a week, and most people visited their branch much more rarely than this. The survey clearly shows the impact which electronic banking services had already made by 1994, and there is a clear suggestion that the number of people visiting their branch more than once a week would be likely to decrease in the future. (See Figure 1.1.)

■ The vast majority of the people surveyed said that they did not know their bank manager. Such people can reasonably be presumed not to regard themselves as obtaining any particular personal benefit from visiting their branch. We can take this finding further and say that, since the whole essence of the process of virtualization of banking services is one involving a reduction in physical contact with one's bank, it is reasonable to conclude that most of the people surveyed were already, in effect, making use of virtual rather than actual banking services. (See Figure 1.2.)

FIGURE 1.1 *Extract from market research findings – I*

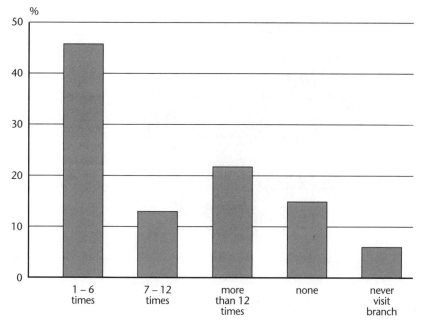

Q: How many times in the last 3 months have you gone into a branch in connection with your account?

(Source: Girobank)

■ A significant proportion of people surveyed thought that using a telephone banking service would be more expensive than running an account at a branch (i.e. expensive to them, the customer). This question was, as is clear from the figure, posed in a carefully unbiased way. The belief that telephone banking will be more expensive than running a branch-based service is interesting and might be taken to suggest that people have an expectation that a new type of electronic banking service with which they are not familiar is likely to be expensive for them to use.

■ By 1994 several telephone answering schemes had been launched in Britain but the take-up was relatively low; most of the respondents to this survey were therefore probably not already users of telephone banking services. In fact, the question of whether using a telephone banking service or visiting one's branch is the more expensive depends, as we might expect, on a number of factors, in particular the distance between the customer's residence and the branch. However, for most people it is much less expensive, both in terms of time and money, to obtain details of their account via the telephone and to effect certain transactions by phone. (See Figure 1.3.)

FIGURE 1.2 *Extract from market research findings – II*

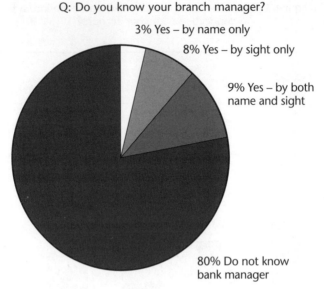

Q: Do you know your branch manager?

3% Yes – by name only

8% Yes – by sight only

9% Yes – by both name and sight

80% Do not know bank manager

(Source: Girobank)

The Visa survey of 1996

In September 1996 the international payments organization Visa commissioned the market research organization Gallup to conduct a wide-ranging survey of a representative cross-section of 1900 British people on their thoughts on what life in Britain would be like in 25 years' time (i.e. by the year 2021).

As with so many of these surveys, some of the questions were fairly trite and clearly geared around the desire to generate coverage in the consumer press. For example, 47 per cent of respondents said they expected that in 25 years' time people would travel in electric cars, while 14 per cent said they expected that people will be living in outer space. Leaving aside these banal conclusions, the survey did, in fact, come up with some useful findings about people's attitudes towards new types of technological tools and the general impact of computers in the home.

Particularly interesting findings in these respects were as follows:

■ 74 per cent of respondents believed that new technologies, such as the PC and the Internet, would continue to revolutionize the way people work and live.

■ 56 per cent thought that the pace of technological change would increase dramatically over the next 10 years.

FIGURE 1.3 *Extract from market research findings – III*

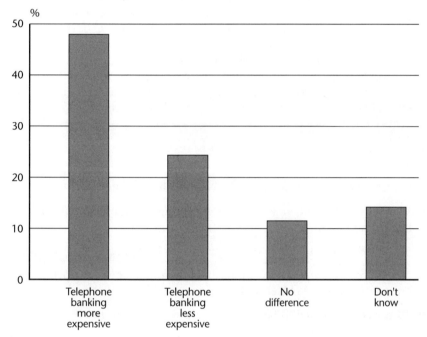

Q: Do you think telephone banking would be more or less expensive than an account run at a branch?

(Source: Girobank)

- 84 per cent thought that children would in the future be as familiar with using modern technology as with reading a book.

- *66 per cent believe that in 2021 we would not need to carry cash around with us* (my italics).

- 67 per cent expected to see a growing trend in shopping from home via a PC or the Internet.

As one might expect, the pace of change was most sharply anticipated by those aged between 25 and 44, compared with just over half of 16 to 24 year olds. Younger people probably take the pace of change for granted, while people already well into their careers are likely to be more conscious of how technology has affected their lives since their childhood. Young people certainly agreed with questions illustrating a vision of greater ease and leisure in the future (as mentioned above, this might indicate some prompting, but the survey results are useful anyway), while people in the 35 to 44 age group are more ambivalent about whether technology is making their lives easier.

When the survey took place, more than six million households in Britain had a personal computer – this figure roughly represents a quarter of all homes in the United Kingdom – and reliable industry sources anticipate that the figure will rise to at least 14 million households by the turn of the century. Visa was keen to find out what owners of home-based personal computers expected to be able to use their computers for in the future, and what the most popular applications were likely to be.

According to the survey, people expected that the prime use of a PC in the future would-be to 'pay bills and manage one's bank account' (70 per cent), followed closely by 'working from home' (69 per cent). The third most popular use would be to use a PC to 'shop from home' (62 per cent).

Other findings were as follows:

■ 57 per cent expected to use their PCs to reserve restaurant tables and book meals.

■ 54 per cent expected to book holidays from home using their PC.

■ 51 per cent thought they would be using their PCs to communicate with family and friends.

■ 51 per cent expected to be using their PC to help educate their children.

■ 39 per cent assumed they would be able to use their PC to find more information about hobbies and interests.

■ 33 per cent expected to be seeking medical advice via their PC.

■ 51 per cent thought they would communicate globally with work colleagues via their PC.

It says a great deal about the pace of change in using technology that many of these developments are already happening now. It is perfectly possible that within two or three years, the findings of this survey will be substantially superseded by the sheer pressure of events.

Finally, the survey asked questions about the use of a PC or some other electronic device (telephone banking is clearly included here) and respondents' attitudes towards this. Interestingly, while it is often thought that women are more prone to 'technofear' than men, given the opportunity today to use a home computer or a similar device to buy things rather than go out to shop, four out of ten men (40 per cent) and nearly a third of the women surveyed (32 per cent) said they definitely would buy goods electronically. Typical spontaneous reasons (i.e. not prompted by Visa) given by women for shopping electronically or the prospect of doing so, were as follows:

■ 30 per cent said it would be 'simpler, easier and less effort.'

■ 21 per cent said it would be more convenient.

- 17 per cent said they expected it to save time and be quicker.

- 11 per cent said it would save the need to travel into town.

Overall, the Visa survey was an interesting and important analysis of customer attitudes towards PCs in a leisure and personal finance/shopping context. If the findings of the survey are only what we would expect anyway, this merely confirms the point made above: that we can make considerable progress in understanding customer attitudes towards electronic banking by thinking about our own attitudes and using common sense to extend this thinking to how other people are likely to use electronic banking and the attitudes they will probably have towards it. Some caution is necessary here: as a reader of this book you will already have a vested interest in electronic banking of some kind and you should not forget that the majority of people have no vested interest in it but simply want an easy banking life so that they can do what they really want to do: that is, enjoy their work and their leisure and be able to buy the things they both need and would enjoy.

The PSI Global survey of 1997

In 1997 the international market research organization PSI Global conducted a detailed survey of 1079 United States households to investigate their attitudes towards electronic banking services. PSI Global kindly allowed me to quote from this survey in depth. While I am grateful to them for this privilege, I can't help commenting that it seems somewhat unfortunate to me that they deliberately chose to confine the survey to those households which were what they described as 'on-line' households: that is, households which either make use of an on-line banking service and/or the Internet at home.

This is a by no means inconsiderable proportion of United States households – it is in fact about 17 per cent of all households. However, the sample clearly suffers from the problem that these households have already made a decision to opt for some kind of virtual service and can consequently be expected to be sympathetic to that service from the outset. It would in many respects have been more useful for the survey to have covered households which do not have any on-line service and to ask the family members about what their attitude to starting to use such a service would be. At the very least, such a survey would have been a useful accompaniment to the survey as completed.

That said, the findings of this survey are certainly very interesting, and PSI Global has at least sometimes made comparisons with ordinary (i.e. non-on-line) US households. I now provide some of the findings that seem to me the most interesting.

First, Table 1.1 shows an age/income distribution of on-line consumer households. Its findings as regards the age range of these on-line households are what we might expect. Note also that the average income of these

TABLE 1.1 *Age/income distribution comparison on-line consumer households*

Age Distribution	Random Sample	Income Distribution	Random Sample
18–24	3%	<$5K	5%
25–34	29%	$15K–$24.9K	8%
35–44	26%	$25K–$34.9K	9%
45–54	26%	$35K–$49.9K	17%
55–64	9%	$50K–$74.9K	27%
65–74	5%	$75K–$99.9K	18%
75+	2%	$100K–$149.9K	12%
		$150K +	5%
Average			
43		$69,971	

(Source: PSI Global)

households is, at $69,971, clearly significantly greater than the average income of most US households. Figures for the average household income in the US are not readily available, but the average national income per capita is $24,294 for 1996, the last year for which a figure is available. (Source: US Bureau of Census)

The research also found that on-line consumers utilize the full range of delivery options, but that the vast majority depend on ATMs and traditional branches for meeting their banking needs.

Interestingly, despite the fact that on-line households generally position themselves in the survey as less branch-reliant, a surprising 79 per cent continue to visit a traditional branch facility regularly. In fact, this finding is not one that could be extrapolated to households around the world, whether or not on-line households, because (as I explain later in this book) the much lower relative cost of land for branch premises in the United States compared to, for example, Europe and Japan means that American banks do not have quite the same incentive to go virtual as do their counterparts in many other countries. Furthermore, there is in the United States something of a 'frontier' mentality towards bank branches, which are regarded with much the same respect, and even with the same mystical reverence, which is often seen in movies about the Wild West.

Despite all this, however, it is true that even people who are highly conversant with virtual delivery services and perfectly happy to use their bank in this way will still often visit branches. Sometimes, though, this is to make use of lobby machines, and so the visit is not really a true branch visit at all. On other occasions, the purpose of the visit is to discuss matters face-to-face with a human cashier; matters which simply cannot be addressed via a virtual service.

FIGURE 1.4 *Delivery channel transaction distribution (among on-line consumer households who are debit users)*

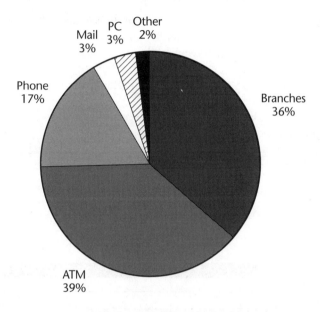

Averaging Total Number of Transactions/Month: 17.7

(Source: PSI Global)

Figure 1.4. shows the delivery transaction distribution among all on-line consumer households. Note that the item 'PC' refers to remote banking systems making use of a personal computer in the customer's home.

Other findings relating to transaction distribution are:

■ 92 per cent of all retail banking transactions conducted by on-line consumers originate from three channels: branches, ATMs and the telephone.

■ The transaction distribution of on-line consumers varies significantly from that of all United States households. While 36 per cent of on-line consumer transactions are generated from branches, the 'all United States households' branch portion accounts for 52 per cent of the total. PSI Global points out, however: 'this disparity gives the appearance that on-line consumers are less branch-dependent than average. In actuality, on-line consumers incidence and frequency of branch use is comparable to all United States households. However, the vast number of transactions which on-line consumers conduct at other outlets serves to decrease their portion of branch transactions.'

■ On-line consumers conduct an average of 17.7 transactions each month versus 12.5 for the national average.

Figure 1.5 shows the use of point of sale (POS) debit (this is how the Americans describe Electronic Funds Transfer at Point of Sale) at different merchant locations. It illustrates what the reader's experience will probably confirm, that by far the most popular place in which to make use of debit is the supermarket. People don't like having to juggle with cash when they are juggling with their shopping.

My review of the findings of this survey concludes with its results relating to ATMs and telephone banking. There is also some useful material on PC banking, but as this is rather specialized, I prefer to include it in the subsequent chapter on remote banking.

FIGURE 1.5 *Use of POS debit by merchant location (among on-line consumer households who are debit users)*

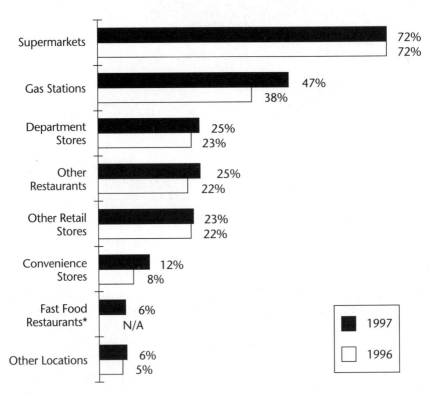

*1996 sample size less than 30.

(Source: PSI Global)

FIGURE 1.6 *Use of ATMs by type of function (among all on-line consumer households)*

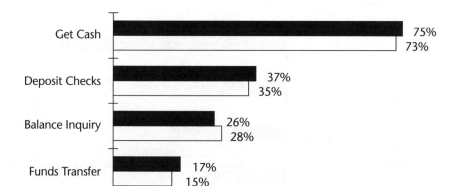

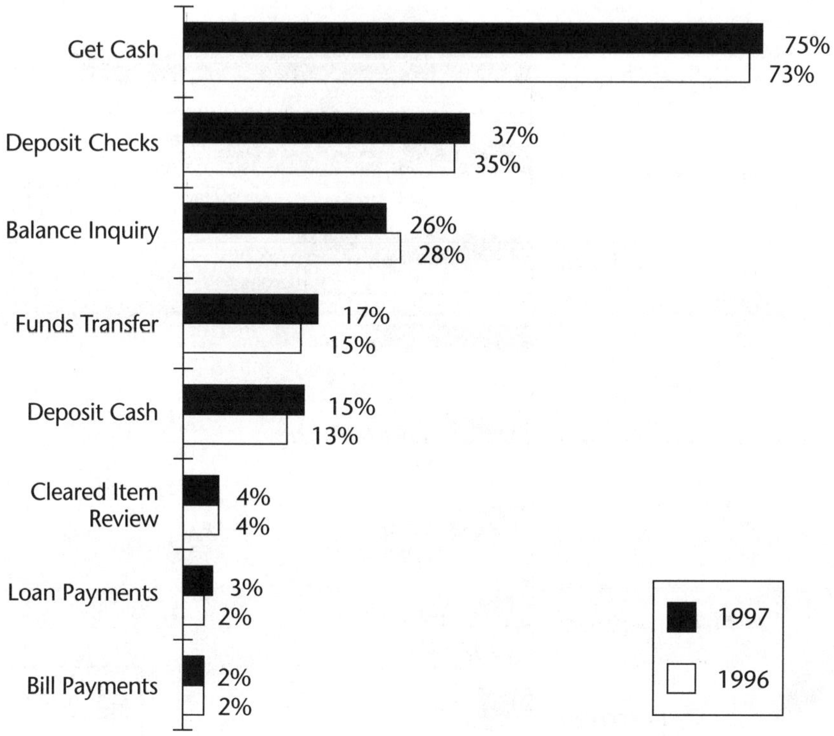

(Source: PSI Global)

Figure 1.6. shows the use of ATMs by type of function. It is self-explanatory. The survey also showed that during 1997, on-line households have expanded their use of ATMs. Incidence of ATM use for obtaining cash, depositing, and transferring funds increased slightly from 1996 to 1997, while a faint portion of balance enquiries appears to have migrated to the telephone or the PC.

As far as telephone banking is concerned, more than one-half of on-line consumer households contact their banks on average three times per month via telephone, conducting an approximate total of five financial account transactions.

Figure 1.7. analyses telephone banking use by type of function.

Overview of customer attitudes towards banking

Generally, it is perfectly feasible to assemble a series of conclusions about customer attitudes towards banking and towards their money as a whole.

FIGURE 1.7 *Telephone banking use by type of function (among on-line consumer households who are telephone banking users)*

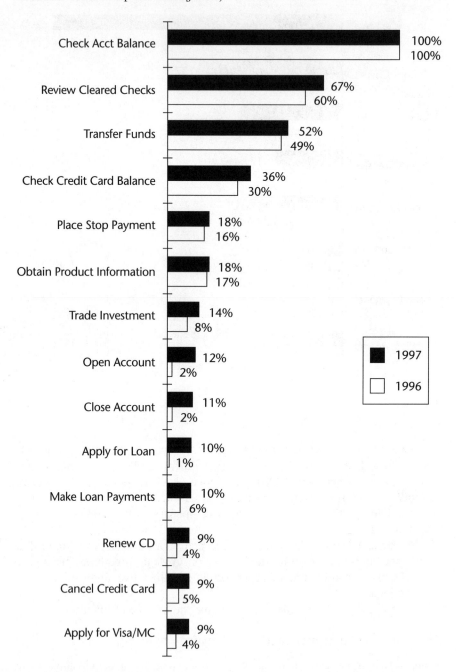

(Source: PSI Global)

These conclusions follow. Note that I have drawn several of them from survey material which, while relevant to the conclusion in question, did not seem sufficiently well targeted to be included in detail in this chapter. With the exception of the last conclusion below, these points are not listed according to any hierarchy of their importance; I have simply put the more straightforward conclusions closer to the start.

1   Consumers want to put money aside as savings wherever they are able to do so while remaining financially comfortable.

2   About half of consumers would rather visit their branch as rarely as possible.

3   About one in every two consumers say they have never met the branch manager of their bank.

4   There is a great willingness on the part of consumers to use remotely delivered banking services, especially ATM services and EFTPoS services. Telephone-delivered services are also increasingly popular.

5   Consumers are highly susceptible to banks' mass market corporate or brand advertising campaigns. Generally, the more straightforward the message, the more likely the campaign is to be effective. A campaign delivered via a visual icon to which consumers can readily relate, appears to have the best chance of success. Furthermore, any campaign which is aimed at reaching the largest number of people must be delivered via television.

6   The average consumer has little or no inherent interest in the technology which drives the service, but is only interested in its results for him or her.

7   For consumers, money is only of secondary importance compared with the primary importance of the goods and services which the customer can buy with the money.

8   Demogeographic factors have a huge influence over people's spending and savings habits. Banks seeking to maximize the appeal of their products and services – and particularly the appeal of innovative electronic banking services – to consumers must therefore pay considerable attention to targeting their marketing at selected classifications of consumers. More details of how to achieve this particular objective are given in the case study at the end of this chapter.

9   Despite the perception among consumers that telephone banking can bring them considerable benefits, there remains something of a gap in the precise awareness among consumers of the benefits of telephone banking services. This almost certainly explains why the take-up of telephone banking services is much lower in all countries than that of ATM and EFTPoS services.

10 Many consumers find insurance and investment products difficult to understand, and frequently feel that these are sold in an intimidating way. Consumers are therefore highly susceptible to buying these products from a large, well-known bank.

11 Consumers are increasingly choosing their bank by recommendation from family and acquaintances. Banks should therefore devote effort to converting consumers into 'brand advocates' who will not only use the brand themselves, but recommend it to family and acquaintances. Generally, consumers appreciate a letter of thanks for making a recommendation, but some kind of incentive to do so is not necessary.

12 The popularity of plastic cards among consumers shows no sign of abating. Certainly, the cards are more convenient to carry around, and offer consumers higher levels of security, as well as access to their funds and payment facilities nationwide, and even abroad. However, it is impossible not to conclude that a big reason for their popularity is that consumers regard them as conferring status.

13 Many consumers feel that they are subjected to unreasonable fees and charges from their bank, most notably from arranging and using overdraft facilities. The most common cause of dissatisfaction with an FSO is excessive charges.

14 The two most important priorities for taking out insurance are attaining financial security for one's dependants and the desire to achieve income in retirement.

15 Even in today's highly virtual insurance industry, where companies such as the UK insurer Direct Line, and its imitators, have achieved great success through remote delivery of these services, most consumers still prefer to buy their life and health insurance through traditional outlets: i.e. real people rather than via the telephone. However, even consumers who do prefer to buy these more 'personal' types of insurance through face-to-face channels are increasingly likely to be prepared to buy non-life and non-health insurance through telephone contact. In time, it seems likely that consumers will be happy to buy all types of insurance via remote channels.

16 Where consumers have already bought insurance and investment products from a remote delivery channel, they are more likely to do it again. The various surveys seem to lead to the conclusion that once consumers have 'crossed the bridge' of using remote facilities for buying insurance, they are likely to continue using these facilities.

17 Despite the high – and growing – levels of competition among banks, there are surprisingly extensive opportunities for banks to seek to create

loyalty, even lifetime loyalty, from consumers. This phenomenon seems to stem from the emotive nature of financial services in consumers' lives, which means that where consumers feel secure with a particular supplier, they are likely to stick with that supplier and regard themselves as having a relationship with it.

18 Once a household becomes familiar with using on-line banking services, it is likely to continue to expand its use of these services and to become something of a connoisseur of the art.

I have left what seems to be the most important conclusion of all until last. This is that consumers today are more likely to open accounts with a bank for reasons of the *perceived quality of the product or service*, rather than for convenience and geographic proximity to home or work. This, beyond doubt, is incontrovertible evidence of the importance of the virtual banking revolution to changing patterns of consumer demand. Perceived quality of service is what matters; physical location is increasingly unimportant. This fundamental fact has created an entirely new type of retail banking industry, and it is this new type of retail banking industry that this book explores.

How virtual banking can enable you to achieve your overall commercial objectives

Having now gained some insight into customer/consumer attitudes towards banking in general and electronic banking specifically, we can now return to the commercial objectives listed earlier in this chapter and set down how virtual banking can enable these to be achieved.

Objective: increase customer bases for all profit centres

It should be clear from the above that, by giving customers what they want – that is, access to better banking services at remote locations which suit their own needs rather than those of the bank – a bank is maximizing the likelihood that its overall customer base will be as wide as feasible.

This basic point holds good, even though some profit centres will still be geared around getting the customer into the branch. An example of this would be an insurance or investment department, where sales were mainly made face-to-face in the branch. However, the huge and increasing success of the direct type of insurance and investment organizations clearly shows that the virtual banking revolution vigorously impinges on these profit centres, if not perhaps quite to the same extent as it affects the retail banking division.

Objective: Increase overall breadth and quality of services

There is little doubt that virtual banking greatly improves a bank's overall services. True, this will not so much apply where the customer likes to have a friendly chat with a human teller at the branch as part of his or her banking routine, but while there will always be such customers, the vast majority prefer to make their visit to the branch as brief as possible – proof of this is the invariably bad-tempered nature of a long queue at a bank – and if possible to be able to avoid going into a bank branch at all.

When electronic banking services were first offered in the 1960s and 1970s, the range of services provided was very narrow. For most banks it was confined to the provision of remote cash withdrawal via a cash machine: at that point it was not really possible to call these automated teller machines because they only provided this one function.

Today, however, the range of services available electronically is extremely wide, and while it is usually theoretically possible for many of these services to be provided by a human teller in a branch, in practice this would take a considerable time and in any case, the human teller would only be using the bank's front-office computer to do the job. The customer would be better off doing the job himself or herself. Furthermore, there are always going to be some extremely important services which a human teller cannot possibly provide: a facility for withdrawing cash at an overseas ATM, for example, an EFTPoS facility, or a telephone banking resource.

In the future, the range of services available via a virtual banking facility is bound to increase, while the branch-based facilities offered by a bank seem similarly bound to contract. Indeed, several new banks do not have branch networks at all.

Another key point here is that services delivered to the customer via electronic delivery channels will always be provided more rapidly and more accurately than those delivered by a human teller. From the point of view of the particular commercial objective to maximize quality of service, it is incontestable that virtual banking has a major role to play.

Objective: Decrease the proportion of routine transactions carried out in the branch

It should by now be clear to the reader that virtual banking radically alters the bank/customer dynamic and is, by definition, geared around enabling customers to use banking services without visiting their branch.

Virtual banking enables customers to avoid visiting their branches because it provides them with a wide range of alternative banking facilities delivered via electronic networks. In essence, virtual banking acknowledges the fact of the secondary nature of the utility which banking services have for people compared with retail outlets which actually sell the things people want. Virtual banking minimizes the customer's interaction with the bank while ensuring that the customer gets what he or she wants.

Note, incidentally, that quite apart from the advantages virtual banking offers in terms of improving customer service – and which are detailed both here in this chapter and later in the book – from the bank's perspective, there is also a very strong cost justification for moving services out of the branch and onto virtual delivery channels. This justification is explored in detail in Chapter 4.

Objective: Increase proportion of profitable sales transactions (e.g. sales of loans, mortgages, insurance, investments and pensions)

On the face of it this is not necessarily an area where virtual banking has a key role to play, because in the past such financial services as these have tended to be sold via face-to-face sessions with customers in the branch. However, even given that many consumers do still prefer to buy certain types of insurance and investment products from real people rather than via a direct, remote sales delivery system that uses the telephone or even an electronic network, there is little doubt that the *trend* here is in favour of people buying an increasingly high proportion of these services directly rather than in the branch. The virtual banking revolution therefore has a great deal of relevance to the selling of these products, too.

Objective: Improve general customer satisfaction

Some aspects of how virtual banking enables a bank to achieve this all-important objective have already been touched upon above. There is in practice no doubt that moving towards a more virtual type of operation – given that this does not necessarily mean dispensing with the branch network entirely – greatly helps a bank improve the level of general customer satisfaction with its services.

Customers who have access to virtual banking services will benefit from a greater range of such services; more rapid access to cash; easier access to payment facilities; more accurate and timely information about their accounts, more overall convenience (not having to visit the branch is a major part of this), improved status and – very importantly – a greater perception that the bank's services are *personalized* to their own needs. Of course, much of this perception is a kind of illusion caused by the remarkable ability of electronic banking services to be targeted very precisely at the customer's own requirements and account details. Indeed, the security system used to ensure that only a bona fide customer gets access to the information concerning him or her naturally guarantees that the service will be highly personalized. From the customer's perspective, however, the fact that the personalization is basically an illusion doesn't matter: the customer gets what he or she wants, and is perfectly happy.

Finally, following on from the discussion above, virtual banking services allow customers to spend the minimum amount of time on the secondary level of utility which a bank provides and more time on actually obtaining the things the customer really wants.

Objective: Increase speed of response to customer requirements

As we might expect, this is an area where virtual banking completely triumphs over more traditional types of banking service provision. The advantage to the customer from the speed perspective is twofold: not only does he or she obtain the facility required (e.g. cash withdrawal, payment system, account information) very rapidly, but the actual delivery of the service is itself very rapid. The reason is, simply, that the whole service delivery process depends on electronic functionality, and this is by its nature the most rapid type of process that modern technology has devised.

The rapidity of the process is particularly emphatic where the customer wants to gain access to cash. Traditionally, in order to do this it was necessary to visit the bank's branch and to cash a cheque: a process that might easily take 15 or 20 minutes if carried out during the peak times for bank branches (usually lunchtimes and Saturday mornings). If the customer withdraws funds via an ATM, however, the process need take no more than 20 seconds. Furthermore, where the ATM is used in a country different from the one where the customer's account is held, the process of delivery takes hardly any longer than at a domestic ATM, but the time saving will be even greater. This is because in this case the alternative for the customer to obtaining local currency would be to cash a traveller's cheque (admittedly these can be used as cash in some countries, such as the US) or even to obtain funds by the highly laborious process of having the bank wire details of these to the foreign bank.

Objective: Reduce overall risk of the institution incurring financial loss

Virtual banking helps here in two respects. First, it tends very significantly to reduce cheque fraud – a major cause of loss to a bank. Second, it helps a bank keep a detailed record of all transactions, because everything being handled by the virtual banking system will, by definition, be computer-controlled and will therefore be subject to an electronic audit trail, which is recognized as the best form of internal control.

The precise security of a virtual banking service is, as might be expected, very much a matter for continuing debate within the banking industry. The problem is that experience has shown that the only practical way to enable a customer to authenticate their identity and authorize an electronic service is to use the PIN (personal identification number) system, which is all very well if the bona fide customer and only the bona fide customer knows the PIN, but this is often not the case.

Customers are alarmingly lackadaisical in how they make use of their PIN, sometimes writing it down on a piece of card or paper which they keep in their wallet next to their plastic card, and also often giving it to a third party (such as a close friend or a member of their family) so that this person can visit the cash machine on their behalf. It is, perhaps, to some extent understandable that for some customers one of the benefits of using an ATM is that they can get someone else to undertake the transaction for them if they are ill or simply too busy to visit the ATM themselves, but this practice is of course a huge security risk. It is likely that most of the cases of so-called 'phantom withdrawals' (where the customer claims a withdrawal from an ATM charged to his account was not one he actually made) stems from this practice, which in any case involves a breach of the bank/customer agreement.

Plastic cards are also highly vulnerable to theft, and the need for a bank to cultivate good customer relations means that there is a limit on the financial burden it can expect a customer to bear if the card has been lost or stolen. In most national jurisdictions, once the customer has notified the bank of the loss or theft, the customer is then no longer liable for any withdrawals made by a third party, although sometimes the liability remains if the customer has disclosed the PIN to somebody else.

Even so, virtual banking carries an additional big advantage in the risk reduction arena, because it facilitates accurate classification of customers according to many criteria, especially those relating to the customer's personal credit history and track record for sticking to, say, loan agreements and mortgage arrangements. Modern methods for evaluating customers in this way lend themselves exceptionally well to incorporation within a virtual banking system. The case study at the end of this chapter looks at one organization that provides credit evaluation services.

Generally, and particularly as a consequence of this last point above, it appears to be the case that virtual banking services certainly do reduce a bank's overall level of risk in providing retail banking services to customers, but the question of plastic card loss, theft or even fraud is still somewhat unresolved. That said, the introduction of the chip card or smart card is already helping to tip the balance of the plastic card security problem back in favour of the banks. This matter is examined in Chapter 9.

Objective: Increase penetration of under-18 customer market

All that really needs to be said here is that this market is extremely important for banks because these young people are the adult customers of the future. Experience shows that if they can be captured when young, there is at least a reasonable chance that they will stay with the bank in the future, although certainly the days when a bank could be sure of this happening are over.

In any event, there is no doubt evidence that the highly computer-literate younger generation is adept at using virtual banking services and prefers to do so rather than visiting a branch. Proof of this is that younger people are relatively rarely seen in a bank's branch unless they have a particular problem which needs dealing with. In conclusion, therefore, virtual banking certainly helps a bank reach this particular market.

Objective: Increase quality of the institution's marketing initiatives

Here, too, the argument that virtual banking helps to address this particular challenge seems clear. The range of services which can be provided rapidly and accurately via a virtual banking system is a huge marketing bonus for a bank. Furthermore, experience shows that a bank does best by launching new types of accounts and banking service which incorporate the electronic banking facility rather than only using these as add-ons to existing accounts and services.

Another important point here is that marketing messages can frequently be incorporated into the actual delivery via a virtual banking system, given that the message is not going to irritate the customer or slow down the transaction. Finally, the plastic card itself on which so many virtual banking services depend is itself an ideal token for marketing messages relating to the name of the account or facility, and/or of the name of any shared access networks (such as Link, Plus or Cirrus).

Objective: Increase retention rates of staff and perceived staff morale

Virtual banking plays a key role here in reducing the proportion of routine and dull transactions which must be processed by branch-based staff, thereby freeing them for more interesting, interpersonal types of activity such as those relating to sales and general provision of customer advice.

Objective: Reduce overall operational costs of the institution

This is an important motivation for using virtual banking services. As already mentioned, this matter is covered in Chapter 4.

Objective: Increase overall revenues in line with the requirements of the institution's business plan

Generally, and by way of a summary, there can be little doubt that the virtual banking revolution helps to meet this fundamental objective by making the bank's services more attractive both to existing and potential customers; allowing the delivery of a wide range of services, and reducing the bank's overall operational costs of delivering these services.

Case study: Experian Group

I conclude this chapter with a case study of the activities and objectives of the Experian Group (formerly the CCN Group). This organization has always played an important role in providing banks and other types of financial institutions around the world with manual and computer-readable information about customers: especially relating to credit ratings, and consequently it must be seen as a leading pioneer in defining how the bank/customer relationship is likely to develop in the future.

Based in Nottingham, in the UK, the Experian Group develops sophisticated techniques for maintaining records – within legal strictures – of the spending habits and financial creditworthiness of individuals and companies.

The Group was formed in 1980 in response to a need from its parent company, Great Universal Stores plc, for an organization which could handle the need to provide reliable information on personal creditworthiness. At this stage, Experian was simply a credit reference agency: that is, it collated publicly available information (such as the Register of County Court Judgements), and combined this with information about creditworthiness obtained from organizations which have granted money to consumers and businesses in the past. Experian merely re-presents and collates this information, it cannot modify it because it belongs, strictly speaking, to the public source or the lender in question.

The one qualification to this is that in accordance with the provisions of the Data Protection Act 1984, Experian allows individuals to obtain details of their credit information and gives them the option of inserting a modification to some aspect of the record on their behalf.

Today, Experian has evolved considerably from simply acting as a credit reference agency. It still performs this function, but also performs a range of other functions, principally in the areas of risk management, target marketing and account processing.

Its risk management services include providing clients with consumer information, business information and vehicle information, as well as processing applications for credit and selling decision support software which lets customers make their own decisions about prospective consumers. In other words, Experian seeks to offer a comprehensive service for the management of credit risk.

The target marketing services are of great importance for the scope of this report. Experian offers services relating to segmenting customers according to a wide range of criteria, targeting prospects and customers, analysing marketplaces, planning the activities of a retail organization, and direct mail services.

Finally, the Group also offers a wide range of account processing services, including customer loyalty programmes, an arrears management service, and transaction management. There are currently 2300 Experian staff around the world and the Group has offices in Africa, Australia, Belgium, Canada, France, Germany, Hong Kong, Italy, The Netherlands, Spain, the United Kingdom and the United States. Experian has customers in 40 countries world-wide.

As might be expected, technology is essential to the Experian service. The Group has two computing centres in the UK, with a total of four IBM-compatible mainframes running MVS, CICS, VTAM and JES3. There is also a computer centre in Germany, based on AS/400 technology which provides local card processing.

Altogether, Experian has mainframe computing power of 428 MIPS and 1.5 terabytes of online storage. It has a telecommunications network supporting 70,000 customer terminals and 24-hour customer support. It features full disaster recovery and 'hot' stand-by services, i.e. services which will come onstream immediately if the principle facility goes down for some reason.

The Group also has print and mailing centres which can handle more than one million mailings per week.

It is an indication of the scale of the business of storing and business information, that Experian's facilities are nothing more than what is necessary to be a major player in this business.

It must be emphasized that Experian complies in every respect with legal rulings on handling information about individuals. However, this does not detract from the fact that the detail of information it holds is remarkable.

As far as the details of personal credit information are concerned, Experian retains details of all credit agreements entered into, even where the account was settled promptly with no arrears, and where the balance has been settled a long time in the past. In fact, Experian holds details of such satisfactory agreements for six years from the time when the account was settled.

From the banks' perspective, Experian's next most important work after the provision of credit information on individuals (and corporations) is in the area of target marketing: which can be described as the process of matching sales and marketing information most precisely to the needs of customers who might wish to purchase the services. Experian provides the direct marketing industry in the UK and around the world – including many banks and 'direct' types of financial institutions) with a fully integrated range of services founded on the company's core skills in name and address recognition and direct mail production. People and companies who are poor credit risks can be weeded out of the mailing at the outset.

Even more interestingly, Experian has pioneered a system of analysis of consumers' needs and lifestyles by overlaying electoral data with what it refers to as 'geodemographic overlays to the lists'. Basically, what this means is that consumers are segmented according to a variety of factors, in particular neighbourhood type, the stage they have reached in their lives, aspects of their behaviour as consumers and credit risk. If, for example, a financial institution wanted to market a new product that combined a mortgage facility with a gold card and an overdraft facility, it would naturally wish to market this to customers who needed such facilities but who also were likely to honour commitments.

Electoral rolls do not contain any information about salaries, and so Experian has developed an intriguing system of analysis which is based, logically enough, on the type of housing in a particular area. There are a total of 12 categories of housing: all tallying with a specific category of person living in them. It is not purely a simple categorization by housing type. But a general guide which can then be overlaid with additional information, such as creditworthiness. For example, if the new mortgage/ gold card/loan facility were to be marketed to category L1 of CCN's classification, which is known as 'high income families', a creditworthiness overlay would weed out from the mailing potential consumers who were felt to be poor credit risks.

The system Experian uses to categorize households in this way is known as Mosaic. By way of illustration of Mosaic's detail and the depth into which the analysis goes, consider Tables 1.2, 1.3 and 1.4. Note that the percentage figures next to the descriptions of households simply refer to the rough percentage of households in the country which fit within this category.

Note also that the variables are different attributes of people in these households, with the figures reflecting a relationship with an index of 100 which represents the average figure for the UK as a whole. For example, in the 'Stylish Singles' classification, the index for County Court Judgements

TABLE 1.2 *High income families (9.9 per cent)*

High Income Families are found in the more affluent and leafy suburbs, where only professionals and wealthy business-people can afford the premium prices of large, owner occupied housing.

These are typically family areas, where houses have four or more bedrooms and generous gardens. Such areas are frequented neither by first time buyers nor by fragile pensioners, but by two-income, two-car households where children as well as parents are performance and achievement oriented.

Variables	L1	Variables	L1
Aged 0–4	85	Unskilled	28
Aged 5–14	110	Manufacturing/	
Aged 15–24	94	mining	75
Aged 25–34	75	Services	113
Aged 35–44	121	Agriculture	53
Aged 45–54	125	Outright owners	135
Aged 55–64	107	Mortgaged owners	139
Aged 65+	89	Private rented	60
Singles	58	Local authority rented	12
Families	122	Detached	299
Cohabitees	64	Semi-detached	86
H/hlds with		Terraced	30
children	110	Flats	35
Professional/		Company directors	325
managerial	194	CCJs	39
Skilled Manual	55	Credit searches	98

(Source: Experian)

TABLE 1.3 *Stylish singles (5.2 per cent)*

Stylish Singles attracts people for whom self-expression is more important than conformity to any external set of social standards.

Typically very well educated and very involved in their work, people are highly interested in the behaviour of different social groups and enjoy living in a diverse, cosmopolitan and sometimes multicultural environment.

People are often too busy experimenting and experiencing life to want to get married early and postpone as long as possible the responsibility of looking after homes, gardens and children. These people prefer the vitality of the large city to the tranquillity of outer suburbs and spend money freely on fashion, foreign travel, the arts, entertainment and eating out.

Variables	L8	Variables	L8
Aged 0–4	80	Unskilled	51
Aged 5–14	62	Manufacturing/	
Aged 15–24	127	mining	50
Aged 25–34	156	Services	123
Aged 35–44	101	Agriculture	15
Aged 45–54	86	Outright owners	73
Aged 55–64	78	Mortgaged owners	89
Aged 65+	83	Private rented	390
Singles	184	Local authority rented	33
Families	54	Detached	16
Cohabitees	183	Semi-detached	25
H/hlds with		Terraced	78
children	60	Flats	276
Professional/		Company directors	192
managerial	174	CCJs	110
Skilled Manual	53	Credit searches	121

(Source: Experian)

TABLE 1.4 *Mortgaged families (6.2 per cent)*

Mortgaged Families consist mostly of areas of newly built private housing, typically lived in by younger households often burdened by high levels of mortgage repayment.

Whilst most of these areas contain young families living on the outskirts of town and cities, we find an increasing number of young single people, cohabitees and childless couples in this group, often living in in-fill housing in older areas.

The furnishing and decoration of homes and gardens is a key focus of their leisure activities and shopping trips are undertaken by the entire family to retail multiples in newly developed retail parks in out-of-town locations.

Variables	L10	Variables	L10
Aged 0–4	135	Unskilled	58
Aged 5–14	111	Manufacturing/	
Aged 15–24	108	mining	104
Aged 25–34	158	Services	102
Aged 35–44	119	Agriculture	44
Aged 45–54	79	Outright owners	58
Aged 55–64	57	Mortgaged owners	169
Aged 65+	44	Private rented	65
Singles	95	Local authority rented	33
Families	95	Detached	107
Cohabitees	216	Semi-detached	123
H/hlds with		Terraced	101
children	128	Flats	65
Professional/		Company directors	94
managerial	107	CCJs	108
Skilled Manual	98	Credit searches	152

(Source: Experian)

(CCJs) is given as 110, which means that the average here for Stylish Singles incurring CCJs is about 10 per cent greater than the national average.

There is no doubt that the depth of analysis represented by Mosaic is the way ahead for understanding consumers, whether this understanding is required by the financial industry or by other major industries. Some sources refer to this categorization as 'behavioural scoring', but this seems to imply a respect for it which it does not entirely deserve. It can never be a substitute for a real understanding of the psychology and needs of a customer, and suffers from the basic drawback that it is essentially an analysis of past customer behaviour, rather than a considered verdict on what is likely to happen in the future. Many stylish singles are in fact much more solvent than high income families whose breadwinners have reached the peak of their earning power, but it is difficult for the categorization to reflect these social trends.

It is true that social commentators might agree that the categorizations are somewhat irritating and tend to reduce the excitement and variety of modern life to the trite platitudes of lifestyle features in glossy magazines. However, it is perhaps inevitable that an attempt to categorize people is bound to wind up generating platitudes. The real point is that commercial organizations find these categories helpful and useful. Furthermore, generally, the categories help to ensure that details of the right product go to the right households. Ultimately, whatever one thinks of the categorization process inherent in behavioural scoring, there is no doubt that such scoring is now an essential part of modern marketing activity, and – just like computer-based credit records – here to stay.

Setting the virtual banking revolution in its strategic context

Introduction

No analysis of the virtual banking revolution will be of much practical use unless it recognizes that the opportunities presented by virtual banking are only one – albeit an extremely important one – of the commercial challenges facing banks today.

Consequently, before proceeding with our examination of the virtual banking revolution, we need to set the revolution in its strategic context, and look at the other commercial challenges facing banks today. To be more accurate, we need to create a balanced perspective in which the challenge of the virtual banking revolution is *only one* of the commercial challenges facing banks.

Unfortunately, most books and conferences about virtual banking don't make any real effort to look at the virtual banking phenomenon in its proper strategic context as just one of the challenges faced by retail banks. Instead, they tend to focus on the phenomenon of virtual banking as if it were something isolated and even remote from the many challenges facing retail banks. Certainly, it is easier to analyse virtual banking in this way, but treating the phenomenon as something isolated is a little like drawing conclusions about all the water-based and land-based life in the world on the basis of examining the life in one continent.

Identifying the major commercial challenges currently facing retail banks isn't on the face of it easy, because the range of commercial challenges facing retail banks today is extremely wide. Selecting the most pressing ones appears at first sight to involve any writer in making fairly arbitrary decisions which carry the danger that, if they are anything other than immaculately formulated, they may be less than helpful – even misguiding – for the reader.

However, I have not relied solely on my own experience of the retail banking sector. I have also discussed strategic issues in detail with a variety of highly experienced consultants working in the retail banking industry. The result has been something of a consensus, and the following list of major commercial challenges can therefore be presented with some confidence.

The final preparatory point to make here is that, as these challenges are all so important, it would be ill-advised, as well as certainly misleading, to suggest that one particular pressure was more obviously important than the others. Consequently, instead of listing these challenges according to some possibly spurious hierarchy of importance, they are listed in alphabetical order. The main commercial challenges can therefore be identified as the following:

- The banks' fear of *disintermediation*.

- The banks' need to maximize the depth and breadth of *electronic delivery channels*.

- The banks' need to display *increased cost-efficiency*.

- The banks' need to obtain a comprehensive view of their overall *risk exposures*.

- The challenge of the *single European currency*.

- The *Year 2000 problem*.

Discussion of the major commercial challenges

These commercial challenges are now discussed in turn.

The banks' fear of disintermediation

For a bank, disintermediation can be defined as

> the notion that in the changing financial services arena of the future, an organization which can only provide a secondary rather than primary degree of usefulness may be left out of the equation altogether.

Implicit in this definition is the belief that banks may be abandoned by customers completely if the customer is able to meet the need for obtaining access to funds from another source: such as a large retailing organization.

Disintermediation is a very real fear for all banks, and especially for traditional ones. The core reasons are that, as we have seen, customers are far from interacting with banks because of the inherent pleasure of doing so, but rather because they need to get access to their money (a secondary degree of usefulness) which can then be spent on products and services provided by retailers (a primary degree of usefulness).

A secondary reason why the fear of disintermediation is so real for banks is that not only do large retailers offer attractive goods and services to customers whose loyalty derives from having obtained such goods in the past and been pleased with them, but in most cases retailers also have better credit ratings. Large and well-established retailers such as major supermarket chains and major high street shopping chains have among the highest credit ratings of any organizations in the countries in which they operate. The possession of such higher credit ratings has important benefits for them on the wholesale money markets, including less expensive access to funds and higher credit ratings for bonds (such as Eurobonds) which they may issue.

Faced with the facts of retailers having large bases of loyal and satisfied customers and enjoying high credit ratings, and with the even more pressing problem that large retailers are adopting an increasingly enterprising attitude towards selling financial services, it is difficult for traditional banks to avoid sliding into a state of panic. Some banks may even feel that their own demise as specialized providers of financial services is inevitable and that they can do little more than wait for this to happen.

However, falling into these ways of thinking is unproductive. Banks need to look on the positive side, and to reflect that as traditional banks they themselves have built up loyal customer bases (albeit customers who have been delivered secondary rather than primary satisfactions) as well as an enormous body of knowledge and expertise in the provision of financial services. These two attributes will not protect them against the full dangers of disintermediation, but will certainly put them in a position where they can compete furiously with retailers.

Certainly, *the time to compete is now.* For banks, the best defence against the challenge of disintermediation is to take steps to maximize one's competitive position now, not wait for it to be eroded. Large retailers with the financial muscle to deal with the inevitable early years during which high profits are usually not obtained, can switch to offering financial services with alarming ease and speed – alarming from the perspective of the traditional bank, that is – and can milk their own customer bases and brands to the full to create a loyal customer base.

This process is greatly facilitated by technology, which allows a direct financial service marketing facility to be set up and also facilitates the identification of customers according to precise parameters, with marketing operations then being readily focused on desirable customers.

Essentially, the fear of disintermediation presents a traditional bank with a basic dilemma: should it spend money and incur risk in developing new areas of activity which may protect it against competition from retailers and other non-financial organizations, or should it devote resources to protecting its existing customer base? The existing base certainly does need to be protected in the race to create new initiatives, but my advice here is to follow the principle that the best form of defence is attack.

Alternatively, take the analogy of the famous board game, Monopoly. In this game, you don't get anywhere by buying a few isolated properties and hoping you won't land on other people's property and incur rental charges. Instead, if you want to win, you need to assemble sets of properties as quickly as you can and build houses and hotels on your own property without delay in order to obtain rental income from other players. There is consequently no easy option, but traditional banks have to go out and deal with the fear of disintermediation by pre-empting it.

How can they do this? We can identify three main options.

■ *Create their own retailer network.* There is absolutely no reason why a bank should not go into the retailing business itself, whether by purchasing an existing operation or by creating its own outlets. This option is not as farfetched as it might initially appear to be: several banks are using branches to display attractive 'primary' benefit products and services such as cars, details of houses, and illustrations of holidays in order to promote loans and mortgages. It is not such a giant step from mounting these displays to go into the business oneself. As we have seen, Barclays Bank has bought up a large car dealership chain and promotes its car loans through this as well as selling cars. Some banks have – with varying degrees of success – purchased their own chains of estate agents and used these chains to promote their mortgages. Generally, most banks have already broadened their activities to offer the widest range of financial services; there is no reason why they should not successfully operate other types of retailer organization, make the organization a profit centre in its own right, and use it to deliver financial services.

■ *Enter joint ventures with existing retailers.* This means liaising with an existing retailer to offer a joint product, with the idea being that the customer gets the best of both worlds, involvement with a retailer who provides primary benefits, and also the secure backing of a long-established bank. For example, in the UK the Abbey National bank and Safeway supermarket chain launched a special Visa card in 1996 which also functions as a loyalty card for Safeway. The card is essentially a debit card connected to a bank account which is set up at the Abbey National via Safeway. It enables customers to obtain cash-back when paying for their shopping, lets them set up standing orders and direct debits, and gives them interest on their funds held in the account. It also bears the logo of the Electron EFTPoS scheme, and can therefore be used to pay for goods at all shops displaying the Electron logo. Ironically, for reasons no doubt best known to Safeway, the supermarket chain did not accept Electron when the Visa card was launched, but did from the start of 1998. Banks are ideally placed to assist retailers with loyalty cards, as the banks have in-depth and lengthy experience of developing financial facilities – such as credit cards, debit cards and shared ATM networks – which the retailer could not necessarily access itself. Another example of such a link-up in the UK is the creation of Sainsbury's Bank, a joint venture between the Sainsbury supermarket chain and the Bank of Scotland. Full details of this joint venture are provided in a case study in Chapter 5.

■ *Move out of offering specialized financial services altogether.* A final option is for the bank to move out of its specialized role of offering only financial services and to create a new organization which operates under a single brand and offers primary benefit retail services as well as financial services. This, in effect, is to beat the retailers at their own game, for what they are doing is moving out of being solely retailers and offering secondary benefit financial services products. No major bank has yet taken this radical step, but there is no reason why one should not at some point. Public perceptions of large organizations are usually easier to change than many senior managers believe. For example, the hugely successful retailer Marks & Spencer was originally solely a clothes shop. It is now also known as a leading vendor of quality food and indeed operates some shops which only sell food. Furthermore, Marks & Spencer is also known as a major vendor of financial services, although to date only via its existing branches and via a direct telephone access service. Generally, banks which want to guard against disintermediation should not be hidebound by notions of how they operated in the past. After all, a large organization – whether retailer, bank or whatever – is essentially in the same position as an individual person seeking to make their mark in the world. Just because someone has had moderate success with one career path does not mean that they cannot achieve even greater success by embarking on another, as the bodybuilder turned movie star Arnold Schwarzenegger, the barrister turned politician Tony Blair, and the schoolteacher turned pop idol Gordon Sumner, alias Sting, would all, presumably, testify.

The banks' need to maximize the depth and breadth of electronic delivery channels

This is where virtual banking comes in. We have already seen in the previous chapter how virtual banking allows a bank to meet a wide range of extremely important commercial objectives.

Most of this book is about the practicalities of how virtual banking manifests itself and specifically how these commercial objectives can be met. At this particular point I will not repeat or anticipate that material but rather point out some fundamental observations about virtual banking.

The first necessary observation is that no virtual banking system will be any use to a bank unless it works properly. This is an obvious enough point, but it's often not accorded enough respect by banks, especially in developed countries where virtual banking services are getting underway.

If customers are to use these services they need to be confident that the service will be available when they want it. For example, a tourist travelling abroad is only going to cut down on the number of traveller's cheques he takes with him if he can be confident that when he is abroad there will not only be an ATM available for him to conduct an international ATM transaction, but also that the ATM will have money in it and will work.

In practice, a virtual banking service must be available around the clock. After all, the whole point of using a virtual banking service is that you can do so at your own convenience time-wise. It must also be available every day of the year. People are as likely to run out of cash on, for example, a Sunday or Christmas Day as they are at any other time. Indeed, they may be more likely to. Few things are more dispiriting and demoralizing to a customer than trying to use an ATM which has no money in it.

Furthermore, the virtual banking service must be error free and accurate. It is certainly a fact that most phantom withdrawals turn out to be due to the customer having totally breached the card-issuing terms by disclosing the PIN to a third party. Additional evidence for this is that most phantom withdrawals take place at ATMs located close to where the customer lives. (If these withdrawals were really taking place because they were spontaneously generated by some fault within the network, it is likely that the transaction would be recorded at any of the bank's ATMs throughout the country or region). Even so, banks must accept that they are under constant pressure to demonstrate that their services are completely reliable and trustworthy and that there is no danger of the customer's account being compromised by some withdrawal or other virtual banking transaction taking place across it which the customer did not, in fact, initiate.

Second, it has to be recognized that the need to focus on virtual banking services is in many respects a relatively new preoccupation for banks. If virtual banking merely required a bank to adopt a new attitude towards technology and to think of technology as a much more dynamic tool than simply some means of automating accounting, the newness of virtual banking would not matter so much. However, the real challenge to a bank arising from virtual banking is not so much a purely technological one (in any case, banks are increasingly tending to outsource much of their technological resources connected with providing a virtual banking service) but rather a challenge to their entire conception of how they manage the relationship with the customer. Not only must they put their customer first and think of him in a new light, but this particular requirement must become central to their entire culture.

Third, the virtual banking revolution tends to require banks to recruit different types of people compared with those who were most suitable for bank work in the past. This is especially true of senior managerial government, but it applies to all staff.

The old days when bankers had above all to be numerically literate and not necessarily particularly skilled in dealing with customers are over. Today, interpersonal skills are extremely important for bankers, given that numeracy will always also be an important factor. Staff recruited to work in branches need to be able to deal with people with ease and also able to demonstrate a genuine interest in the customer's needs and problems.

And what is true of staff recruited at branch level is even more true of senior managers. The days when the senior management of a bank was likely to consist of people who had been working at the bank for 20 or 30 years and who had made their entire careers there are generally past. Many of the most able senior executives of banks today are young people with a highly entrepreneurial attitude to banking. They can certainly read a balance sheet, and in fact have often proved ruthless in adhering to the need for bottom-line profitability, but they have also in many cases shown themselves to be dynamic business people in every sense, with a shrewd understanding of the need to focus on what the bank does best, and to use the resources of the virtual banking revolution to minimize the cost and difficulty of handling routine aspects of retail banking.

The fourth point is that virtual banking clearly forces a bank to think of its branch network in a completely different light. For some banks this may actually mean reducing the number of its branches right away, or otherwise imposing stricter criteria for the volume and profitability of branches if they are to stay viable. It will always involve seeing branches less as locations for routine transactions (although there will always be customers who insist on using a branch for this purpose) but rather as places where customers can be sold more profitable products, such as loans, mortgages, insurance and investment products.

In most developed countries the trend for bank branches increasingly to be used primarily for the sales role has already manifested itself, and the trend will surely accelerate in the future. Anyone walking down the main street of almost any town or city in a developed country will be struck by the number of banks which have their offices there. Streets in the UK are particularly crammed with banks – where, in some cases, it is quite routine for every third or fourth retail outlet to be that of a bank – but this problem is by no means confined to the UK.

To some extent the problem is being slowly solved by the increasing tendency for banks to merge with each other and to take each other over, in which case superfluous branches in a town are likely to be closed. However, the success of direct types of bank which deal with customers via the telephone, without any branch infrastructure at all, makes it likely that in the future banks will be spontaneously closing a large proportion of their branches unless there is a very strong justification for keeping them.

Note, incidentally, that there are even technological solutions which automate as far as feasible the entire concept for visiting a branch. An example of this is the system called Interact, designed by leading management consultancy Andersen Consulting and designed to provide a customer with a reasonable simulation of a visit to a branch. Customers would typically use the system in the lobby of the branch, and thereby benefit from a rapid and compressed branch visit which gives them access to most of the services provided by the branch via the screen, without making them interact with branch personnel. Interact is therefore a time-saver from both the bank's and customers' point of view. Interact can also be delivered via a telephone line to a customer's own PC. Further details of the system are now provided in this case study.

Case Study: The Nationwide Building Society's 'Interact' System

Introduction

The Nationwide is Britain's second largest building society. It is the third largest mortgage lender in the UK and the eighth largest retail financial services organization. Its assets exceed £30 billion, and it has 7.7 million customers and 700 branches. In 1997 there was considerable public speculation that the Nationwide would give up its building society status and elect to take a listing on the Stock Exchange and become a bank. These speculations led to a phenomenal amount of activity by 'carpetbaggers': people who start an account with a building society and thereby become members who may qualify for free shares if the society converts to a bank. However, the Nationwide responded by closing new account entry applications for a while, increasing the deposit thresholds to key accounts permanently, and then announcing a commitment to remain a building society for the foreseeable future, although in the banking industry this can, as experience has shown, be comparatively short.

Nationwide has a history of innovation. For example, in the mid 1990s, it was the first building society in Britain to introduce automated passbook handling systems in its branches. These systems mean that customers can even make cheque withdrawals from their passbooks using the machines sited in the branches; there is no need for them to queue in order to see a human cashier. Nationwide also introduced the first Visa Delta debit card in 1991.

Competition within the retail financial services market is putting increasing pressure on UK building societies to improve not only the levels of products and services sold to their existing customers, but also their ability to retain those existing customers and to win new ones. It is, incidentally, precisely this pressure which is causing some societies to convert to banks, seek stock exchange listings, and thereby broaden their capital base. It must be remembered that many organizations which formerly had nothing to do with financial services, are now major players in this sector themselves. Examples are Marks & Spencer, the food and clothing retailer, and Virgin, the international record and aviation group. Both of these are using their own reputations for trust and quality to move into and gain market share in financial services. Similarly, existing financial services banks are taking advantage of new virtual delivery channels to sell their products and deliver these to new customers.

Despite Nationwide's attempts to redefine its products and inject them with a certain uniqueness, the increasing public perception that all building society products are commodities which are much the same whichever society is supplying them.

Clearly, the big drawback to a society of its products being perceived as commodities is that it is restricted to competing on anything but price, which will generally mean its profit margins are lower than it would like. By way of illustration, Paul Feldman, head of management services at Nationwide, told me:

> Retail financial service companies such as ourselves are having to compete on price and service accessibility far more than they used to. Automation can clearly reduce costs and improve service (24-hour availability, shorter queues) but it risks weakening the quality of the relationships we have with our customers. You must also bear in mind that to succeed, we need to sell our customers high-value products such as investments and mortgages, not just process transactions more efficiently.

How did the Nationwide decide to respond to these pressures? It decided it needed to improve its sales effectiveness by facilitating all of the following:

- Allowing customers to spend time in the branches of Nationwide exploring their financial needs without incurring high costs.

- Establishing a new level of service and trust in terms of the quality of information made available to customers.

- Enabling staff to concentrate on the customer rather than having to remember details of every product or the administration of every product.

- Finding ways to deliver services to customers in places they previously could not reach, while being able to present Nationwide's brand image and product range.

Bernard Simpson, Nationwide's group services director, commented:

> Basically there are too many companies in the financial sector looking for the same customers. We need to differentiate, we need something that sets us apart. So while we had our specific business objectives, we also wanted to obtain them by developing something that would really make a difference.

The solution Nationwide developed was designed by Andersen Consulting – the leading management consultancy and systems house – which developed a prototype of a 'virtual branch' which employs a wide range of multimedia techniques and technologies. The impact of this prototype on Nationwide's senior management and subsequently on customers through market research was enormous. It offered an apparently simple way for customers to understand and explore their financial needs and how these could be satisfied. Beyond that, it offered a vision of how an organization could present itself to its customers in an increasingly virtual world dominated by a wide variety of electronic delivery channels.

Work started in January 1994 to turn the concept into reality. A year later, Nationwide went live with the new system at a pilot branch in the town Eastleigh in Hampshire. The system, now branded as 'Interact' has been installed at a further six branches in and around Southampton, with another installed in Swindon, and three at non-branch locations. Early in 1996, the author was shown Interact by Rob Baldock, an Andersen Consulting partner who played a principal part in designing the new system. Interact is fascinating to use. Essentially it is a virtual reality experience which makes use of the traditional computer screen rather than a virtual reality headset. Note, however, that the screen is much flatter on the table than a typical computer screen. The flatness (in practice, it is at an angle of about 30 degrees) is designed to maximize the facility with which users can touch the screen to activate various elements of its interface.

The presentation of the system is that the user starts by seeing a typical high street and a Nationwide branch pictured on the screen complete with street noise. To enter the branch, they must physically push against the doors on the screen. The doors then open and admit the customer into a virtual branch. Now, the customer faces the entrance lobby of a virtual branch with various elements of the branch – such as the customer lounge, homes and mortgages and savings and current accounts – presented both visually on the screen and with small text descriptions to make it clear what each element represents.

An interesting feature of the screen is that the user is introduced to the branch by a 'receptionist' who is presented in video format so that she looks like a real person rather than a computer image. The receptionist, whose speech is that of a real person rather than a computer-synthesized voice, welcomes them to the branch and gives them an explanation of the different parts of the branch. The user cannot talk to the receptionist – clearly this is a major limitation on the realism of the system, but it is precisely the sort of matter which will be improved in such systems in the future – but can proceed through the branch by touching different areas of the branch. As these areas are clearly labelled, there is not much danger of the customer getting lost.

The system allows users to find out about, experiment with, and apply for Nationwide's products and services. As customers proceed through the system, they can talk to staff at any point in a central call centre, (Nationwide Direct) using a discreet video conferencing link or request quotations or application forms which are printed on the spot. As Rob Baldock explains:

> In my view, the most important element of the Interact system is that customers obtain the sense of being in compete control. The interface is so intuitive, and the touch screen technique so natural, that no one needs any training and customers feel that the system is specially tailored to their own needs.

Figure 2.1. illustrates a typical Interact screen.

FIGURE 2.1 *A representation of the 'welcome' screen of the Interact system*

There is no point pretending that Interact is a kind of substitute for actually talking to branch staff. It is, however, an excellent system for allowing customers to obtain information about the different products and services which Nationwide has available. Because the system is easy to use, and also entertaining, it is reasonable to suppose that customers will enjoy getting access to this information. It is, however, only an extremely limited type of virtual reality system. Like so many banking systems which are billed as offering 'virtual reality', the level of realism is strictly limited. For example, the system does not anticipate more than an extremely limited range of queries and the way in which the customer navigates through the system is rigidly controlled with no real flexibility being available to the customer. Obviously, even the computer technologies of the mid to late 1990s severely restrict the level of realism which virtual reality can offer, but there is, clearly, far more that retail banks can do in order to give their customers an exciting virtual reality experience.

In particular, any sales system or branch simulation system has got to provide for far more queries and problems than even a relatively advanced system such as Interact provides. The system should ideally anticipate not only the most obvious queries which the customer *will probably* have, but also those which customers *might* have. Customers enjoy using systems which anticipate queries because it gives them the confidence that the system is really 'on their side'. Indeed, some of the best software in the world which does offer customers this feeling, is not billed as virtual reality, but does none the less let customers feel that they are interfacing with a sympathetic and helpful system. To take an example from the world of office computer systems, the version of Microsoft Office which runs on Windows 95 embodies a wide range of anticipated queries and a correspondingly high level of help for the user.

It is relevant to mention Microsoft's Windows 95 here, as Interact was built with the first beta version of Windows 95 and was, according to Microsoft, the first and most sophisticated production implementation of that environment. However, it is not realistic to expect Interact to provide the same level of user querying response as a software product like Microsoft Office which cost many millions of dollars to develop.

Based on the initial results of Interact, Nationwide considers that it will, in the future, play a crucial role in delivering the following benefits:

■ increased sales to existing customers;

■ gains in terms of new customers;

■ reduced costs per sale;

■ greater effectiveness in the use of branch staff time;

■ enhanced staff confidence in their ability to help customers to select the right product;

■ improved customer satisfaction, retention, and cross-sell rates.

Major developments in the implementation of Interact

6 February 1995	Interact pilot officially launched at the Nationwide branch in Eastleigh, Hampshire.
24 April 1995	Pilot extended to six further branches in the Southampton area.
19 May 1995	Interact introduced to Swindon branch alongside other technology innovations to create a completely new type of building society branch environment.
27 September 1995	Interact arrives at Victoria Station, the first pilot in a remote location. (Interact currently unavailable at Victoria as the system is being re-sited).
26 October 1995	Interact and other banking services introduced into Chesterfield Royal Hospital for the use of hospital staff, patients, hospital visitors and the general public.
29 February 1996	Interact introduced at Richmond Railway Station. (Videophone and printing facilities not available at Richmond).

February/March 1997   Interact introduced in Guildford, High Wycombe and Luton Branches.

June 1997   Nationwide opens new 'Online Branch' in Guildford. The new branch offers visitors the opportunity to use the Internet, Interact and SelfService machines. It is the first such collection of innovative customer services under one roof in the UK.

To bring the Interact story completely up to date, the Nationwide has currently deployed 32 Interact terminals in its largest branches (defined as largest in terms of throughput of transaction and size of customer account base).

The original idea, that Interact might be deployed at remote locations (e.g. in shopping malls) has been scrapped in favour of this branch deployment, as Interact has been found to be extremely useful as a way of helping customers – especially new customers – familiarize themselves with the services Nationwide offers.

Nationwide expects to have deployed about 50 Interact terminals in its branches by the end of 1998: a figure which appears to indicate steady growth of the Interact idea rather than astounding success. However, the idea behind Interact is probably one which customers have to be educated into liking and using: it is a much more complex proposition than, say, an ATM.

The final point to make about electronic distribution channels is that we should not let ourselves be hidebound by our knowledge of what channels are currently available. The pace of development in this area has been so rapid in the past 10 years that it would be naïve not to anticipate other sweeping changes in the nature of electronic delivery systems.

At present, the most obvious type of delivery system likely to become more prominent in the future is the Internet, which is rapidly becoming not only a major part of individual consciousness but also being used more and more. At the time of writing it is still principally a business resource rather than a personal resource, but this is changing all the time, and there can be little doubt that by the year 2000, Internet use among private individuals will have become so substantial that it will have attained the status of being a major delivery system for banking services. Even now, there is one purely virtual bank which operates across the Internet; details of this are provided in Chapter 5.

As global communications become ever more a part of daily life, a larger proportion of people will be assessing their telephone banking services from their mobile telephones. This is already happening on a widespread basis. Television-delivered services may also become more popular, but in the past the use of the television has suffered as a distribution channel for personalized services by virtue of it being a form of dumb terminal, that is, something which has no onboard processing power. However, the advent of digital television may start to change this and give manufacturers the opportunity to put greater processing power into televisions. If this happens, we may expect to see the television playing a greater role in the distribution of electronic banking services. It is, after all, the electronic service with which the vast majority of people are most familiar.

The banks' need to display increased cost-efficiency

Cost-efficiency has always been something to which banks have paid careful attention, but in the past they have mainly tended to see it as requiring them to take great care about incurring unnecessary expenses in any part of their operations.

This point will be clear to anybody who remembers visiting bank or building society branches before the early 1980s. The branches were notoriously dull and dowdy, the staff often paid the bare union minimum, and the bank often lamentably short on customer facilities. For example, many banks did not have fax machines – which business customers could use to communicate with them – until the late 1980s, and some still don't even today.

Modern approaches towards cost-efficiency are more creative and subtle than this, instead of simply trying to minimize costs throughout the organization, banks have cottoned on to the notion – familiar in all other commercial sectors – that you have to speculate in order to accumulate. In other words, banks know that they are not going to win sophisticated, well-paid career professionals by deploying electronic services which don't work reliably and by having branches full of demoralized staff and grey interiors. Banks are nowadays ready to invest in order to win business.

Even more importantly, banks have become intensely aware of the importance of maximizing the profit they obtain from a customer, and understand that cost-efficiency is not only about minimizing costs generally but also about maximizing profit from a particular customer. Unfortunately, there is a basic problem in so doing, and it affects all banks to some extent. The problem is that banks labour under the difficulty that some customers are far more profitable than others. This is a problem, because in order to ensure that the most profitable customers have access to the necessary facilities, the bank must spend money on facilities which will also be used by less profitable customers.

There is, of course, no reason why a severely unprofitable customer could not be terminated. For example, a customer whose account is continually overdrawn when there is no facility for this available, and who consumes large amounts of staff time, even though his deposits may be small or even non-existent, and who visits the branch frequently to make the most routine and small transactions, is clearly not going to be profitable. The bank or other bank may decide to terminate such a customer; a radical resource which carries with it the danger not only of bad publicity (if the customer complains to the media) but also that the customer is unlikely ever to return to the bank if his or her circumstances improve.

Logically, a bank which is willing to rid itself of unprofitable customers ought to do as much as it can to keep *profitable* customers happy, but too often this doesn't happen. As Rob Farbrother, managing director of UK-based bill payment network, PayPoint, mentioned to me, many banks adopt a clumsy approach to this. He commented: 'They may offer a lapsed profitable customer incentives for returning to the bank, but will not offer a profitable customer who has *not* lapsed similar incentives for staying at the bank'. The parable of the prodigal son, in which the wastrel son who had strayed was praised for returning to the straight and narrow, with the continually loyal son being largely ignored may make sense in religious terms, but doesn't make much sense in today's banking climate. Banks should not simply set up incentives to induce those who have left *and who are desirable customers* to return, they should encourage desirable customers who have not left to want to stay.

Incidentally, just because a customer is a large organization does not mean that it will be a profitable one. Many large organizations are actually close to being completely unprofitable for banks.

The unavoidable hub of the cost question is this: generally, the mathematical proportions here are that for most banks, 20 per cent of their customers will bring between 150 to 180 per cent of overall profits; 20 to 80 per cent of customers will bring about 10 per cent of overall profit, and the remaining 20 per cent of customers will incur overall losses of about 50 per cent.

These are disconcerting figures, whichever way you look at them, and certainly there are few commercial organizations in other sectors which would be in any sense comfortable about them. It is hardly surprising that in the highly competitive financial scenarios of today, new chief executives of banks often seek to make a quick impact in their new jobs by seeing what can be done to terminate large numbers of unprofitable customers. However, as we have noted, there can be drawbacks to this approach.

For most banks, it does make some sense to terminate chronically unprofitable customers, but a more sensible approach – and one less likely to alienate the media and customers – is to take every step to maximize the overall efficiency of the organization and to minimize the cost of handling accounts of customers whose money on deposit is low and who demand a lot of staff time. Very likely banks in the developed world could learn something in this respect from banks in developing countries. For reasons of politics and social responsibility, these can rarely terminate customers. Instead, they have to make large numbers of small deposit accounts profitable. They do this by minimizing the range of facilities available to such persons and to taking every step to induce them to use electronic facilities rather than expensive branch facilities.

Banks in developed countries have a long way to go here, because it is, unfortunately, often the profitable, highly-paid customers who prefer to use electronic facilities due to time constraints, and the less profitable who like to go to their branch for a cosy chat.

What else can banks do to maximize cost-efficiency?

They must certainly remember at all times that the average cost of handling an electronic transaction is currently about 5p, while the cost of handling a branch-based transaction (taking into account the cost of premises, staff costs, training costs and the cost of branch equipment) is about £10. Clearly, by joining a shared facility such as LINK – which provides access to numerous banks to a national network of ATMs, or to a shared EFTPoS system, a bank can maximize the number of terminals available to its customers and thereby encourage them to put the larger number of transactions through the more cost-efficient electronic network. Any steps a bank can take to reduce transaction costs is extremely welcome.

As I have already pointed out, this ability to reduce transaction costs is, in fact, a major reason for banks switching to virtual banking. This subject deserves an entire chapter, and gets it in Chapter 4. In the meantime, the additional point should be made that it is likely in the future banks will outsource an increasing part of their virtual banking resources to some kind of central utility which can handle a wide range of routine banking transactions and take over responsibility for these, thereby allowing the banks to concentrate on their key task of risk management and building customer relations.

Such a third party organization has in fact already been created. It is known as the Integrion Financial Network and was launched in September 1996 by IBM and 15 banks which claim as customers more than half the households in North America. Integrion went live in the second quarter of 1997, and is now underway with a programme of expanding its activities.

The aim of Integrion is to attract new banks to the world of on-line banking. In US terms, on-line banking does not only mean electronic banking but also the processing of transactions which were formerly manual but which can be automated to some extent by electronic means, such as cheque processing and the handling of money transfers. The concept behind Integrion is of an organization which acts as a secure, standardized third-party resource that in effect allows banks to outsource a large proportion of transactions, and provide a facility through which their customers can talk to them. Axiomatic in the creation of Integrion is the use of an industry standard by which banks can communicate. Integrion will also allow participating banks to brand their own on-line products on the screen.

Customers will be able to use Integrion to check their bank balances, write cheques, transfer funds and send e-mail to their banks. The expectation is that in due course, customers will be able to use Integrion to trade securities and obtain stock quotes, gain access to their mutual funds and apply for loans. As far as the subject matter of this book is concerned, we can view Integrion as representing banks' latest efforts to assert themselves in the banking services business and to maintain their competitive edge. The launch of Integrion can therefore be seen not only as a weapon in the battle to become more cost efficient, but also as a powerful resource in the battle against disintermediation.

Historically, the origins of Integrion can be traced to the consternation caused within the financial industry in 1994 when the Microsoft chairman, Bill Gates, declared that banks were 'dinosaurs'. Since then, Gates has, admittedly, tried to dispel the notion that his company will try to steal banks' customers. None the less, one indication that the US financial industry was still smarting from Gates' remark came in a reference to it by Robert Gillespie, president and chief executive of Cleveland-based KeyCorp, at the Integrion launch news conference on September 9, 1996. 'If we are dinosaurs, as some have said . . . I would suggest that today, we're putting our competitors on notice that it's a new breed that is evolving', Gillespie said.

Exhibit 2.1 is Integrion's description of itself. This profile is sufficiently objective and balanced to be useful as an exhibit.

Exhibit 2.1 Profile of Integrion

Integrion Financial Network is a newly formed limited liability company created through an equal partnership of 16 North American banks and the IBM Corporation. Integrion's founders share the following vision:

The financial services industry needs an efficient channel for the processing and delivery of bank-branded electronic financial services. It is imperative that ownership and control of this channel remain within the financial services industry.

The lack of industry standards is impeding development of the market for electronic financial services and is enabling software companies and third-party processors to gain control over the payment system as well as position non-bank brands between banks and their customer bases.

A large-scale collaboration will create the critical mass to speed development of open standards, provide economies of scale and counter the encroachment of non-banks into the payment system.

Integrion, through the Interactive Services Platform, offers banks a network through which electronic transactions flow from multiple consumer access points to the banks host systems and/or processors. The Integrion owners, who collectively provide services to over 60 million US households, are committed to creating an open platform with standards available to any and all providers. Equally important, the owners have made a commitment to provide access to Integrion to all banks on an equal basis. Banks which are not owners of Integrion will receive the same services, pricing levels and support as will owner banks.

Integrion is a complete electronic delivery solution, providing four key elements:

First, an efficient core processing foundation to spread the operations and development cost and share the scale benefits across the Integrion bank customer base. Through its transaction delivery manager, Integrion will cost-effectively move message and transaction requests between banks and their end-user customers. The core processing platform is designed to be manageable and support rapid growth of the market. It provides the transaction logging, error recovery and authentication services to assure reliable and secure movement of financial information and transactions. All information movement associated with the Integrion core processing platform uses the 'Gold' standard message structure developed by Integrion.

Second, flexible client connectivity and third, simplified bank connectivity to share development costs, attract developers, and enable a high degree of customization by individual banks. Through the development of the Gold end-to-end standard message structure, Integrion has greatly simplified connectivity issues at the client-side and back-end.

Fourth, market-driven applications will reside within Integrion allowing its bank customers to share development and operating costs for these applications. Under development today are core banking account support (deposit and loan account information), core transaction support enquiries, transfers, updates) and bill payment and presentment applications.

Establishing 'Gold' as the Industry Standard

Integrion has taken a leadership position in establishing a standard in the handling of financial transactions across the electronic channels. Integrion and each of its owner banks are fully committed to the Gold standard. Representing more than 60+ million of the retail banking customers. This support brings to the Gold standard a critical mass to assure its viability. However, Integrion is supportive of Gold gaining acceptance beyond its owner base and becoming an industry standard.

Finally, Integrion recognizes that any industry standard must evolve as the market matures and needs of consumers and banks change. Integrion intends to be open and inclusive in maintenance of the Gold standard, while retaining a business perspective to assure management of the standard is not slowed by a cumbersome committee structure. Accompanying the publication of the Gold standard will be a process for review and input on the Gold standard documentation.

(Source: Integrion Financial Network)

The banks' need to obtain a comprehensive view of their overall risk exposures

No bank can make money without taking on board a level of risk. This point is more true now – in today's highly competitive financial industry – than it ever has been in the past.

Furthermore, it make sense that the ideal customer for the more profitable products a bank is offering – that is, loans, mortgages and credit card facilities – is someone who can afford to make repayments on time but who is not so well-off that they don't need the facility in the first place. It follows logically from this that managing exposures to these kinds of customers is always going to be a difficult matter, as their finances will inevitably embody some element of precariousness compared to someone sufficiently wealthy not to need the facility. On the whole, customers tend to be more optimistic about their personal financial prospects than is warranted; they usually reckon positive future developments into the equation (such as receiving a salary rise) and discount negative developments (such as a health problem) which are in fact often as likely to happen.

For a bank, managing credit risk is an essential part of successful operation, but banks are increasingly coming to understand that a principal commercial challenge facing them is the need to obtain a comprehensive and, as far as possible, integrated view of *all* their risk exposures. Clearly, they can't do this unless they first know what these exposures actually are. Table 2.1 provides a comprehensive listing of all the main types of risk facing a bank.

The challenge of knowing about risk exposures on a comprehensive basis is a major commercial challenge, and one that is by no means easy to solve. As will be clear from Table 2.1, the variety of elements of risk that must be dealt with is vast. Simply obtaining the basic information to make reliable risk assessments is far from easy.

Modern technological tools help to some degree in this process. There are many packages now available which use a range of extremely ingenious mathematical formulae (usually known in this context as algorithms) that give a bank the opportunity to obtain a surprisingly good handle on risk management. An excellent journal which provides more information about these subjects is the UK magazine *Risk*.

However, it will be clear from the extensive range of risk issues listed in Table 2.1 that many of these issues do not readily yield themselves to mathematical analysis. This is either because the tools for such an analysis are simply not available, or because the data which would need to be input into the equations is simply too complex to be quantifiable in purely mathematical terms.

Where some reliable assessment can be made of risk factors, there is an increasing tendency for banks to use packaged or custom-built software to integrate these risk findings into a comprehensive picture of risk throughout the organization. A full discussion of this is beyond the scope of this report, but readers may, again, wish to peruse the magazine *Risk*, which regularly has information about software and systems available for this purpose.

TABLE 2.1 *Main types of risk facing a bank*

External risk	environmental risk	compliance
		contamination
		employment theft
		public health
	country risk	civil disorder
		economic shock
		expropriation
		natural disaster
	fiscal risk	change of government
		corporate tax rate change
		sales tax change
	government risk	consumer demand
		effect of government change
		inflation
		anti business ethos
	litigation risk	product liability
		safety
		side effects
	regulatory risk	capital adequacy
		competition policy
		tariff barriers
		expropriation
		parallel imports
		reference pricing
		trade policy
	security risk	intellectual property theft
		physical property theft
		sabotage
Fund management risk	dealing risk	market information
		inappropriate internal information
		market collapse
		personnel
		rogue dealing
		unit selling branch
	processing risk	collusion
		dealing error
		fraud
		input/output error
	statutory risk	financial regulation
		legal entity
		taxation treaties

	trading risk	documentation
		execution accuracy
		product complexity
		settlement
		valuation methodology
Infrastructure risk	human resource risk	lack of staff
		quality of staff
		strike action
		lack of training
		succession planning
	organizational risk	objectives
		policies
		alliances
		market image
		authority limits
		audit
		sales force profile
	planning risk	accuracy of situation appraisal
		incorrect budgeting
		poor quality of data
		forecasting inaccuracies
	reporting risk	accounting policies
		data flow
		complex management hierarchy
	systems risk	inadequate performance
		alignment to business strategy
		availability of systems
		data integrity
		disaster planning
		programming quality
		project management
		security of network
		systems availability
		telecommunications
		verified algorithms
Liquidity risk	cash flow risk	business interruption
		customer confidence
		forecasting quality
		access to finance
	counterparty risk	default risk (credit risk)
		financial performance of counterparty

		credit rating
		bank confidence
		liquidity
		supplier confidence
	rating risk	market confidence
		market sector re-rating
		shareholder risk
Operational risk	logistics risk	delivery mechanism
		global distribution
		handling of shortages
	procurement risk	alternative source identification
		quality of parts
		stock shortages
		supplier profile
	production risk	cost
		make versus buy
		process problems
		quality reviews
		technology
Position (market) risk	currency risk	non-convertibility of currency
		economic factors
		transaction risk
		translation risk
		basis risk
		mismatches
		volatility
	interest rate risk	basis risk
		parallel yield curve shifts
		twists in yield curve
		movement and direction
		yield curve construction
		incorrect day count basis
Proposition risk	competitive risk	competitor product action
		inferior product
		product imitation
		patent expiry
	economic risk	client pricing
		competitor pricing
		market share
		market developments
		product expiry

strategy risk	business portfolio
	communication
	development methodology
	efficiency
	human resource profile
	initial pricing
	lack of competitor knowledge
	poor marketing strategy
	poor market identification
	reputation
	research focus
	tracking against plan

Source: IBM

Risk management is always going to be a major commercial problem for a bank, and the broader the range of the bank's activities the more complex the problem. However, a bank which at least recognizes this problem as a major commercial challenge, and which is constantly striving to get better risk-related information, is certainly taking two important steps to move towards finding a solution for this problem, insofar as this is possible.

The challenge of the single European currency

European Monetary Union (EMU) is an important challenge for all banks, and the challenge is extremely pressing. Whether or not the country in which a bank operates will be part of EMU from the outset, at a later stage, or not at all, the institution still needs to make provision for the introduction of the Euro. The EMU challenge implies a need both to create a facility which will deal with the new currency and also to ensure that the possibility of returning to the traditional national currency is retained. The prospects for EMU and the effect it will have on national economies is, to say the least, unclear. Some commentators believe there to be a real danger that EMU will not work as planned and that countries will be forced to return to their national currencies at some point in the future, whether or not on a permanent basis. Against this is the obvious commonsense argument that EMU makes sense from a logical perspective and will surely happen eventually anyway.

The Year 2000 problem

The computing and administrative problems caused by the imminent switch to a new millennium have been greatly hyped in the media but this doesn't mean that they aren't important. No doubt some of the computing implications have been exaggerated, but the fact remains that there is abundant evidence to believe that the majority of computer systems used by banks today – including some famous operating systems which are used as a standard throughout the world – are unlikely to be able to be able to cope with the fact that the two digits at the end of the numbers for the years of the new century can in fact be years subsequent to 1999.

The reason for the existence of this problem is that when, about 20 years ago, the numbering protocols for today's computer systems were standardized, computer memory was extremely expensive. As a result, computers were programmed to identify a year simply by looking at the last two digits of it, rather than by looking at the whole year in its entirety. Dealing with the Millennium problem is – at least in theory – easy enough; it simply requires the computer to be programmed to look at the entire number of the year rather than just the last two digits. However, in practice matters are rather more complex than that. The job now facing institutions – and other large organizations – is a major one, because the mainframe and mini computer systems they are currently using, and which have to be viewed conceptually as 'legacy systems', are all programmed in the old manner.

The Millennium problem is, in fact, already an issue for banks because millions of bank cards are already available which expire in the year 2000. Unfortunately, many of these cannot be used automatically in an electronic system but must have details keyed in manually.

This being so, makes sense to end this chapter with an analysis of how to approach the challenge of solving the EMU *and* Millennium challenges. This case study has been provided by Terry Bourne, chairman of leading UK financial systems house Total Systems plc.

Case study: Mastering the Challenges of Year 2000 and the Euro

Unless you've spent the past few years on an ice-floe somewhere, or exploring the rain forest, you'll know that many financial organizations use computer systems which can't deal with the year 2000. After all, national newspapers and the financial trade press have for many months been stuffed full of features about what is frequently known as the 'Millennium Problem'.

Does this mean there is nothing else to be said about the matter? No. Indeed, I even think a great deal of published coverage of the problem has actually been *unhelpful*.

For one thing, the coverage tends to belong to the school of journalism which might be described as 'horror for horror's sake', in other words, it sets out to frighten and even shock the reader rather than provide much in the way of helpful advice.

Second, what's been written so far usually focuses attention on the Millennium Problem rather than the problem of the Euro, which in reality is equally important, especially for financial organizations, which are so heavily involved in cross-border investment involving Continental Europe.

Here, I want to adopt a sober and objective approach to both the Millennium and Euro problems, and demonstrate not only how they can be solved, but that these problems can be transformed into important opportunities.

One term that needs defining at this stage is the *legacy system*. Often the definition of what is and isn't a legacy system depends on who you're asking. I prefer to define the term specifically, as

> any computer system which has been inherited from an earlier generation of technology, and especially a computer system which does not feature Year 2000 and Euro functionality.

Defining a legacy system from a functional standpoint has the advantage that the definition focuses on what needs to be done to make the systems suitable for the current business environment, and how solving these problems should be made to fit in with a financial organization's strategic business plan.

Not that you really have much choice about the matter. The simple fact is that after 1 January 1999 you're going to need Euro functionality if you want to stay in business. Similarly, after January 1 2000 you're going to need Year 2000 compliance. Ideally, you'll have both these already. The matter really is as simple as that.

Even if you're running packages, you can't assume your packages will contain these functionalities as a matter of course. Many do, and it's fair to say that over the past year vendors have been working very hard to produce new versions of existing packages which do fit the bill from the Millennium and Euro standpoint, or else supplying customers with enhancements that can be connected to existing software. Even so, if you're running a package, you need to be very tough indeed with the vendor and insist that Year 2000 and Euro functionality are either added to the package within the shortest possible time-frame, or that you are given – or can buy for a reasonable price – a new version of the package before long which does indeed contain the requisite functionalities.

Moving on now to address the problem of an in-house system which doesn't contain the requisite functionalities, this is, clearly, a much more complex issue.

As always in business, it's important to start out by focusing on where you want to arrive. In this case, you want to end up with a computer system which contains the Millennium and Euro functionalities you need but which goes beyond that and becomes a powerful tool for the development of your organization in the future. Generally, the features of your new computer system – we'll leave for the moment the question of whether this should be a completely new system or a modification of your existing one – should, as a minimum, include all of the following:

■ Facilitates maximum speed of product development and maximum speed to market of new products. This means that the system helps with the design of new products, including all relevant parameters, and is able to adapt to include the new product in all its accounting and administrative functions.

■ Can handle the crucial year 2000 and years beyond this.

■ Contains an in-built multi-currency facility and is able to adapt to the Euro.

■ The system must be easy for end-users to operate.

Note that I am only proposing these as a minimum: you may want to include other features that you regard as crucial for your future success.

The next step is *not* to plunge ahead with working out how you can translate your objectives into technology that works accurately and reliably, but rather to use this crucially important time when you are planning your upgrade from a legacy system as an opportunity to analyse and think about your entire way of doing business. This part of the methodology is known as re-engineering. I certainly think there is no sense whatsoever in a financial organization of any kind making modifications to its current legacy system or enhancing this system without first turning to the challenge of examining its current business activity to try to identify ways in which its activity can be made more efficient, cost-effective and more likely to result in the creation and marketing of products – and services, where applicable – which are attractive to your customers.

Once you are satisfied with your efforts in the re-engineering direction, it is time to look at the general options for operating a legacy system.

There are basically three options, as follows:

1   To upgrade your existing software but keep that software in place (given that it's been upgraded) and keep it running on the same hardware as before.

2   To add desired new functionality to your current system by connecting it to new applications, with these applications being designed in-house or bought in as packages.

3   To dispose of your current legacy system and replace it with something else entirely.

Option 1: Upgrading existing software

. . . .

In practical terms, this particular option is more of an emergency measure than a reliable long-term solution. It does solve the basic problems of a lack of Year 2000 and Euro functionality, or at least it should do, but it's unlikely to provide much in the way of additional functionality to provide a competitive edge. As such, it delays the need to provide a more radical solution to the legacy system problem rather than removes it.

The option involves rewriting or modifying existing software in order to provide Year 2000 and Euro functionality.

Option 2: Adding new functionality

. . . .

This is a kind of intermediate solution between the emergency measure of rewriting or modifying existing software and the most radical measure of all of replacing the current legacy system entirely. Even though this option *is* an intermediate measure, it is often popular, because it has the big advantage of allowing the additional functionality to be added while keeping the current system intact and allowing it to get on with the company's day-to-day activity.

Option 3: Replacing the current legacy system entirely

. . . .

In this case what is happening is that the legacy system is being thrown out completely and the new system is replacing it.

Legacy systems contain data which is almost invariably both good and bad data: that is, it is typically a combination of useful data stored in a useful format, useful data stored in an outdated format and data which is obsolete in some way. The latter type of data should be distinguished from archive data which may be obsolete but which you still wish to retain, so that, for example, you can handle a contract, transaction or security initiated some time ago.

An important task of the migration process when a package or bespoke new system is being used is only to migrate *quality* data, which means useful and accurate data that you are likely to need again in the future.

How do you make the migration process happen?

Clearly, you need to draw up a detailed, systematic and methodical project plan with realistic time-frames and budgets. In most cases it's also best to face the need for bringing in some external technical assistance with the process of migration. It's very important to devote care and thought to selecting that technical assistance, because decisions made now in relation to the computer system will have an impact on the business for at least a decade and probably longer.

I do, however, think that financial organizations need to keep firmly in mind that they should retain control of the project management process and to maintain all external parties on a tight leash. That way, they can oversee the whole thing from start to finish and minimize the danger of being involved in cost and time overruns. In few other areas of the financial sector is careful central control so important as in the project management of the migration of an obsolete legacy system to a truly powerful modern computer system which, all being well, will be winning a competitive edge for you for many years to come.

(Source: Total Systems plc)

The origins and competitive implications of the virtual banking revolution

Introduction

The virtual banking revolution has come about because banks wanted to provide virtual banking facilities and customers were happy to use them.

This chapter looks at how the virtual banking revolution originated, and details how banks need to respond to it in order to stay ahead of their competition.

Early history of banking

The virtual banking revolution is an extremely recent development in banking compared with the entire history of banking. Even so, we can better understand what prompted virtual banking to originate – and why virtual delivery systems are so important for the banking industry as a whole – if we start by taking a brief look at how banking evolved in the first place.

It is difficult to believe that banking can be anything other than of ancient origin, although little is, in fact, known about it prior to the thirteenth century. Many of the early 'banks' – whose activities are to some extent detailed in medieval writings – carried on a form of business that had presumably been in existence since classical times: dealing in coin and bullion, changing money between different currencies, and supplying foreign and domestic coin of the correct weight and fineness.

Another important early group of banking services was provided by the merchant bankers, who dealt both in goods and in bills of exchange: providing for the remittance of money and payments of accounts at a distance but without shipping actual coin. The business arose from the fact that many of these merchants traded internationally and held assets at different points along trade routes. The merchant bank has of course survived until today: normally denoting a bank which provides financing for large companies and which is usually heavily involved with bringing companies to the stock market and with trading various types of securities.

The origins of modern banking can be traced to the sixteenth century, when European goldsmiths – who had long offered a service providing safe custody of their customers' valuables – started to allow customers to make payments to third parties by giving the customers transferable notes of title to gold which the goldsmith was holding. The customer would give the note to the third party, who could either then present it to the goldsmith and receive gold in exchange, or else – which was more usual – use the note to pay *another* third party.

The precise moment when an individual goldsmith became a primitive bank by the simple expedient of devoting more time to issuing notes than to traditional goldsmithing activities is, obviously, difficult to ascertain. What is clear is that by the seventeenth century, many goldsmiths spent all their time on banking activities.

Indeed, London bankers had by that point developed a system featuring most of the essentials of modern banking. They issued notes of title, dealt in foreign exchange, paid interest to attract coin deposits and – discovering that only a fraction of depositors would demand their cash at any one time, given confidence in the bank prevailed – they loaned the balance at interest.

Banking in the eighteenth and nineteenth centuries

Banking did not change significantly throughout the eighteenth and nineteenth centuries, other than that individual banks became larger, built up significant asset bases, and started to become much more involved in international activity. They were ultra-formal, even pompous organizations which operated according to rules and procedures as strict and regimented as those applying in the military. Banking procedures, like those in nineteenth-century commerce, were applied with an almost religious reverence.

For example, the Swiss industrialist Johan Konrad Fischer recalls in his diary a visit to the branch of a London bank in the summer of 1851. The entry describes a place of meticulous formality.

> When I returned to the bank a little before nine o'clock I was shown to a seat facing a counter where five cashiers conducted their business. At five minutes to nine the official to whom I had to give my cheque took his place behind the counter. I had it in my hand and showed it to him. He did not say a word but emptied several little bags of gold coins into a drawer. Then he produced the well-known little cash shovel that is used for coins in banks. And then he just waited. At the stroke of nine he asked me if I wanted gold or banknotes. I said I wanted gold. He did not count any of the sovereigns and half-sovereigns but simply weighed them on his scales and then put them on the counter without taking any further notice of me . . .

Banks operated with this type of customer service culture for a surprisingly long time. They operate like this today in developing countries, and even did so in developed countries until the 1950s and early 1960s. Thereafter, however, two things started to happen which dramatically changed how banking worked.

Why things changed

The first change was the development of more egalitarian social structures. In this situation, having a bank account came to no longer be seen as the exclusive privilege of the upper middle classes or the very wealthy. People from all walks of life saw the advantages of owning a bank account and wanted one.

It is true that a significant proportion of people in developed countries do not have a bank account (even today, in most developed countries, including the United Kingdom, the unbanked proportion is between about 15 and 20 per cent of the entire population) but generally the benefits of keeping one's money safe and being paid interest on the surplus above what is necessary for day-to-day living, are seen as so enormous that the majority of people want to enjoy them.

These changes in social structures arose from a variety of factors, not the least of which was the more widespread use of technology throughout industry and commerce. This tended to remove many of the formerly completely unskilled jobs in society and required more skills and education from the working population. This in turn lead to children staying at school longer and to the overall level of education rising. Not surprisingly, better-educated people were less willing to accept inferior positions in society and saw no reason why they should not enjoy what more prosperous classes could enjoy.

Another important factor was the increase in importance of the media. This gave people a greater knowledge of society as a whole and of the opportunities within it. Furthermore, governments were elected on a mandate to create fairer societies with opportunities for all. Even right-wing governments helped to speed their countries towards a more egalitarian framework because they operated according to a strict philosophy that merit should be rewarded, although it is certainly true that their policies generally did little to help the poor.

The importance of technology throughout commerce and industry was certainly a factor in social change generally, but in the banking industry, banking technology was the second reason for the great changes that have come over banks in, the last 30 years or so.

Until the 1950s, banking even in developed countries was an almost entirely manual process. Some calculating devices were used – even today, visitors to Japanese banks will be surprised to see how important the abacus is as an aid to calculation – but generally all aspects of account keeping were carried out manually. The enormous expenditure of labour on this task almost defies belief, for any mistake in calculations could, clearly, involve the bank in loss or even a compromise of its legal position, and calculations had to be rigorously checked.

Not surprisingly, computers were implemented in banking almost as soon as they were developed: indeed, it has always been the case that the banking and financial sector is the commercial sector which is the most hungry for new technology. It is second only to military applications in this respect.

The origins of virtual banking

Computers started to be implemented in the banking sectors of the developed world in the 1950s and early 1960s. From the outset, they played an essential role in automating formerly manual calculations and processes. The banking technology industry has moved on so far from those early days that it is easy to forget how exciting these first applications were. The case study below reminds us of this early excitement.

Case Study: The Bank of America's cheque-processing system

In the 1950s, the Bank of America, headquartered in San Francisco, was the largest bank in the world. By the middle of the decade it was processing 12 million cheques every day. Sorting and recording these cheques – a low-status job mostly done in those antediluvian days by female high-school graduates – was extremely tedious. Cheques had no numbers, only signatures, and were filed alphabetically. The work was so dull that, on average, a girl stayed only nine months. Naturally enough, because the work was boring, mistakes were common.

Quite apart from wishing to do something about the problem of staff turnover, the Bank of America wished, for purely business reasons, to expand the volume of personal checking accounts it handled. It was aware that in order to do this it would need to automate its cheque processing resources, otherwise – as the Bank estimated – within five years or so it would have to hire one third of all high-school graduates in California just to sort cheques. For the Bank of America, the computer turned out to be the answer to its prayers.

The Bank decided to hire the Stanford Research Institute as a consultant. The Institute helped the Bank of America to devise what the Institute called the Electronic Recording Method of Accounting (ERMA). With EMRA, account numbers discreetly placed on each cheque were printed in magnetic ink which could be read and sorted by machine.

The first EMRA system was completed in 1959 by General Electric. It was launched by a popular movie star called Ronald Reagan – later to achieve greater fame in a somewhat different guise. Announcing EMRA's debut, the future President said:

> This is Los Angeles and I'm Ronald Reagan . . . A competent experienced book-keeper using conventional mechanical equipment is expected to do the cheque sorting and account updating for about 250 accounts an hour. EMRA can handle the work for 500 accounts a minute.

Automated cheque sorting was a tremendous success. By 1967, eight years after EMRA's launch, 95 per cent of all banks in the United States made use of computers to handle the routine processes connected with their checking accounts. In 1961, the Bank of America stopped hiring book-keepers; EMRA had replaced 2332 of them.

Such statistics alarmed people, promoting a national debate about the impact of computers on society. No amount of debate, though, could detract from the fundamental point that computers could be used to process routine transactions with immense speed and accuracy, and were far better than people for doing this. There was to be no escape from the knowledge that computers were the way ahead; for the military, for banks, and for millions of other users across a range of commercial and industrial sectors.

One person at least had the right idea of how to calm the public's fears about computers. Tom Watson Jr, who had committed IBM's future to the computer – the paragon of automation – tried to calm the public's fears: 'A lot of people are calling these machines giant brains,' he said. 'When I hear the term I shudder, because these machines are giant tools, not giant brains. If you install giant tools you are actually upgrading men, not downgrading them.'

The automations whose origins are traced in the case study continued throughout the 1960s and the 1970s, but by about the middle of the 1970s the nature of the automation started to change, with this change being spearheaded in the United States.

By the mid-1970s, if not a little earlier, computers had to a large extent already been implemented in banks to about their fullest extent: at least as far as their use as tools to automate what would otherwise have been manual calculations and manual processes. The use of computers as tools to automate a bank's accounting systems and day-to-day banking activity processes was close to complete, given that future improvements in hardware would of course always be used to replace less powerful devices.

The next development was that it gradually dawned on some bankers – especially those in high-population density areas of the United States – that using computers as tools for accounting was only one way to use them.

These bankers saw that there was another, completely new and potentially extremely exciting, set of applications. These applications related to the use of computers to expand and improve customer service in a very direct sense.

Of course, the bankers were not being entirely altruistic in making this conceptual breakthrough. They saw that the need to provide a resource to customers for routine banking transactions was both costly and time consuming. Anything which could reduce the burden of this obligation would, surely, be an extremely important innovation.

There is no obvious evidence to suggest that bankers had at this stage a grand vision of a virtual banking revolution where technology was exploited to the full to give customers automated facilities for obtaining access to cash, account information and payments services. Instead, the virtual banking revolution gathered momentum relatively slowly, with new applications being launched tentatively by far-sighted but none the less cautious bankers.

The first such application was the cash machine, later to be known as the automated teller machine (ATM). This could offer the enormous advantage that it could provide customers with cash withdrawal facilities outside branches in a physical and also temporal sense. That is, the machines could be located in the walls of a branch rather than in the lobby and could also be made available for business at times when the bank was itself not open.

Indeed, some of the early cash machines were actually only available for business outside branch hours and were closed whenever branches were open. However, the obvious advantages of providing customers with cash withdrawal facilities, even when the branch *was* open soon led to cash machines being available both during the day and into the evenings. However, at first the machines were not open around the clock – partly for technical reasons (round-the-clock computing was not yet a widely accepted concept), and also for security reasons.

Initially banks only made the cash machines available to their best and wealthiest customers. Ironically, these people usually occupied professional positions which gave them opportunities to visit the bank branches during the day, either because they could to some extent choose their own working hours, or because they tended to work near the city centre, or for a combination of these factors.

Blue-collar workers who had neither of these privileges were precisely the people who most needed cash machines because they could not visit their branches during the day. Fortunately, after a relatively short period, the importance of making cash machines available to all a bank's customers was understood and became the norm. Similarly, the importance of ensuring that cash machines were open for the maximum period was also recognized.

The cash machine was not an instant success; people needed to get used to the idea. However, once they had, the cash machine rapidly became an essential part of the customer service armoury of any bank with any serious aspirations to provide retail services to a wide range of customers.

Naturally, the opportunity to deliver these services via a cash machine assisted and reinforced a bank's inclination to offer banking facilities to the widest range of retail customers. By the mid 1970s, the cash machine was well-established in the United States. The idea had already started to spread to other developed countries, and by the end of the 1970s was well-established in most of the world's developed banking industries.

The great success of cash machines inspired banks to look at other forms of electronic banking service. Banks started to realize that installing dedicated teller machines *inside* their branches could dramatically reduce the volume of routine banking transactions carried out even by people who weren't inclined to use a through-the-wall ATM.

Furthermore, the use of bank cards accelerated dramatically in the 1970s and 1980s, as both banks and retailers saw the advantages of speed and security of transaction which bank cards offered. Bank card transactions tended to increase at the expense of cheque transactions, which were always slow and potentially risky for retailers, who would have to bear the burden of bad cheques or cheques which were not properly processed.

As well as this, bank card transactions carried the huge advantage that they reduced the amount of cash a retailer would have to handle. People who do not work in the retail business often fail to understand just how troublesome cash is for a retailer. It is an obvious security risk, as well as being time consuming to handle and count, and the retailer's bank always charges a comparatively high fee for processing it.

In this book, the principal types of virtual banking service – ATMs, EFTPoS and remote banking – are all given their own chapters. I also devote a chapter to the smart card or chip card. While this is not, strictly speaking, a virtual banking service, it features so many exciting opportunities to develop state-of-the-art virtual banking services that it seems to me to deserve a chapter to itself.

Even though these different elements of the virtual banking revolution are considered separately, it is useful here to provide a summarized overview of the main types of virtual financial services.

Principal types of virtual financial services

Automated teller machines (ATMs)

ATMs are automatic machines for dispensing certain banking services to customers. The services most commonly delivered are as follows:

■ cash withdrawals;

■ 'fastcash': this is a rapid cash withdrawal facility permitting the customer to select one of several pre-programmed accounts;

■ details of most recent balance of account;

■ 'mini-statement', i.e. a statement showing the most recent transactions to have passed through the account;

■ statement ordering facility;

■ deposit facility (but where the ATM is being shared with another bank, the deposit facility is usually only available to users whose accounts are with the bank operating the ATM in question);

■ payments to third parties (which will typically be such organizations as utility companies, large retailers where the cardholder has a current account, and so on).

ATM networks

A bank's ATM resources will usually consist of a number of ATMs linked to a host computer which – generally in real-time (i.e. instantaneously) – authorizes transactions and relays details of the completed transaction to the customer's account. The precise number of ATMs operated by a bank varies widely. A small bank with a customer base restricted to one town may install no more than half a dozen ATMs. A large bank, however, with a dominant position nationwide may wish to install several thousand ATMs.

Shared ATM networks

An unavoidable fact about ATMs is that they are relatively expensive to buy and install. The cost of deploying them varies with the number deployed at any one time, but is unlikely to be much below £30,000 sterling or the equivalent per ATM. Banks will inevitably be engaged in a constant struggle, from the outset, to profit from their capital expenditure on ATMs by using the machines to win more business and more revenue, which means attracting more customers.

Clearly, the capital expenditure of deploying even a modest-sized ATM network is such that banks have every incentive to reduce it significantly by sharing the cost with other banks. This practice has been pursued with enthusiasm by banks ever since ATMs started to be popular in the mid to late-1970s. Quite apart from the cost advantages, there are other significant benefits of participating in a shared ATM network; and in other consortia organizations – including those which brand plastic cards. These additional advantages are discussed below.

Electronic funds transfer at point of sale (EFTPoS)

EFTPoS is an electronic payment method involving goods and services being paid for at the point of sale through electronic debit of the customer's account. The formal term EFTPoS is often replaced by 'debit card system' – note, however, that credit card transactions are also increasingly authorized and enacted via EFTPoS.

The transaction is usually initiated through one of two methods:

■ The EFTPoS card is swiped through a card-reading device to 'capture' the transaction, which is first authorized by means of a PIN being keyed into a hand-held pad by the customer.

■ The authorization and transaction capture processes take place electronically but the transaction is confirmed manually, by means of the customer signing a paper voucher. Note that in this case, the funds are not debited electronically and the transaction is not, therefore, strictly speaking true EFTPoS. It is, however, routinely seen as such.

In the long term – which for the purposes of this discussion can be regarded as by around the year 2005 – it is likely that all EFTPoS terminals in developed countries will use real-time means to:

■ Verify cards (i.e. to check that the card has not been lost or stolen).

■ Check that sufficient funds are available in the customer's account, or that the existing credit line extended to the customer is in order.

■ Authorize the transaction by ensuring that the PIN is the correct one for the customer in question. Note that the information relating a PIN to a particular customer (or, more accurately, the numerous customers who have the same PIN) is held in fully 'end-to-end' encrypted form in the computer system, which means that the encryption is total throughout and that no user – even one employed by the bank in question – could see which PIN goes with which customer.

■ Capture details of transactions.

Types of EFTPoS debit

There are usually four different ways in which the debit can be made:

■ Real-time (i.e. instantaneously) against a current or savings account, using a debit card.

■ Debit after the usual clearing period (e.g. three days in the UK) against a current or savings account, using debit cards.

■ Real-time debit against a credit account, using credit cards.

■ Debit after the usual clearing period against a credit account, using credit cards.

Remote banking

Many industry sources call remote banking 'home banking' but research has shown clearly that customers are, in fact, about equally likely to access their banking facility from the telephones where they are working than from those at home. One of the most reliable examples of research into this matter comes from the highly successful remote bank First Direct, which says that about 50 *per cent* of phone calls it receives are made during conventional office hours.

In a remote banking interaction, the interface between customer and bank usually involves some kind of automated voice-response system that may be activated either by the customer's own voice or by the customer keying in various numbers on a touch-tone phone. There are, however, other alternatives, namely:

■ Interactive television, which allows the customer to obtain the requisite information on the television screen and instruct the television to display a particular page of information.

■ An Internet terminal. Internet is the interactive, global, shared computer-based information service. It is ideally suited to providing customers with a remote banking service, although the Internet will only be able to do this widely and reliably when there is a foolproof method of displaying a screen containing personal information, without letting any non bona fide person view it.

■ Screen phone: this is a dedicated computer terminal which connects to the bank's computer in real-time and allows information passed to the screen phone to be displayed on the screen. (Note that the screen phone is not the same as the video phone, which lets users view whoever is on the other end of the line.)

■ Personal digital assistant (PDA): this is a hand-held computer which gives the user access to a wide range of functions. If the PDA is connected by radio waves or cellular technology to the user's desktop terminal, then the user should be able to get personal banking information displayed on the PDA.

■ Other people provide the information. This simple solution to the challenge of managing the customer/bank interface for the remote banking arrangement has been used with great success by First Direct, the UK's first virtual bank: a case study of which appears in Chapter 5.

A remote banking service generally offers customers the following facilities:

■ balance enquiry;

■ statement ordering;

■ funds transfer (payment) to third parties;

■ funds transfer between customers' different accounts;

■ ordering traveller's cheques and other financial instruments, which can subsequently be collected from a branch of the bank in question.

Despite the immense usefulness of remote banking services, it is important to bear in mind that the very nature of the service means that certain functions are never likely to be capable of being offered by these means. These functions are:

■ cash withdrawal;

■ cash/cheque deposit;

■ sale of the more complex types of financial services such as life assurance, mortgages and pensions.

Smart cards

These are bank cards which instead of (or in addition to) containing a magnetic stripe on which some information can be stored, also contain a silicon microchip. An alternative term for the smart card is the chip card, although the former term is more appropriate as it emphasizes the *function* rather than the *technology* and it is therefore the preferred term in this book.

The enormous potential of the smart card stems from the chip it contains, which allows far more extensive personal customer-related information to be contained than can be held on a magnetic stripe. The chip also has the great advantage from the security perspective that the information it contains cannot be copied, whereas the information on a magnetic stripe can be.

With one important exception, the smart card cannot, strictly speaking, be said to amount to a virtual financial service itself. Rather, it offers banks the opportunity to enhance greatly and develop the range of such services by making use of the added security and much greater range of personal information that can be held on the card.

The exception is the stored value card.

Stored value card (SVC)

The SVC gives the customer the facility to 'pre-load' the card with spending power (usually expressed in its cash equivalent) which can be off-loaded – spent – at any compatible terminal.

A cynic might find it difficult to believe that the SVC would be regarded with much favour by customers, who do not usually expect to pay for goods and services *before* they have obtained them.

Another apparent drawback to the SVC is the difficulty of organizing a refund to a customer who loads the card and then loses it. If the customer's bank gave the customer a refund (or replaced the card with one loaded with equivalent value) the bank would, clearly, have given two sets of spending power for one payment.

The extent to which this would involve the bank in loss would depend on how the debiting process took place: whether a card that was loaded was regarded as containing value that has already been debited from the bank's account, or whether the debiting process only took place after the card was 'spent'. In either case, though, the bank would clearly suffer a loss if the mislaid card were found and used.

None the less, despite what are on the face of it obvious drawbacks to SVCs, those pilot projects which are taking place at present and which have taken place in the past suggest that SVCs are popular with consumers, who seem happy to regard them as a convenient form of cash. An interesting issue is to what extent the sense of privilege many customers may feel at being able to take part in a pilot scheme may be distorting consumer acceptance of SVCs.

This may, all the same, be a red herring, and it may be that the public acceptance of SVCs indicated by trials that have taken place so far is representative of general consumer acceptance of them. Certainly, in the use of traveller's cheques we see a long-established precedent for the principle of laying out money in advance to purchase spending opportunities, and season tickets for use in such applications as travel and parking are also arguably specialized examples of the same principle. It is probably reasonable to conclude that the SVC represents a major step forward in the creation of the cashless society.

Chapter 9 contains details of some state-of-the-art smart card projects, as well as an interview with Glenn Weiner, a vice-president of Amex's Electronic Commerce 'Centre of Excellence'.

In addition to the SVC, smart cards can also offer benefits to banks and their customers by being used in the following ways:

■ *As an information library:* the smart card can be used as a convenient, portable and secure method of storing a wide range of information about a cardholder.

■ *As an identification tool:* the smart card can provide an exceptionally secure means of positively identifying bona fide cardholders because of its information-carrying capacity and the difficulty of copying it.

■ *As a combined plastic card:* many people nowadays carry more than one plastic card. The storage power of a smart card makes it easy for it to be used to embody the functions of several plastic cards. Where it is used in this way, however, the branding issue needs to be sorted out by the different banks involved.

Such is the widespread agreement within the retail financial sector of the benefits conferred by smart cards that most countries with developed banking infrastructures (and several countries without) have launched pilot smart card projects. Furthermore, some of these pilot projects are turning into (or being about to turn into) limited implementations.

However, progress to date in creating nationwide smart card infra-structures has been relatively slow, with long evaluation periods being the rule. The main reason for this is that magnetic stripe technology – and especially the terminals for reading magnetic stripe cards – has been established for about 20 years, whereas smart card technology is only now becoming available. In many countries – such as the UK and the US - changing from terminals capable of reading and processing magnetic stripe cards to those capable of reading smart cards will cost banks literally billions of dollars.

Which is not to say that the process will not take place – the manifest advantages of smart cards means that it inevitably will – but some way needs to be found to share the burden of costs among all participating banks. The task is certainly too substantial for one or two banks – even giant ones – to undertake unaided.

A major exception to the general lack of national smart card infrastructures is France, where all bank cards are already smart cards. The French use of smart cards places France firmly in the vanguard of progress in this region.

The 'super-smart' card

An interesting extension of the smart card concept is the currently experimental 'super-smart' card. This is essentially a smart card with a manual input facility – which would typically operate like the tiny keys of a credit card sized electronic calculator. This facility allows the customer to input a wide variety of data into the card, including details of balance updates which might themselves be obtained from a remote banking terminal.

A super-smart card, used in conjunction with a home-based remote banking terminal, could one day create the equivalent of a bank branch in the customer's own home. Indeed in the Mondex SVC pilot – detailed in Chapter 9 – various accessories have the effect of turning the Mondex card into a kind of super-smart card.

Virtualization and a bank's new vision of itself

It should by now be clear to the reader that virtualization compels a bank to see itself in a completely different way to how it might have been entitled to regard itself in the past.

Historically, a bank was very much exemplified by its physical location. The buildings in which banks accommodated themselves – and which, indeed, they frequently owned outright – were large, often stone-built and usually looked more like government offices rather than the offices of a commercial organization. As the reminiscence above of visiting a Victorian bank suggests, the people who worked in such buildings displayed about as much charm and ability at interpersonal communications as the stone used as cladding for the buildings. Of course, some of the staff *may* have had these skills, but the job didn't encourage their deployment.

The whole traditional idea of banks regarding themselves as solid edifices, and inhabiting buildings to match, stems from their origins as goldsmiths, which needed solid edifices to ensure, and advertise, the security of their business activities and the protection of their strongrooms.

Even today, banks need strongrooms and other secure locations. Even so, the vast reductions in the proportion of routine transactions conducted within branches compared to the proportion conducted via virtual banking services means that the interior environment of branches can be transformed into a much more friendly, hospitable environment – more like the lobby of a hotel than the traditional interior of a bank.

Today, many banks do not even make use of security glass between the cashier and the customer, instead relying on the use of cash dispensing machinery which keeps the cash reserve secure from any thief. Bank interiors often have attractive displays of items which could be bought with the money saved with, or dispensed by, the bank (again, we see the notion of banks trying to overcome the problem of the secondary degree of utility) and many branches even have areas where children can play.

There are also usually machines in the lobby which give customers access to a range of services including cash withdrawal, statement ordering, cash and cheque deposit and even foreign currency conversion. Most banks make use of highly experienced interior designers to create a style for all their branches. Clearly, while the importance of the bank branch has declined, banks are doing their utmost to ensure that their own branches are very much worth spending time in. The reason is not because banks want to encourage customers to conduct routine transactions via the branches (although certainly banks know that as long as they operate a branch network, there will always be customers who want to use it for such routine purposes), but rather because banks need to be able to sell more profitable types of products and services within their branches and do not want to exclude customers from their branches completely. A cynic might object that banks are trying to have their cake and eat it, and certainly there is something in this view.

Yet a bank's new vision of itself now that virtualization has become such an important factor in banking is much more than a vision of itself as an organization which uses friendly and hospitable branches as the point of contact with customers.

What the bank must do is see itself as an organization that is very much composed of two types of customer delivery channels: the physical channel and the electronic channel.

In theory there is no reason why a bank should not market its physical delivery channels (i.e. its branch network will) and its electronic (i.e. virtual) channel separately, rather as insurance companies have done which have set up 'direct' organizations. However, the view of most banks seems to have been that the bank should present a seamless connection between its physical and virtual elements.

The reason for this appears to be that banks want to be seen as a unified brand incorporating everything they can offer to their customers. Besides, there is certainly no logical reason why a bank needs to float off its virtual delivery services into a separate division, because there is nothing *intrinsic* about the banking activity which presupposes that it needs to be associated with a physical branch infrastructure, and to float off the virtual division would give customers the idea that this was the case. Instead, banks nowadays prefer to see themselves as entities composed both of physical and electronic delivery channels. This idea is shown in Figure 3.1.

Note, however, that this rule that banks prefer to market themselves as a combination of physical and virtual delivery channels does not apply when the virtual bank is a completely new one that has been created from scratch. For example, the UK virtual banking First Direct has never had a branch network and never will do, even though it is nominally part of the Midland Bank (itself owned by the HSBC Group).

If we now turn to Figure 3.2, we see that this presents a more detailed view of the precise way in which banks generally (including of course insurance companies and investment firms) are tending to interact with their customers in the new virtual banking scenario.

FIGURE 3.1 *Virtualization explained*

Virtualization explained

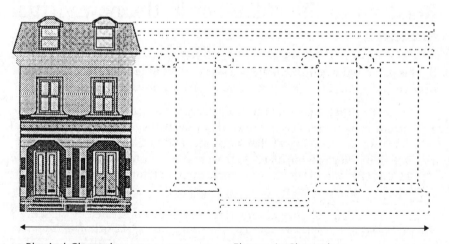

Physical Channels   Electronic Channels

(Source: Andersen Consulting)

FIGURE 3.2 *Virtual interactions*

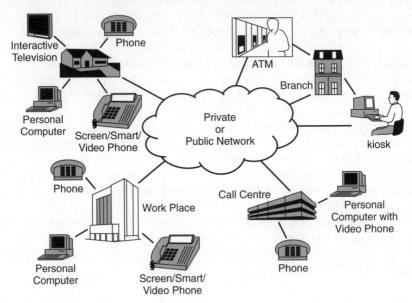

Ways in which financial institutions interact with customers
in the new virtual banking scenario

(Source: Andersen Consulting)

Relating to the customer in the new virtual scenario

By this point in the book it should be clear that relating to the customer in the new virtual scenario is, at heart, straightforward. It can be summed up as:

> Remember that there is abundant evidence to suggest that customers like virtual banking services. So give them what they want, and make sure that your services are reliable, accurate, and available around the clock. But don't neglect the need to ensure that customers have access to facilities for purchasing more complex types of financial services, too.

What is true of a bank's customers as a whole is particularly true of younger customers. Among the several important points demonstrated by Figure 3.3 are that there is a clearly greater propensity for younger customers to prefer using virtual banking services to using the branch. An additional point that should be made here, though, is that when these younger customers grow up it is hardly likely that they are going to want to return to the bank's

FIGURE 3.3 *Matching the virtual service*

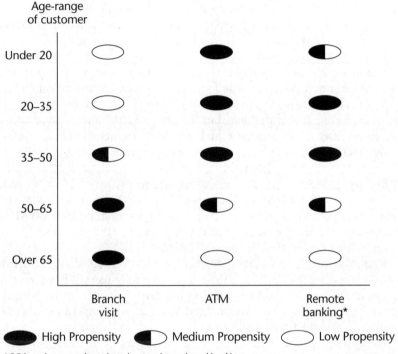

Matching the virtual service to the customer by age group

Branch   ATM   Remote
visit   banking*

● High Propensity   ◐ Medium Propensity   ○ Low Propensity

* PC-based, screen phone-based or touchtone-based banking

(Source: Andersen Consulting)

branches to any great extent. The figure therefore should not be seen as demonstrating a constant difference in customer preferences for using virtual or physical facilities depending on the customer's age, but rather as depicting the tail end of a period when older customers preferred to use a branch.

Winning a competitive edge from virtual banking

We now move to the most important implication of the virtual banking revolution. This is that banks need to exploit the revolution to their own ends: that is, they need to win a competitive edge from it.

The remainder of this chapter looks at how they can do this. The first conceptual step is for the bank to be clear about *when* it should be embarking on its virtual banking initiative.

Technology, almost by definition, is in a constant state of change. Even when a major new technological application becomes available – such as, for example, the television or the personal computer – these new applications are never fixed and static: they become ever more powerful, adding more functionality and more flexibility.

Take the microchip itself, for example. When the world's first mass-produced personal computer was launched back in 1979, the microchip it featured had a processing speed of 330,000 instructions per second. This seemed incredibly fast at the time, but the Intel 80286 chip – first produced a mere three years later – operated at 1,200,000 instructions per second.

By this time processing speeds were being expressed in 'mips' (millions of instructions per second). The Intel 80386 (first sold in October 1985) and the 80486 (April 1989) offered, respectively, 5 and 20 mips. Then, in March 1993, the ultra-fast 80486 was superseded by the Pentium processor, which operated at 100 mips. Successive versions of the Pentium processor have now brought this beyond 200 mips, and the days of the 500 mips processor will certainly come during the life-span of this book.

Naturally, this kind of technological power is not for the faint-hearted. Properly managed, and intelligently and resourcefully used, it is a power that can transform our lives, bringing unprecedented levels of flexibility and control over the way we live, as well as a huge competitive edge to a commercial or industrial organization.

Banks which seek to gain a competitive advantage from the deployment of virtual financial services cannot expect simply to be bystanders in the banking technology business. Instead, banks which wish to steal a march on the competition, technologically speaking, must become technological trend-setters themselves.

They must, in other words, constantly monitor advances in computer technology and look at ways of bringing these to the service of their customers.

This does *not* mean that a bank should necessarily commit itself to substantial speculative expenditure on technology. Not only are some forms of expenditure (e.g. for changing the banking infrastructure of a country from that suitable for magnetic stripe cards to one suitable for smart cards) beyond the financial capabilities of any one bank, however large, but the bank must be on guard against the cardinal sin of being carried away by the excitement of a new technology and not stopping to pause to ask whether there is a market for it.

Within the retail banking industry as in other industries – what matters is not the inherent sophistication of technology but the usefulness it offers to customers and, by extension, the commercial advantage it provides to banks.

Ideally, a bank should aim to start its technological initiative at the crucial point *after* the viability and feasibility of the technology and its associated applications has been demonstrated but *before* the technology and applications have been delivered so widely to customers that there is little or no opportunity for the bank to gain a competitive advantage from deploying it.

If achieving the correct balance between these two extremes sounds difficult, that is because it is. In practice, the only way to have any chance of achieving the balance is for the bank to keep intimately in touch with technological developments in retail financial technology and with the needs of their customers. The importance of this last point must never be underestimated. Most triumphant breakthroughs from winning competitive advantage from implementing new types of virtual financial services are really triumphs of understanding what customers want from their retail banks.

Criteria for success

Generally speaking, only financial technology applications which meet *all* of the following five criteria will offer banks the likelihood (but not in any sense a guarantee) of successful implementation.

The applications must offer:

- The opportunity to create a closer relationship between the bank and its customers.

- Better protection for both the bank and its customers against fraud.

- Greater speed and convenience for the customer.

- Substantial cost savings and profit potential for the bank.

- Opportunities for the customer to enjoy enhanced status by using the application. Enhanced status is, admittedly, difficult to quantify in advance, but at the very least the bank should feel confident that the customer will want to use the application.

The three evolutionary phases of virtual financial services

Useful assistance with understanding the way in which virtual financial services evolve and provide opportunities for banks to win competitive advantage is gained if these services are categorized into one of three phases of technological evolution.

These three phases represent, in effect, the impact the particular application has achieved within the industry to date.

The phases are:

- *The inception phase* – where the technology behind the application is still being developed and some technical problems still need ironing out, and where a substantial speculative investment will be required by any bank which seeks to develop the application.

■ *The growth phase* – where the application is increasingly acceptable to the bank's customers and the technology behind the application is widely available commercially.

■ *The maturity phase* – the principal characteristic of which is that customers are likely to be dissatisfied with any bank that does not offer the application, and that as a result any such bank not offering it is likely to be under a severe competitive disadvantage.

Figure 3.4 shows the phases which specific applications of retail financial technology currently (as of March 1998) occupy, with the vertical axis representing general volume at penetration, and the horizontal axis indicating the approximate period that has elapsed since the application was first launched.

This analysis shows that *smart cards and SVCs* are in the inception phase. Another application in the inception phase is *virtual shopping/banking*.

PC-based remote banking (i.e. banking via a PC or screen phone) is also in the inception phase. It has already been launched in the UK but has still not gained widespread acceptability.

FIGURE 3.4 *Evolutionary phases of virtual financial services – United Kingdom*

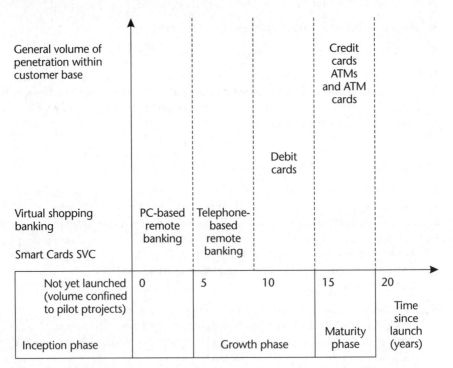

Telephone-based remote banking, on the other hand, is in the growth phase. It has unquestionably won an edge over PC-based home banking. This is due to the simple fact that telephone-based home banking does not require the user to obtain any special technology other than the telephone.

Debit cards (also called payment cards) which operate on EFTPoS systems are also in the growth phase, but are farther advanced in this phase than telephone-based home banking. They are, indeed, on the verge of the maturity phase.

Applications which are definitely in the maturity phase are *credit cards, ATMs and ATM cards*. No retail bank that hopes to compete in the marketplace can seriously expect to do so without offering their customers credit cards and ATM cards. This is, indeed, a useful indication that an application is in the maturity stage: that a bank will need to offer this particular application if the bank is to avoid falling by the wayside from a technological perspective.

Deciding on the appropriate level of technological expenditure

It might be asked how a smaller bank can possibly compete with larger banks over the implementation of multi-million pound technology applications. This is a crucially important question. It should ideally be seen in relation to another question: how can large banks know when they ought to start investing money in a new application of banking technology?

The truth is that investment in a new technology application represents a problem for smaller banks *and* large banks. Even a relatively modest pilot project of a new technological application can be extremely expensive: smaller banks may simply not be able to afford even this type of trial.

Large banks, on the other hand, will in most cases be able to afford such trials, but will very reasonably ask *which* type of applications deserve their attention.

To some extent the answer is that they ought to investigate any application that is currently in the inception stage. However, this is not a complete answer, for decisions as to which specific applications are in the inception phase must to some extent be arbitrary. Besides, the bank still has to decide what level of investment is appropriate for an application which – as it *is* in the inception phase – must inevitably to some extent represent a speculative investment.

The benefits which card branding organizations can offer members

An important subsidiary point to make at this stage is that much of the burden of uncertainty and potential anxiety of investing in new technological applications can often be removed or reduced by those organizations which operate and support the major card brands of the retail financial sector.

Examples of such organizations are the international payment systems and card branding organization Visa International, the UK shared ATM network LINK, and the US shared networks PLUS and Cirrus.

These type of organizations vary in the extent to which they support their members' technological initiatives, but most branding organizations do in fact have a built-in reason for taking the initiative in technological matters.

The reason is that they are perfectly aware that their members need to use networks, systems and card brandings in order to operate virtual financial services, and that if the networks, systems and card brandings are not perceived by the member to embody state-of-the-art technology and to be highly reliable and effective, as well as being backed up by an ongoing marketing campaign that promotes the brand world-wide, the members will soon wish to go elsewhere.

One card branding organization which adopts a particularly dynamic approach towards supporting its members in a technological sense is Visa International. With about 20,000 member banks world-wide, Visa – whose origins as a payment system operator go back to 1970, and which took the name Visa in 1977 – clearly has every incentive to ensure that these members remain happy with the quality of its network and branding.

To this end, Visa takes technological and application-related initiatives across all areas of members' activities in order to ensure they have support with their provision of virtual financial services to their customers. The nature of these initiatives is such that Visa is spearheading several new pilot schemes in virtual financial services at any one time.

Not surprisingly, under the circumstances, Visa is concerned – some might say to an almost paranoid extent – that its members do not come to conclude that it is itself interested in competing with them as a provider of virtual financial services in its own right.

The principal method it uses to combat this suspicion is communication. Visa communicates to its members in a variety of methods: chief among them being various newsletters and other corporate literature. Exhibit 3.1 is an excerpt from such literature. While this could not be described in any sense as an objective document, the usefulness of the information it contains justifies its inclusion here.

Note in particular how Visa argues its case by emphasizing the benefits its systems can offer over members' own proprietary systems. Visa makes its points decisively, while emphasizing the collaborative nature of the relationship it seeks with its members.

Incidentally, Visa uses the term 'electronic banking' rather than the more up-to-date expression 'virtual banking'. Note, too, that Visa's confidence in its own brand is such that it did not apparently occur to whoever wrote the following copy that Visa itself is, strictly speaking, itself a 'third party'.

Exhibit 3.1: Today's limited options for electronic banking

None of the options available today provides a complete electronic banking service. For most banks, technologies that go beyond simple touch-tone access are prohibitively expensive to develop. And third-party-branded products can weaken bank–customer relationships.

The proprietary route

With a proprietary approach, the bank keeps control of the customer relationship and can customize the service to meet its needs and those of its customers. The bank is able to make sure that the communication at the point of transaction (usually a personal computer), screen phone or touch-tone phone) reflects its brand identity.

Costly to develop, maintain and update

Unfortunately, the development of proprietary solutions for high-tech electronic banking has proven expensive for all banks. What's more, because of the fast-paced technological advances, solutions that banks invest in today may be obsolete tomorrow. In some cases, banks that have tried the proprietary approach have found these technologies difficult to bring to market.

The third-party-branded alternative

The technological aspects of electronic banking are opening up opportunities to a wide range of third parties, ranging from telephone and cable companies to software vendors and on-line service providers.

Third-party-branded products may weaken member–customer relationships

With a third-party-branded product, the third party – not the bank – has the primary relationship with the customer. This third-party provider may actually be the one marketing the financial service to the customer.

For instance, there are PC software firms and third-party service providers that offer electronic banking services directly to consumers under their own brands. The consumer's bank's name never appears at all.

Other issues associated with third-party-branded electronic banking are:

■ the bank cannot ensure access security;

- the bank may bear the burden of customer service without the compensation of a revenue stream from the third-party access;

- the bank may have no control over the third party's use of customer data or account data.

These issues present financial risks which can affect profitability – and threaten member banks' relationships with their customers. This could ultimately be the most expensive option of all.

The Visa electronic banking solution

For over 20 years Visa and its members have led the industry by anticipating – and meeting – customer needs. Today, by establishing standards in the marketplace, Visa is developing a complete electronic banking solution – one that provides all of the benefits and none of the drawbacks of other options. The Visa solution helps you:

Build stronger customer relationships

Because members market the additional services and convenience customers want within the framework of the members' own brand identity, members can increase customer loyalty.

Add value to your current card products

Your existing cards will evolve into 'relationship cards' which give your customers access to electronic banking and other financial information services.

Benefit from standards and rules

Visa establishes industry standards, thereby ensuring that control of electronic banking is in the hands of banks.

Offer profitable electronic bill payment

Visa is developing new standards and operating rules for electronic bill payment services that will lower operating costs, improve service both to the consumer and to the organization issuing the bill, and leverage the strength of the existing Visa member network.

Simplify the start-up process

Members can deliver electronic banking services to their customers by building upon the Visa world-wide payment systems infrastructure already in place.

Compare the Visa solution to any other electronic banking option and the choice is clear. Other options provide limited benefits. Visa provides a complete solution with the greatest number of benefits both to member banks and to their customers.

The Visa solution simplifies electronic banking now and will carry the industry well into the twenty-first century. What's more, it helps build long-term customer relationships – the key to member profitability.

Build stronger customer relationships

The Visa electronic banking solution enables Visa members to strengthen their customer relationships while providing the wide array of services which customers want. It allows each member to differentiate its electronic banking capabilities from competitors by branding and customizing the services offered.

Electronic banking branded with your bank's name

With the Visa solution, a member does not have to use any third-party name – or even the Visa name – on its service, but can brand the service with its own identity. Member branding provides several advantages:

- *You keep ownership of the customer relationship.* Your bank remains firmly at the front of the customer's mind.

- *You strengthen your image.* Customers associate the convenience and high level of service with the member – not with a third-party provider.

- *You can better cross-sell additional financial products and services.* Whenever your customers review the electronic banking menu, they see the unique names of your bank's products and services – and are reminded that your bank is the single most convenient source of financial products and services for them.

(Source: Visa International)

Table 3.1 provides corroborative evidence for the points raised in Exhibit 3.1. We can now look more deeply at the practical business requirements surrounding the implementation of virtual banking services.

The main rules for successful implementation of virtual banking services

These are:

- Never deploy technology for its own sake, but only when the application has some kind of track record for utility and customer acceptability.

TABLE 3.1 *Analysis of features of virtual financial services and advantages branding organizations can offer*

Features	Proprietary Products	Third-Party Products	Visa
Customizable	Yes	Yes	Yes
Member-branded	Yes	No	Yes
Reduced up-front costs	No	Yes	Yes
Quicker to market	No	Yes	Yes
Establishes industry standards	No	No	Yes
Accommodates technological change	No	No	Yes
Prevent risk of obsolescence	No	No	Yes
Quality control	Yes	No	Yes
Access security	Yes	No	Yes

(Source: Visa International)

- Remember that customers are basically indifferent to the nature of the technology that is delivering the service to them, but are looking for convenient and round-the-clock levels of *information* about the state of their accounts.

- Opportunities to pay for goods and services in more convenient ways.

- More access to banking facilities from their houses.

The main question should not be 'how state-of-the-art is the technology which we are able to implement on our customers' behalf?', but 'to what extent does this technology allow us to meet the above customer requirements?'

- Do not proceed towards full implementation of a new virtual financial services without first testing the application thoroughly in a pilot project.

- Plan from the outset to ensure that the overall customer appeal and marketing impact of the new service are maximized by designing new products (e.g. new types of accounts and new types of plastic card products) around the new virtual service. This exploits to the full the utility of the new service, dramatizes its launch, and should ensure that the benefits of the new service are communicated to customers in the most effective way.

As long as a bank keeps these fundamental principles in mind, it should not have any real difficulty outperforming new entrants to the market which will be implementing the same kind of technology as the bank will be implementing, but which will not have the bank's track record. Other things being equal – which in this case means assuming that the bank is not prepared to allow itself to be outcompeted in terms of deploying virtual applications – the well-established bank should always outcompete the new entrant which has no track record (or, no track record in the new market area) of operating in the retail financial arena.

Specific guidance for making the most of virtual banking services from a competitive perspective

This section provides *practical* guidance about how your bank can make the most of the virtual banking revolution from the point of view of maximizing its own competitive impact on the market.

Main business challenges

These can be regarded as:

Customer pressures
There are two kinds of pressures here, namely:

- The need to deliver virtual services that are more attractive to customers than those delivered by competitors' banks.

- The sheer business need to ensure that those virtual services already implemented by the bank work reliably and accurately, are secure from external fraud, and are open and available for the periods of time that offer the customer most convenience: which, in practice, means operation 24-hours a day, seven days a week.

Competitive pressure
This is the pressure to outperform competitors in implementing virtual services which attract and retain customers.

Apart from the competitive issues which have already been addressed in this report, the other key point to make here is that managing competitor pressure will always require a combination of shrewd marketplace business sense plus a knowledge of the precise levels of competitive advantage that can reasonably be expected from deploying a particular virtual financial service.

In effect, a bank has to seek at all times to strike a careful and dynamic balance between not wanting to fall behind its competitors in deploying these services (which means that it must at the very least keep up with its rivals in this respect), and not wanting to waste money on unrealistic or unattractive services. Managing this dynamic balance is the most important task facing the bank's information technology team.

Technological pressure
This, too, is a pressure that must be managed with an awareness of the carefully balanced dynamics involved. As we have seen, implementing a technology

merely because it represents a state-of-the-art technological development is likely to prove a disastrous motive because inevitably what will be under scrutiny is how advanced the technology is rather than what it can offer customers.

On the other hand, a bank obviously cannot remain oblivious to the onward march of technology, or neglect the need to keep a watching brief on ways of using new technological developments to deliver more convenient and more useful virtual services to the customer.

What is required is an innovative and enterprising approach towards technology on the part of the bank that never allows itself to be distracted from putting the customer's needs first.

Financial pressure

The financial aspects of virtual financial services are an essential consideration. The cost issue is discussed in detail in the next chapter. Here, I simply provide a summary of the business case relating to cost.

There are certain basic points which can usefully be made about the financial side of operating these services. The points depend to a large degree on what type of virtual service is under consideration and are discussed below.

The overriding reason for implementing virtual financial services should be to make tactical and strategic competitive gains over rivals.

In the case of ATM services, banks can gain revenue from these services in either of three ways:

■ By charging its customers (i.e. debiting the customer's account) for every transaction or some transactions (e.g. some banks only charge for an ATM transaction when the customer's account balance falls below a certain threshold). Note that electronic banking transactions made by a bank's own customers on its own equipment and system are known as 'loyal' transactions.

■ By charging its customers for using its ATM network via some shared network. Whether or not the bank decides to do this, it will itself need to pay for each and every transaction carried out by its own customers on another bank's system and routed to itself via the shared switch, so whether or not the bank decides to pass on the charge depends on how merciful it feels towards its customers.

Note that electronic banking transactions made by a bank's own customers via another bank's equipment and systems are known as 'disloyal' or 'not on us' transactions.

■ By charging other banks when their customers use the bank's network.

In practice, the revenue a bank can gain from ATM transactions can often be surprisingly high, particularly if it is a large bank whose ATMs are likely to be used extensively for 'not on us' transactions.

There is also a significant indirect financial benefit of deploying ATMs in terms of the likelihood that numbers of front counter staff can be reduced, the number of in-branch staff employed to process routine transactions such as cash withdrawals can be reduced, and the number of bricks-and-mortar branches can be slashed.

There are, however, various ways in which revenue from ATM transactions will be eroded or completely offset. These are:

- The reluctance on the part of the bank to pass on the cost of loyal or disloyal transactions to the customer. Obviously there can be a competitive price for passing these charges on, namely the possibility that the customers may go elsewhere.

- The cost of establishing, operating and maintaining the ATM network.

In the case of remote banking services, whether these use an ordinary telephone, a PC terminal or a screen phone, these services are still too little used by the largest proportion of the population for a general picture to be formed of the cost basis that customers will accept.

Furthermore, the banks which do operate these services differ widely in whether, for example, they give or lease a terminal to the customer or expect him to buy one, whether they in fact charge for the service, and whether they subsidize telephone calls or not.

In time, it appears that the most likely scenario – which increased competition over the provision of remote banking services will probably hasten – is that banks will bear most of the costs of running their remote banking services themselves, and seek the payback in terms of:

- further reduced costs of operating the branch network;

- increased numbers of customers meaning increased deposits and increased profits from holding these deposits.

In terms of smart cards, these applications are in most countries in too embryonic a stage for the likely cost implications to be clear. However, two principal observations here seem reliable:

- Where smart cards are used as plastic cards giving access to a wide range of virtual financial services, some way will need to be found for banks to recoup the cost of the cards, which can cost banks up to about £5 each, although this cost will continue to come down as the technology improves.

   It is likely that smart cards will first be introduced to controlled cardholder bases (e.g. country clubs, sports clubs, gold-card holders) where there will be a prospect of the customers being prepared to pay for using the cards.

- Where smart cards are used specifically as stored value cards (SVCs), the cost of the SVC is likely to be more than for the ordinary smart card. The bank will need to pass this cost on. Furthermore, the relationship between customers and bank will, by the very nature of the SVC, need to be a strong one. Again, SVCs will be launched initially to controlled cardholder bases.

■ Where the use of smart cards to activate ATMs is widespread (as it is in France already), the cost issues here will probably wind up being similar to those observed today where plastic cards are used.

Regulatory pressure

This will depend on the nature of the virtual financial service and on the legal status of the organization delivering the service. It is essential for a bank to keep a watching brief on regulatory changes and how these will affect its ability to deliver virtual services and/or may create new competitive opportunities.

Possible overall responses by the bank

Faced with these different pressures, a bank has basically three different options for how it can respond to the virtual scenario in order to maximize its profitability.

The first option is for it to seek to become solely a low-cost commodity provider: meaning that it offers the largest number of customers a simple, inexpensive virtual service without frills.

The option of becoming *solely* a low-cost provider is unlikely to be attractive to long-established banks, which will be more likely to want to see ways of offering more complex services that give them a real opportunity to offer a competitive advantage.

On the other hand, a newcomer, such as a telecommunications company, which would be well placed to maximize profit from supplying a high volume of straightforward services, might find the low-cost provider route a useful one to take.

The second option is to innovate, and seek to steal a march on the competition by implementing new kinds of attractive applications before a rival does.

The third option is to base the entire range of virtual services around the customer relationship: that is, to seek customer intimacy.

There is also a fourth option, which is that the bank aims to achieve all three of the above: that is, to minimize the cost of its virtual financial services, to be a low-cost provider, and to seek customer intimacy.

Aiming to achieve all these objectives is the course recommended in this report, and everything that follows should be seen as having been written with these objectives in mind.

The different ways to interact with customers

It is important at this stage to set down the different ways of interacting with customers in the new virtual scenario.

Matching the virtual service to the customer

It is also important to bear in mind that different types of customers will have more of a propensity to use certain virtual services than others. As we have already seen, one of the most reliable criteria on which to base this kind of analysis is the age factor.

It must be emphasized, however, that while there is abundant evidence that this is an accurate interpretation, it would be unwise for a bank to base a major implementation on this interpretation without first undertaking its own research into the acceptability of virtual financial services by different age groups of customers.

Matching the product to the customer

Once the bank has decided which type of virtual service it wants to offer customers in a particular age-range, it should design and market the product in order that the product has the widest appeal to the target customers. To re-emphasize a point made earlier, *the product should be closely designed around the virtual service,* in order that the outlay on the service has the maximum chance of being translated into return arising from enhanced use of the service.

Relevant product design factors

The following are the principal design factors of a new product, with comments about the appeal of different aspects of these factors to different categories of customers.

Type of account(s) involved

The options usually facing a bank here are either to make the account a current account – where the emphasis will be on the convenience of an account which may not have any interest element attached to it – or else to make the account a deposit account, where the interest rate that goes with it will be a major competitive factor.

Generally – although there is no hard and fast rule about this – current accounts are more popular with younger age-range customers, and deposit accounts with older age-range customers.

Type of virtual service attached

The product will have at least one of the three principal types of virtual service (ATMs, debit function, remote banking) attached to it. Often the product will provide all three, *or* any combination of two.

Generally, the more virtual services that are attached to the product, the more attractive it will be, particularly to customers in the younger age-ranges.

Brand name of product

The way in which the product is branded is a crucial factor in its success, or otherwise.

Generally, banks tend to err towards choosing brand names which are too obviously fashionable, and which insufficiently acknowledge the gravity with which most people – even younger ones – regard their financial affairs.

Sometimes, indeed, the brand names are of the type which have been clearly chosen by a fashionable, and possibly overly trendy, name-branding agency. These agencies are generally good at choosing names for fast moving consumer goods (fmcg) such as washing-powders and chocolate biscuits, but experience has shown that they are often much less effective when selecting a brand name for a financial product. They tend to choose distinctive, user-friendly names which appear superficially impressive, but which don't tell the prospective customer what the account does for him. Names such as 'Orchard', 'Vector' and 'Matrix' – all of which have been used by UK banks in recent years – clearly suffer from this particular fault.

It is better to ensure that the brand name makes clear what the account has to offer customers. The name of the highly successful Nationwide Building Society 'FlexAccount' goes a long way towards achieving these objectives, as does 'Cardcash', the similarly successful Halifax Building Society account which was the first UK banking account designed specifically to be used with an ATM.

Probably the best solution of all to the brand name dilemma is simply to give the product a name which tells the customer what it is. If, for example, the new product is a current account, the bank could name it Current Account or The [name of bank] Current Account. Several UK banks have indeed adopted this approach to their branding, and have been pleased with the results. For example, in the UK the Halifax bank has changed the name of its main current account from 'Matrix' to 'the Halifax Current Account'.

Incidentally, while younger age-range customers do tend to like products which give them a high level of access to virtual services, it is a mistake to assume that they will readily fall for crassly youth-orientated brand-names. Not only are younger people highly sensitive to the feeling that they are being manipulated or patronized by older people, but they like to feel 'mature', and will usually prefer a product which they feel other grown-ups are using rather than one which is obviously targeted towards them as youngsters.

Design of the plastic card

As we have seen, the plastic card plays an essential role in the bank/customer relationship. Its design should therefore be taken with extreme seriousness by the bank.

An increasing number of design elements – such as holograms and logos – are prescribed by security and shared branding considerations, but even so the bank has considerable scope for branding its cards distinctively.

Such branding is likely to appeal to all age-ranges of customers, but with particular force to those customers for whom the product is their first bank account. Such customers will, of course, inevitably tend to be in the younger age-ranges.

Advertising the new product

This is not the place to go into the highly specialized discipline of advertising financial services in great detail. Instead, the bank should seek out the assistance of an advertising agency which produces work that the bank likes. There is not usually much point in seeking out an agency which already works for other banks, as it is likely that competitive factors will prevent it from taking any more banks onto its books.

One general point worth making about banks' advertising of their new banking products is that the advertisements *frequently contain too little information about what the product offers.* It is all very well basing the advertisement around a comic concept, or using a celebrity to promote the product by association, but ultimately what prospective customers really want to know is: (a) what the product offers them in terms of convenience and range of functions; and (b) what the product offers them that other banks' products do not.

Customer benefits of virtual financial services

These have already been touched upon at several points. They can now conveniently be summarized as:

- more convenience;

- better knowledge of state of accounts;

- wider range of products/services available to the customer; possibly lower cost of accessing banking services.

Benefits to the bank of supplying virtual financial services

Again, these have already been referred to, but can now usefully be summarized as:

- larger numbers of satisfied customers, and consequently higher retention rates;

- possibilities for attracting new customers;

- more scope to differentiate services;

- greater opportunity to cross-sell;

- the opportunity significantly to extend operational base by participating in shared networks and/or brandings which allow customers access to virtual services in locations beyond the bank's normal operating base;

- the opportunity to save on the cost of developing technology initiatives through participating in shared networks and/or brandings which give the bank access to networks and infrastructures which allow the bank to deliver a dynamic range of virtual financial services with much less capital expenditure than would be necessary if the network or infrastructure were proprietary;

■ generally, the opportunity to deliver services at a lower operating cost than if the service were delivered via a bricks-and-mortar branch;

■ the opportunity to make money by charging customers and/or other banks for transactions via a virtual delivery system.

Finally, one particularly important thought with which to end a chapter which has, on occasion, been deliberately provocative.

Many customers, commentators and even senior managers of retail banks ask whether virtualization is, as far as banks are concerned, something they should get involved with now or later.

What is the answer to this question?

The best answer is, perhaps: *it depends whether the bank wants to be a leader or a follower.*

The cost issue

Introduction

This chapter looks at the entire issue of cost in relation to virtual banking systems. This is necessarily a complex issue, with many different aspects, but one point must be regarded as paramount and is therefore emphasized here at the outset:

> Delivering banking services via a virtual delivery service is almost always only about one-sixth as expensive to the bank as delivering these services via a physical branch, and there is ample evidence to suggest that in many cases virtual delivery can be as inexpensive as one-sixteenth of the cost of delivering the service via the branch.

This enormous potential cost-saving stems from the much lower cost of running an electronic delivery network compared with the cost of running one centred around branches.

Quite apart from the sheer savings in the notoriously expensive bricks-and-mortar (whether or not the branch is owned outright by the bank) branches in central locations, there are also huge savings in labour costs, since once an electronic network has been set up, it often only requires personnel to monitor it rather than be fully engaged with it at all times. Even where personnel *are* required all the time — as in the case of telephone banking systems featuring real human operators rather than an automated system — the savings are still considerable.

In addition, if we link these savings with the point already made – that customers like using virtual systems and in many cases prefer using these to making time-consuming branch visits – we see that the business case for using virtual banking is effectively unanswerable.

Later in this chapter I return to this matter of the cost differential between virtual and physical banking.

The need for cost-effective implementation of a virtual banking system

Clearly, a bank must ensure that it implements its virtual banking systems in as cost-effective a manner as feasible. Note that 'cost-effective' in this context is not a genteel synonym for 'cheap'. Cheapness is not the same thing at all, because the concept of cost-effectiveness focuses on the relationship between expenditure to the benefits of that expenditure. On the other hand, the concept of *cheapness* merely refers to the fact that less was spent on the item or service under discussion than one would expect to spend on it.

It follows that any possibilities for cost-savings from implementing a virtual banking system must therefore be considered in the light of the bank's needs to meet its obligations to its customers and to establish and maintain a competitive advantage in the marketplace.

In other words, the cost-effective implementation of a virtual banking system means finding the right kind of balance between cost savings, continued quality of service and competitive advantage.

Some bankers prefer a more formal definition of cost-effective in this respect, along the lines of 'when the application of a virtual banking system adds more measurable value than the cost of the system'. Unfortunately, though, this definition does not accommodate a situation which often arises, i.e. when the benefits of the new system are not precisely quantifiable.

Effective cost management is therefore best regarded as the sum of those management skills which provide the bank with the most cost-effective technology.

Cost-effective management of a virtual banking system is much more than merely a matter of looking for opportunities for cost-savings, but certainly paying due regard to minimizing the basic costs of the system (which in practice means the costs of the delivery technology itself) is essential.

It is therefore necessary to state a rule which is well known to all entrepreneurs, but which some senior bankers ought to take more to heart:

> The rule is: for a bank, one good way to make money from technology is not to spend money on it.

The rule needs stating as formally as this, because experience shows that bankers who are razor-sharp when it comes to controlling costs in other areas of their activity – or who can spot a bad loan prospect a mile off – all too frequently suspend their good sense and budgetary acumen when technology is involved.

The result is that the world's banks waste more money on technology than any other sector, apart from the defence industry.

A good reason for a bank to spend money on technology

This waste could in most cases be avoided by bearing in mind that *the only good reason for a bank to spend money on technology is so that it can function more competitively and efficiently and generate a higher profit.*

Three bad reasons for spending money on technology

There are, of course, also bad reasons for spending money on technology. The three below are the most commonly encountered.

1 'Because I want to impress my superiors and I think that if I buy this system they will be impressed by my foresight and talent.'
   In fact, far from being impressed, if the system turns out to have been a waste of time and money – which it most likely will if the reasons for implementing it have not been thought out clearly – senior management will only see incompetence and the result could be termination of employment.

2 'Because I've read about this system in the press and one bank I read about seems to be having a great deal of success with it.'
   With all respect to the press, the story might be inaccurate, misleading or – as is often the case – only tell half the true story, rather like a newspaper headline which might have said 'Iceberg damaged by Titanic'.
   Banks do not like to admit that they have made mistakes with technology, but will put a brave face on the most disastrous deployment. And even if the bank referred to has implemented and used the new system successfully, it does not necessarily follow that another will be similarly successful as its business aims might well be different. Unless and until those business objectives are precisely defined, no new banking technology should be implemented.

3 'This is a tremendous new development in technology and I want our bank to be first to exploit it.'
   Even if it *is* a major new development, does it work well enough to be the motor behind the kind of reliable system needed in the financial sector? Even if it does, should your bank be the pioneer in its use? The following are a set of guidelines to ensure that bankers spend money on technology wisely, and have in place a stringent policy of cost-effective management.

General guidelines for the good cost management of technology used in a virtual banking system

1 Never forget that a bank can actually *make* money by not wasting money on technology.

2   The business case interests must be put first when assessing whether or not to proceed with a particular virtual banking system. The entire subject matter of this book is how banks can apply technology to further their business interests, earn more revenue and win competitive advantage. It is therefore useful at this juncture to set down examples of specific ways in which technology can help in this respect. These apply in the case of a retail bank; they would be different for a wholesale bank.

(a) By facilitating the delivery of new types of service (e.g. ATMs and EFTPoS), thereby making the bank more attractive both to existing and potential customers.

(b) By helping to reduce the unit cost of handling routine banking transactions.

(c) By enabling the bank to reduce the number of staff it needs to employ in its branches and, frequently, the number of branches.

(d) By facilitating the gathering of more in-depth information about customers, and information on a larger number of customers.

(e) By generating revenue from customers who use the virtual banking system. This is a complex point, because banks are aware there is, not unreasonably, considerable reluctance on the part of customers to pay for transactions they make over a virtual banking system. In practice, however, the utility of these systems to customers is so great that most customers are happy to overcome this resistance to some extent. This is especially true when a customer is using a virtual banking system via a shared network and the access points the customer is using is not owned by the customer's own bank. For example, in the United Kingdom the Abbey National Bank doesn't charge customers for ATM transactions they make via the Abbey National's own machines but it makes a charge of £1 per transaction made via another institutions' ATMs. Making such a charge is often necessary because the bank itself will have to pay for a so-called 'not-on-us' transaction. That said, a large proportion of banks are happy to bear the cost of these. Competitiveness among banks does indeed often lead to a situation where they don't make a charge for ATM transactions on their own machines initiated by individual private customers, but note that most banks do not extend this privilege to business customers who usually have to pay for each ATM transaction they make. Note also that there is an increasing trend to supply remote banking services (such as a telephone-based service) free of charge to customers or via a special local rate telephone call subsidized by the bank. The point is that banks want to encourage their customers to use remote banking services and thereby reduce the burden on branches. The benefits to the bank of this reduced burden are so great that it doesn't usually matter to them that they will have to subsidize the cost of the telephone banking service.

(f) By facilitating the gathering of computer-based information about customer preferences and the relationship between which type of customers want which type of products. This information is of great importance for the purposes of marketing and general commercial development.

3 A hierarchical budget approval system for expenditure on banking technology must be introduced if it is not in place already. Budget decisions relating to technology need to be approved by several people in ascending order of seniority within the bank. Ideally, the bank's information technology team should be obliged to present details of the proposed expenditure to superiors in the form of a proposal; this approach will ensure that the team states the business case clearly and is forced both to analyse the potential benefits of the new system and to state these in detail.

4 People at the bank with authority for financial technology expenditure must be accountable and take responsibility for their decisions. It has to be made very clear to individual staff members that they must take the consequences of their decisions regarding financial technology. People are less likely to make risky or inadequately researched decisions if they feel that their jobs are at risk if things go wrong. However an atmosphere of personal accountability need not necessarily mean a discouraging atmosphere: indeed, management should actively ensure that invention and innovation are not suppressed.

5 A bank's information technology staff should have the opportunity to participate in regular discussions about the bank's attitude towards technology and the role it should play in increasing competitiveness. The more creative, dynamic and commercially minded a team's thinking about technology, the more likely the team is to be successful when implementing a project. Many banks regularly send members of their technology team on conferences and seminars organized by third parties. These events can have their uses but they are expensive and time consuming, often with little tangible benefit. In many cases, a better use of the money would be to organize internal seminars, where technology staff and management alike have a chance to discuss how technology could be applied most effectively, and could occasionally feature an outside expert to stimulate debate or present a paper on a specific subject.

6 The bank should make a conscious effort to recruit technology staff *with acumen in the banking business*. A bank should where possible avoid recruiting staff whose experience lies solely in the technology arena. What a bank ideally needs are technologically knowledgeable staff who have experience in the financial sector and business acumen. They should understand both the dynamic nature of the role of technology in banking

and the concept that technology applications must always be driven by business needs, and not vice versa. Examples of methods by which the right mix of abilities could be obtained are:

(a) By making practical business experience an essential criterion when assessing CVs.
(b) By wording recruitment advertisements in such a way as to require business expertise, rather than merely technological expertise, from applicants.
(c) By instructing in-house recruitment interviewers and external recruitment consultants to tease out specific details of applicants' business experience.
(d) If suitable applicants cannot readily be found, the bank should recruit bankers and train them in technology, rather than recruit technologists and train them in banking.

7   Prospective technology suppliers should be given the incentive to seek a long-term relationship with a bank and to maintain a continuing interest in the successful operation of the technology supplied. Banks must pay particular attention to managing the financial aspects of their relationships with vendors. Banks are coveted customers and the vendor's reputation will be enhanced by association with them. However, banks are not in business in order to give vendors large profits, and must make it clear that a product or service must not be priced to give excessive margins, although the vendor should not be driven down to such a low margin that the bank's business is of no account or the vendor is forced into financial difficulties.

A bank should ideally cultivate a long-term relationship with the vendor that results in the vendor wanting the product or service to be as successful as the bank wants it to be. For example, payment could be made when significant milestones are reached, or the vendor could be given a direct stake in the system, so that some proportion of the profits could be given to the vendor as a bonus.

8   The selection of external third-party consulting or software design assistance for any aspect of a bank's technology-related activities must be rigorous. The following procedures should be pursued here:

(a) A precise specification of what is required from the third party should be drawn up, although those eventually selected for the task should be able to make suggestions regarding how the specification might be modified.
(b) Details of the candidates for selection should be obtained, using published sources, conversations with industry contacts, and information held about possible candidates with whom the bank is already acquainted.

(c) The specification can be advertised in a journal likely to be read by relevant third parties. A bank may not be aware of all possible candidates.

(d) Once the list of third parties has been obtained, all these organizations should be contacted and asked whether they would like to quote for the project.

(e) Assessment starts from the moment of first contact. Methods of assessment include such factors as the speed of response, the quality of the reply and the overall level of professionalism.

(f) On receipt of their replies, detailed specifications must be sent to the third parties under consideration, asking them for a quotation by a set date. The quotation should be for completing the task in question, not for devoting a certain number of consultancy days to it, or the third party will be legally entitled to stop work once those days have been worked.

(g) The decision should not be based entirely on the quotations received. Visits should be made to the shortlisted organizations to watch them working; this gives useful insights about the way they operate and their overall professionalism.

(h) Serious consideration should be given to appointing several third parties to handle various early stages of the project, making it clear that the decision regarding who will handle later stages will depend on their performance. This will maximize competitiveness among the third parties and prevent the bank depending on only one third party.

(i) The bank should start negotiations with prospective vendors before the final selection has been made. This is important if the selected vendor is not to be given a massive advantage in the negotiation process: having been informed that he has been selected, he will be more likely to drive a hard bargain. What a bank should do, therefore, is obtain sample contracts and terms of business from all shortlisted vendors and discuss points of difficulty in the contracts before the final selection has been made.

Using this approach, the main areas of difficulty can be sounded out before the final selection of vendors has been made. This will put the bank in a much better position to start the final negotiations.

A spirit of co-operation and fair play is necessary here: after all, the purpose is to work with the vendor on a collaborative basis, not to crush him into submission. However, it is absolutely essential that the bank protects itself against technology that does not achieve what the vendor promises or leads the bank to expect. The final contract must contain or embody a formal acceptance document which in effect sets out a schedule of payment based upon the delivery and successful performance of elements of the system, such as response times and transaction processing volumes. The bank must be able to test that a certain criterion has been met before authorizing the corresponding part of the payment.

One good way for the bank to create a sense of genuine and mutually beneficial collaboration between itself and its vendors is to incorporate within the contract a bonus for successful performance of the system beyond a certain target. For example, it is common for wholesale banks to negotiate such contracts with vendors who supply front office systems or software. Here, the commission might take the form of a proportion of trading-room profits beyond a certain level.

Another point which must be factored into the negotiations is that the third party must agree not to invoice for any amount higher than that agreed at the outset, without having first obtained written permission from the bank to undertake the additional work incurring the additional cost.

9 During the actual development process of a technology application, costs must be kept down. Precise methods for good cost management during the development process of a technology application are beyond the scope of this book, but they must be carefully attended to.

10 If the bank engages a consultancy to assist with the new virtual banking application, prospective consultancies should be asked at the procurement stage to make suggestions for how *their* engagement would help the bank to keep down the costs of the new virtual banking initiative.

The cost–benefit analysis

No new virtual banking application should be allowed to go beyond the planning stage without a cost-benefit analysis taking place and the results of this analysis being clearly positive. There are two elements to the cost-benefit analysis: the process of estimating the *costs* of the new system, and the process of estimating its *benefits*.

Estimating the costs of the new system

Until around the end of the 1980s, banks used to base their cost estimates for a particular system on the supposition that a certain number of lines of software code needed to be written to complete a particular application (we can call this x), and that in a working day a programmer could write a certain number of lines of code (we can call this y). Since a bank could provide figures for both x and y, and knew the costs of employing a programmer for a day, this was supposed to give the accurate development costs of a new system.

Experience has shown that this approach does not work, because writing the code that a system contains is nowadays only one element of the cost equation. The following are more realistic cost elements that must be added together to obtain an estimate of the new system.

Internal costs

These include:

- the salaries of staff involved with the development;

- the portion of fixed costs (e.g. for premises rental, heating, lighting, electricity etc.) allocated to the development;

- the costs of drawing up both the feasibility study and the functional requirements specification; software licences (if applicable); cost of system testing procedure and the miscellaneous items bought in to assist with completion of project (e.g. manuals etc.);

- the *opportunity cost* of developing the system: that is, those costs that represent profits not earned because those who would normally be earning them are devoting time to the system instead. The extent to which opportunity costs should be factored into the costing process will depend on the bank's general approach to preparing costings.

External costs

These arise from using external assistance and include the fees and expenses of consultants, and payments to vendors of both software and hardware.

The final figure for the estimated cost of the system is obtained from adding internal to external costs. For this estimated figure to be reliable, rigorous control procedures must be in place to compel external suppliers to stick to their initial estimates. The principal justification offered for an increase in final costs is that there was more work than was originally envisaged. The bank should therefore not allow additional work to be done unless absolutely necessary; in any event it ought to insist that additional work can only be carried out with its written approval.

Estimating the benefits of the new system

Given that the bank has arrived at a reasonably accurate estimate of the likely costs, the next stage is to produce an accurate estimate of the benefits.

There are two kinds of benefits, *financial* and *non-financial*, and it is important to distinguish between them. However, before benefits can be properly analysed, the bank must decide on the time period, after full implementation of the system, which will be taken into consideration when assessing the system's benefits.

This time period will vary according to the bank's accounting procedures and policies, but one calendar year is considered to be a suitable period, although it would be unwise to be dogmatic about this and some banks may want to adopt a much longer-term view, even extending over the entire useful projected life of the system, which might be as long as 15 years, or in some cases even longer.

Financial benefits are those that can be quantified financially within the time period under consideration. Their nature will depend on whether the bank's front office or back office is under scrutiny. The assumption below is that the change in state is due to the introduction of a new system. However, it must be emphasized that these financial benefits differ in terms of the extent to which they can be measured, with the specific value depending on the implementation in question.

Examples of financial benefits

These would include:

- overall fee increases;

- higher revenue due to more transactions going through the front office as a result of its greater efficiency;

- higher revenue due to front office staff being better supported (e.g. sales staff might now have access to more effective types of computer-based sales aids);

- higher revenue from more business coming in to the front office generally (and greater income from deposits);

- savings in staff costs due to a more efficient back office system requiring fewer staff, releasing them into other departments.

Examples of non-financial benefits

These would all relate to the improved appeal of the bank to customers, stemming from such factors as increased appeal of the bank's services, improved staff morale and a general perception among the bank's target markets that the bank was more up-to-date and in touch with customer needs than its rivals.

Accounting implications of expenditure on virtual banking

The final budgetary consideration of expenditure on virtual banking is the accounting implications. The following points should be briefly made. These apply to UK accountancy procedures and tax regulations, but most countries have similar rules in place.

- In the UK, from a taxation perspective, expenditure on financial systems is regarded as equivalent to other capital expenditure on a business. As such, the bank is allowed to write down 25 per cent of the overall cost of the expenditure in the first year, and 25 per cent in each of the three successive years.

- Expenditure on labour (whether or not this is involved with implementing the initiative) is 100 per cent deductible for tax relief purposes in the bank's first financial year.

- Note that in some countries there are also tax benefits to be gained from purchasing items on leasing arrangements.

Demonstrating and quantifying the cost benefits of virtual financial services

As we saw at the start of this chapter, the fundamental nature of the cost advantages of virtual financial services consists of the fact that delivering banking services to customers via virtual networks, and carrying out transactions via these networks is always much less expensive, on a unit basis, than delivering similar banking services, and carrying out transactions via a branch.

This cost differential is so important that numerous industry experts have taken the effort to quantify it with some precision. The general view is that delivering banking services and enacting transactions via a virtual network can be up to about one-sixteenth as expensive for the bank as delivering the same type of service, and handling similar transactions, via a branch. Even in the worst-case scenario, delivering banking services via a virtual banking system is unlikely to be more than one-sixth as expensive as delivering the equivalent services via a branch.

The cost to a bank of handling a transaction in a branch is surprisingly high. If all costs of running the branch network (i.e. principally the cost for premises, staff costs, system costs and heating and lighting costs) are totalled and then divided by the total number of transactions processed in (say) a year, it is unlikely that each transaction will cost the bank much less than £30 sterling (or foreign currency equivalent) and it may cost up to £50. On the other hand, the cost differential means that it would only cost about £3 – or even less – to handle the same transaction through a virtual network.

Furthermore, it is also possible to draw a distinction between the cost of a transaction handled by a remote banking system such as a telephone banking service, and through an ATM. Carrying out ATM-based transactions is less expensive than those carried out via a telephone banking service. The precise differential here will also vary from one bank to another, but it is high.

The fundamental cost differential between in-branch processing and virtual network processing applies to the very type of routine transactions which are so well suited to virtual banking systems. Indeed, it is precisely because the nature of the routine transactions makes possible the automation of the service delivery and transaction enactment that the whole process lends itself to virtualization.

The routine transactions which would offer the cost differential if handled through a virtual network rather than through a branch are:

■ cash withdrawal (this corresponds to cheque encashments in a branch);

■ balance enquiry;

■ ordering statements;

■ payment of third-party bills;

■ transfer of funds to another person's or organization's account.

Of these five functions, the first three will be offered by all virtual banks, while the last functions will be offered by some virtual banks but not by others.

Consequences to a bank of the cost differential between virtual and physical delivery

The major consequence to banks of this cost differential between service delivery via a virtual resource and a branch are as follows:

1   The bank will, naturally, want to move as many routine transactions out of its branches as possible.

2   The bank will have a pressing motivation to maximize the usefulness of the virtual resource to the customer. In this context, it is in the bank's interests to ensure that:

   (a) The facilities for making the routine transactions outside the branch should be efficient, since on occasions when these facilities are not working, customers will want to use the branch facilities instead.

   (b) The facilities for making the routine transactions outside the branch are available at all times, morning and night, and seven days a week. This will allow the customer to make the transaction at his convenience, and thereby reduce the chances that he will want to visit the branch to enact the transaction.

   (c) The bank may need to consider ways of pro-actively motivating customers to use the virtual service. Banks in different countries differ in how they enact this pro-active motivation. In the UK, customers have taken readily to virtual services and there has been little effort on the part of banks to motivate customers to use the services other than by marketing and promoting the services widely, and designing new types of bank accounts that feature the virtual service (e.g. the Halifax Building Society's 'Cardcash' account).

In other countries, positive motivation (i.e. actively encouraging the use of the virtual service) or negative motivation (i.e. actively discouraging the use of the branch) have both been used. For example, Citibank offers new customers a small initial financial reward when they carry out a transaction via a virtual service rather than in a branch. On the other hand, a few US banks now impose a charge for branch visits, with this charge sometimes being relatively punitive.

3 The bank will have a clear incentive to use its branches mainly for the more lucrative types of transactions. Just as the bank should do its utmost to ensure that as many routine transactions as feasible are processed outside its branches, it should also do all it can to ensure that those transactions are the most lucrative ones. Such transactions would include:

(a) selling customers pensions, mortgages, life assurance, savings plans and similar products;
(b) contracting with customer for loans and overdrafts;
(c) setting up new accounts for customers;
(d) meeting customers needs for aspects of the banking service where the customer prefers face-to-face contact;
(e) selling new types of products that the bank may start to sell as part of its future development.

A bank which does not make an effort to develop its branches' functionality in the direction of selling more lucrative, high-margin services than standard routine transactions is like a supermarket which only stocks baked beans. The baked beans may be popular, but the low margins available on such an everyday product will make it difficult or impossible for the supermarket to make a profit.

Today's banks will probably need to continue to stock baked beans for some time to come, if not for ever: there will always be customers who will prefer to carry out routine transactions in the branch. However, just as a supermarket can only be profitable by stocking a large proportion of high-margin goods – and will confine baked beans to a small part of its floorspace – institutions must stop seeing their branches as places where routine transactions are conducted, but rather see them as locations for selling to and assisting customers. Routine transactions, like the baked beans, only deserve to have a small amount of floor space devoted to them.

Cost of the virtual banking resource versus the cost of branches

Delivering services and processing transactions via a branch, then, is far more expensive than doing so via a virtual banking resource. But is there not a danger that the cost of setting up the virtual resource will be so high that it will outweigh the cost advantages to the institution of moving from branch virtualization?

The answer is that this is unlikely to be a problem. According to reliable figures made available by Citibank, the cost of setting up for example, a 300-man telephone call centre to provide telephone banking using real staff rather than automated response and operating 24-hours a day is unlikely to be anything more than the cost of setting up and running just two bricks-and-mortar branches a year.

Gatecrashers at the party

Introduction

The twentieth century taught us many important lessons about technology. Two of the most valuable – that technology is ultimately a completely neutral entity and that it is, broadly speaking, available to everybody – are extremely important as far as to the virtual banking revolution is concerned.

Technology, like most great forces, is fundamentally neutral in that whether it is beneficial or positively dangerous depends on the way in which it is used.

In the case of military technology, the question of whether the technology will be useful or dangerous simply depends on which way it is pointing. In much the same way, advanced technology might enable the creation of potentially dangerous devices, but it has also facilitated the construction of devices to help us deal with the danger. For example, new forms of engine design technology and computer diagnostics encourage the creation of motor cars which go much too fast for their (and our) own good. However, advanced technology has also given hospitals life-support systems and health diagnostic tools which can go a long way towards making us better if we are injured in a serious road accident.

Technology is available to everyone. In general terms this point is valid, but it needs some qualification.

For one thing, much advanced technology is patented and will only be available, at least for a time, to the person or organization which developed it. Some technology has obvious implications for national security and will consequently either not be available at all to the general public, or else only available to them in a less effective form. For example, the increasingly popular GPS satellite-based location-funding system is available to the general public, world-wide, but not at quite such a high level of accuracy as the version available to the military.

Other technology is only available to organizations which have a great deal of buying power. This is true, for example, of modern mainframe computers, which typically cost many millions of dollars.

Sometimes this particular point that certain technology is extremely expensive will be deliberately exploited by organizations seeking to prevent unauthorized third parties producing certain types of product. An obvious example – taken from the banking industry – is the increasing use on cheques and bank cards of special features which it is difficult for any person or organization without access to great spending power to reproduce. Holograms and special watermarks fall into this category. Interestingly, this kind of attempt to limit counterfeiting by incorporating features which only official or extremely well-funded organizations can be expected to be able to provide is actually an old-fashioned technique. Banknotes of even 200 years ago featured complex printing patterns which it was reckoned ordinary counterfeiters would be unable to imitate.

Given these qualifications to my earlier statement, I should perhaps modify that statement to say that, *leaving aside special official or military applications, and give the constraints of patenting, technology is available to everyone who has the money to develop and deploy it.*

Today, the virtual banking revolution has led to a form of counterfeiting which is far from illegal, but which none the less threatens the entire traditional banking industry. It is this type of counterfeiting which I address in this chapter.

The reality of the threat of disintermediation

We have already seen, in Chapter 2, that the fear of disintermediation is a major commercial challenge – and a very real threat – facing banks today. It is now necessary to look at this problem and its implications in more detail.

To recap, we are defining disintermediation as

the notion that in the changing financial services arena of the future, an organization which can only provide a secondary rather than primary degree of usefulness may be left out of the equation altogether.

Again, banks are only providing a secondary degree of usefulness because the money which is their prime commodity is only useful for what it can buy, rather than being useful in itself.

Clearly, the threat of disintermediation arises from the facts of technology being both a fundamentally neutral force (it isn't specifically designed to serve the interests of banks) and also being something that is readily available to other organizations which have enough spending power. In this case these other organizations are non-bank organizations which want to move into the banking business.

If banks can use the technology that lets them become virtual organizations, then so can their non-bank rivals. Indeed, and this is the really important point, *non-bank rivals can enjoy the huge cost and efficiency advantage of not starting the competitive battle handicapped by a substantially obsolete branch network.* If a traditional bank can create a virtual banking division (or extension) that makes use of state-of-the-art technology and doesn't rely on the traditional banks branch network to function successfully, why should a non-bank not enjoy precisely the same privilege?

Why not indeed? Especially since smaller banks have for 20 years or so been exploiting earlier stages of the virtual banking revolution to compete at a national level with their larger rivals.

One of the great plus points of shared ATM networks, from the perspective of smaller banks, is that they give these smaller banks the opportunity to offer their customers a nationwide ATM service without the bank itself having to install more than a small number of machines. Technology within the banking industry has frequently demonstrated himself to be a great facilitator of competition in this way. Banks can, therefore, hardly be surprised if newcomers to the market exploit this capacity to their own ends.

Not only is the technological means available to facilitate the newcomer's entry into the market, but the *desire* to make the entry will inevitably be there, too. Banking is potentially a highly profitable business to be in; especially given the fact, already explored, that virtual banking systems enable the delivery of banking services at a much lower cost than is the case when these services are delivered via a physical branch. But it is true that the banking industry generally, and the retail industry in particular, are not areas where a newcomer can expect to make an instant killing. Inevitably, the initial cash-flow is going to be substantially more outward rather than inward, as the newcomer builds up a reputation and an effective presence. However, given that fundamental point, the industry is still highly attractive to well-funded organizations looking to make a profit in the medium to long term.

We now need to look at what types of organizations these newcomers to the banking industry are, and why they are so keen to become bankers.

Who are the gatecrashers?

Gatecrashers generally come in a great variety of shapes and sizes, and so do the particular type of gatecrashers who are entering the banking industry today.

Of course, to call them 'gatecrashers' at all is slightly to beg the question as far as their status is concerned. From *their* point of view they are not gatecrashers but are simply exploiting an exciting and potentially profitable commercial opportunity. However, no traditional type of bank can afford to be so philosophical about the challenge posed by these newcomers: the challenge is a frightening one and most definitely questions the entire assumption of the need for a traditional banking industry.

In terms of the nature of the organizations which are coming into this industry, they could potentially consist of almost any type of organization which has the financial resources to launch a workable virtual banking resource, and maintain it during the first couple of years when profitability is likely to be low or non-existent, and which have the inclination to move into the banking business.

We should not rule any large organizations out as potential entrants. After all, if General Motors can buy and make a success of an organization like Electronic Data Services (EDS), which is in a very different business from that of making motor cars, it should not be difficult for any large organization to move into banking.

As one might expect, the type of organization most likely to move into banking are large retailers with substantial customer bases and a high profile among the general public. After retailers, the next most likely class of organization to move into banking are financial services organizations (such as insurance companies and investment companies) which already have a track record – and often a very lengthy track record – of supplying financial services to the public. The next most likely class of organization to get involved in banking appears to be telecommunications organizations, which already have networks set up through which virtual banking services might be delivered.

Real-life experience suggests that telecommunications companies are unlikely to enter the banking business without first teaming up with a business partner with access to some of the know-how associated with marketing retail or financial services to the general public. However, the first two categories of organization mentioned in the preceding paragraph are usually perfectly happy to enter the banking industry themselves, without forming any joint venture, although they may need some additional expertise. Sometimes retailers do join forces with a bank, in order to provide a major new range of banking services, but where this is the case the retailer will usually avoid promoting the bank which is the business partner but will ensure that the new banking service is seen very much as associated specifically with the retailer's own name.

Whatever the nature of the newcomer, it will obviously have decided that entering the banking business makes sense to it from a commercial standpoint. In order to investigate the nature of the competitive threat posed by these newcomers, we need to confront the precise reasons why they are so well placed to become bankers, and also look at the problems they face in their endeavour.

Reasons why newcomers are well placed to enter the banking business

Assuming that we are talking here about a newcomer which fits into one of the three categories listed above (large retailer, large financial services company and large telecommunications company), the reasons why entering the banking business will probably make sense for them are as follows, in descending order of importance.

The newcomer will have a widely-recognized brand name

It is infinitely easier for an organization to win the public's confidence in relation to a new venture if the organization has already won their confidence with another type of venture. Large retailers have by definition a considerable number of loyal customers who associate them with the generally positive experience of doing their weekly shopping on the retailer's premises. The notion of the experiences being positive is important. The importance of weekly visits to supermarkets and superstores is being increasingly recognized by sociologists as an important part of the fabric of modern life. Some are even going so far as to argue that these visits replace an earlier generation's visits to a church.

In the case of financial services companies, the association with agreeable weekly shopping visits will not be there in the same way, but this should be readily compensated for by the solid reputation the financial services company will presumably have built up.

Telecommunications companies have the least advantage in this respect, since even though their name is likely to be well known to the public, there will be little truly advantageous brand association. Most people take their telecommunications companies for granted and do not think much about the name of the company which supplies this basic utility. One might say that telecommunications companies are handicapped by the facts of their service being supplied in a virtual way from the outset!

The newcomer will have a large customer base and will be ideally placed to market the new service to it

This point is fairly self-explanatory. Next to the brand name, its customer base will be its most valuable resource, both in terms of its entry to the banking sector and in terms of its commercial activities generally.

Furthermore, modern marketing methods – including a variety of methods which enable the buying potential of different customers to be assessed with considerable accuracy (one organization supplying such techniques was profiled in the case study at the end of Chapter 1) – greatly assists with maximizing the success rate from marketing new types of service, such as banking services, to customers.

The newcomer will have considerable financial resources

Entering the banking business is extremely expensive and, as we have seen, is unlikely to produce much in the way of return for the first year or so. It is consequently essential that the organization entering the market is well funded. The organization also needs financial credibility and creditworthiness to a level beyond any suspicion that it would ever default on its liabilities. All developed countries nowadays have extremely stringent regulatory requirements which any organization entering the banking sector, or for that matter already in it, must comply with.

In the case of large retailers, financial services organizations or telecommunications companies, the possession of the requisite levels of financial resources will almost always be in place. Furthermore, as I mentioned in Chapter 2, these types of organization frequently have better credit ratings than many traditional banks (this is particularly true in the United States). While the average customer is unlikely to be aware of the credit rating of a traditional bank compared with that of a newcomer – or, indeed, aware of credit ratings of large organizations at all – organizations with better credit ratings can borrow money (by the issuing of bonds) more cheaply than those with less good ratings, which gives them an in-built commercial advantage.

The newcomer will already be experienced at operating in a highly competitive environment

In the vast majority of developed countries the banking industry has been extremely competitive for at least 10 years. Prior to that, restrictions on who could enter the industry, coupled with the persistence of traditional ideas that having a bank account was some kind of privilege, meant that many traditional banks were not all especially effective at operating in a highly competitive environment.

Even though the time when banking was, arguably, too respectable and uncompetitive for its own good has passed, many traditional banks still to some extent appear to regard fierce competitiveness as somewhat below them and still consider that they have a God-given right to their customer base.

Newcomers to the industry – especially if they are in the three categories identified and consequently used to operating within highly competitive markets (admittedly, this is less true of telecommunications companies but it applies to some extent) – will be adept at competing fiercely and consequently they have an edge over traditional banks in this respect.

Problems newcomers may face

In addition to the advantages newcomers are likely to enjoy from the perspective of competing with traditional banks, they will also inevitably face some problems. These, listed in order of severity, are as follows:

The newcomer will not have a track record of offering banking services

This is an obvious problem for newcomers. It amounts to just about the only thing the traditional banks have going for them in a competitive sense in relation to the threat posed by the newcomers. The public will not automatically associate the newcomer with being a provider of banking services, and consequently the newcomer will have to launch a vigorous marketing initiative to project itself in this way to its customers.

However, there is ample evidence from newcomers which have already started to succeed in the banking industry that customers quickly get used to the idea of a new organization offering banking services, especially if the organization is one with which they are already familiar.

Furthermore, the point that newcomers will not have experience of offering banking services and delivering them is not really a valid one, as the whole point of the virtual banking revolution is that an organization can buy in the requisite delivery technology, as well as specialized banking expertise (from a consultancy or simply by hiring banking specialists), and set up a bank from scratch.

The newcomer may initially be restricted to relatively unprofitable customers

This is not such an obvious problem as the first, but it is likely to be more persistent. The point is that newcomers to any banking industry frequently find themselves landed with customers who are not particularly creditworthy and not especially rich. This is because more creditworthy and wealthier customers are likely to have their banking arrangements already deeply embedded in a relationship with a traditional bank. As such, they are unlikely to want to change those arrangements unless a very good incentive is offered to them for doing so. Of course, newcomers will from the outset set out to market products which provide the very incentive which may be required, but this does not greatly alter the fact that the more profitable types of customers are unlikely to be successfully wooed by newcomers.

There is also the status factor, especially in countries like the United States and United Kingdom, where personal status – and implicit differences in status among different people – is an important part of general culture. For example, a London-based customer of Coutts Bank is unlikely to want to become a customer of Sainsbury's bank without a great deal of persuasion, and while this is a fairly extreme example (as Coutts is a particularly traditional and exclusive bank) the status issue is always likely to be a big factor for people who do not like the idea of banking with an organization they usually see as a supermarket.

Some newcomers might agree that this problem is not as severe as it might seem at first sight, because there is plenty of money to be made from less wealthy customers as long as stringent credit testing procedures are put in place. Furthermore, wealthier customers might move to the newcomer in time if the newcomer is perceived as offering a consistently good deal.

The newcomer's entry will only be credible if the technology it deploys is extremely reliable and its staff are highly-trained in customer service

This is not so much a problem as a warning. Clearly, a newcomer's technology and remote delivery systems will have to work to the highest level of efficiency if the competitive credibility of the newcomer is to be established and maintained.

Similarly, customer service staff deployed by the newcomer must be of the highest personal qualities and must be highly trained in the often difficult and sensitive business of handling bank accounts and providing advice over financial matters.

Fortunately for their customers and themselves, newcomers understand the need for technological infrastructures and staff capabilities to be of the utmost quality. Which is essential. If you are delivering a banking service via remote channels and making use of telephone staff to assist customers, these are your only resources and they have got to be of superb quality.

The competitive power of newcomers around the world

The role of newcomers in competing with traditional banks by using virtual financial services varies considerably around the world, depending on a variety of factors relating to certain commercial and academic conditions in the country in question.

Generally, the factors dictating what level of competitive power the newcomers are likely to enjoy will be as follows:

The extent to which the current traditional banking system has left any scope in the market for newcomers to offer products and services that can be supplied at a profit

This may seem a fairly tautological factor, but there has to be some slack in the banking industry if any newcomer is likely to have a chance. Experience shows that the major area of potential opportunity is simply the relative slowness of traditional banks to offer virtual delivery channels, because they are still too branch based. This unquestionably creates an opportunity for newcomers to move into the market by offering such services, which, for reasons we have already seen, are extremely attractive to customers.

There are also, clearly, opportunities for newcomers to offer services which meet customers' needs more precisely than those being offered by traditional banks, and products – such as new types of account – with benefits (mainly in the area of access, interest on deposits and banking facilities) which, if the product is properly designed, the customer may prefer to existing products offered by traditional banks.

The newcomer's brand strength in the market

We have already seen that the newcomer's brand strength is an essential resource. It is not, clearly, impossible for a completely unknown newcomer to launch a successful market initiative, but this is much more difficult than for a newcomer which already is a familiar name, and the additional financial expenditure necessary to overcome the confidentiality of the name may prove an overwhelming disincentive to the would-be newcomer.

The strength of the newcomer's existing customer base

Similarly, it will be much easier for a newcomer to make an impact in the market if it has an existing base of customers who can be targeted as prospective customers of the new products and services.

A benign regulatory climate

Clearly, no newcomer can make an impact in a country's banking sector if the newcomer is forbidden by law from entering the sector. The fact that in most developed countries the regulatory climate is, generally, favourable for such incursions by newcomers should not blind us to the fact that this is far from the case in every country. In many developed countries – especially areas with lower populations – there are extremely good reasons for the number of service providers in the banking sector to be kept relatively small and for possibly unscrupulous outsiders to be kept out.

It follows from these points that there is no possibility of summarizing the success which newcomers are having in moving into the banking industry generally throughout the world. Instead, we are obliged to investigate each national market as an individual case.

A complete investigation of the role of newcomers in moving into the banking sector in the leading countries of the world would have little clear benefit to the reader. The purpose of this book is to make practical strategic points, and focusing on large numbers of individual cases would no more provide this strategic advice than a telephone directory provides information about the human personality. Another obvious problem is that the scale of the research needed would be unfeasibly large, and that in any case the time elapsing between the undertaking of the research and the publication of this book would mean that the information was out of date as soon as it was published.

That said, some insight into how newcomers are moving into providing banking services needs to be drawn from real life case studies. Furthermore, the reader will understandably want to know in broad terms what success newcomers are having in the major markets of the world. I consequently look in the next section at national trends in the United Kingdom, United States and Continental Europe, and then provide details of representative case studies. The chapter concludes with strategic advice about how banks can fight back.

Major national trends in the success of newcomers from other sectors at penetrating into the banking industry

There is no doubt that the most developed market in the world, as far as newcomers entering the banking industry is concerned, is the United Kingdom. While this might seem too easy a conclusion for a UK-based writer to reach, it is none the less a valid fact.

Why should it be so? A number of reasons can be identified.

First, and perhaps most importantly, the UK has historically had extremely strong and successful retail and financial services sectors. It is from these two sectors that most newcomers in the UK derive. Britain led the world's industrial revolution, and also in the subsequent huge social change which led to the growth of cities at the expense of the rural life of the past. In many respects the most competitive period for retailers in Britain was not the twentieth but the *nineteenth* century, as anyone who has read the advertisements in Victorian magazines and family newspapers will readily see. Retailers who were able to win a reputation for quality and attention to the needs of the customer were able to establish powerful positions in the marketplace even before the end of the nineteenth century. Furthermore, it is difficult not to conclude that there is something inherent in the British national personality – something to do with the love of individual assertiveness and the sense that one's home is one's castle and the seat of one's personal empire – which makes retail a profession well suited to it. Napoleon was not being entirely insulting when he called Britain 'a nation of shopkeepers' – he was also being to some extent accurate.

Similarly, the financial services sector in Britain was already well demarcated in the nineteenth century, with many of today's market leaders achieving a dominant position during the century. This is particularly true of the insurance industry, which by the twentieth century had built up a very substantial capital base.

Second, the relatively large population of the United Kingdom has made the country a potentially highly profitable place to do business for companies which are able to create products and services and appeal to the widest proportion for the population. It is, therefore, generally the case that companies which have done well in this respect have done very well.

Third, and this point is often not accorded the importance it deserves in works analysing the UK banking industry, the whole cultural bias of the United Kingdom is of a country which, while life is heterogeneous in different regions, none the less coheres very successfully into a single national unit. Furthermore, the United Kingdom is small enough in a geographical sense for a company to obtain a national presence relatively easily, whereas in many other countries – notably the United States – achieving a national presence is only possible for the very largest companies, and even they frequently do not obtain true national coverage in the sense that this is possible in the United Kingdom. For example, a British clearing bank would only regard itself as truly national if it had a branch in every major town or city. Such a level of coverage would be impossible in the United States, and in many other countries.

The ready national cultural coherence of the United Kingdom is extremely important for the argument here, because it means that companies have ample scope to project a chosen branding to the entire country. The United Kingdom's public is a ready target for the communication of such a branding, and the process is greatly aided by the relatively few media delivery channels. For example, at the time of writing there are in the UK only two national television channels which broadcast commercials, and the peak viewing times for both these channels are well known, so much so that an organization which wanted to make a large sudden impact on the consciousness of the UK public could easily do so by advertising at these peak periods, such as during the commercial break in the most-watched evening news, *News at Ten*.

Proof of the ready capacity of the UK public to assimilate a new branding was dramatically shown in 1995, when the National Lottery was launched. From a zero standing start, the National Lottery became a national institution within a week or so of its launch, and initial enthusiasm has shown no great signs of diminishing. As a result, the National Lottery is the most popular lottery in the world, and its popularity easily exceeds much longer-established lotteries, such as state lotteries in the United States.

In practice, all the most successful newcomers in the United Kingdom's banking industry had strong brandings even before they became involved with the banking sector, and used these brandings as central focal points for their banking initiatives.

Finally, the regulatory climate in the United Kingdom is extremely amicable to new entrants to the banking industry, given that they have the highest level of credibility and the financial resources to ensure investor protection. The United Kingdom banking industry was, in effect, deregulated to a great extent during the mid 1980s by legislation which, designed to offer much higher levels of investor protection, tacitly accepted that the best way to do this was to set specific requirements which entrants would have to fulfil and thereby create a level playing field for all market participants, whether traditional institutions or newcomers.

As a result of these factors, the United Kingdom is an ideal microcosm to demonstrate how vigorous activity from newcomers can make a serious impact in the banking industry. The effectiveness of the assessment is, however, limited by two factors: first, by the understandable reluctance of actual participants to reveal the precise statistical details of the success in their new markets, and certainly by the reasonable inference that if the United Kingdom is a particularly fertile environment for newcomers wishing to move into the banking sector, that lessons learned there may not necessarily be capable of being duplicated elsewhere.

Moving now to consider the United States, it is – perhaps somewhat unexpectedly – the case that in that country there is little sign of newcomers making moves into the banking industry, at least on anything other than an occasional basis.

The reasons why this is the case are not difficult to identify. For one thing, fewer people hold bank accounts in the United States compared to most developed countries; many working people only visit a bank in order to cash their paycheque. There is also the point that the cost of property in the United States is, with the exception of densely populated cities, much less than in Europe. As a result, banks are rarely under the same cost pressure to reduce the number of their branches that their counterparts in Europe are under.

Another important factor is the relative scarcity of widely recognized retail and financial service organization brands in the United States compared to the United Kingdom and continental Europe. This scarcity has already been touched upon and has a great deal to do with the physical difficulty of creating a truly nationwide infrastructure of any kind.

A more subtle point is that retail organizations in the US tend to focus on a particular social sector from the beginning and as a result tend to become categorized fairly rapidly into certain niche areas which relate to the customer base. Typically a retailer will either be positioned at the lower end of the market (for example K-Mart) or at the upper end (e.g. Patagonia). Retailers who span all social classes in their appeal (such as Marks & Spencer in the UK) are relatively rare.

Another interesting factor in the United States is the 'frontier' relationship which many people have with their bank: the physical identity of the bank is very much rooted in the idea of a solid, reliable building which keeps their money safe and which they can trust. This is a point that is difficult to corroborate, but experience to date suggests that Americans are not particularly keen to switch this solid and reliable type of relationship for a more virtual relationship *with an organization which they do not readily think of as a bank.*

There is no contradiction here with the fact that electronic banking services were first developed in the United States and first demonstrated their popularity in that country. The point is that Americans see these electronic banking services as extensions of their own bank and as part of that banking relationship. There is little evidence to suggest that they would be happy to use a virtual bank – set up by an organization they regarded as being in another sector completely – with such enthusiasm.

Taking our conceptual wander across the Pacific to Japan, we find a much more promising country from the perspective of newcomers from other sectors entering the banking industry.

Japan is very much a cash-based society, and as a consequence of this has the largest per capita figure for ATMs in the world (about 1100 per million people, compared to about 570 per million in the US and just under 400 per million in the UK (Retail Banking Research). To date retailers or financial services organizations have not made much progress with breaking into the banking business in Japan, but evidence that they are looking at this very seriously was provided to me by a senior executive at Sainsbury's Bank in the United Kingdom, who said that the majority of requests for opportunities to visit the new bank and find out how things are going are received from Japan.

Certainly, Japan seems an ideal candidate for giving newcomers from other sectors the opportunity to move into the banking industry. For one thing, property is fabulously expensive in the major cities – it is, indeed, among the most expensive property in the world – and banks therefore have considerable incentives to go virtual. A newcomer offering a virtual banking service would not be seen as anything unusual by customers used to their own banks delivering more and more of their services across computerized networks. Furthermore, Japan has an economy that is famous for its highly visible major corporations, and many of the largest organizations have their fingers in many pies already. There is, additionally, a highly cohesive Japanese national identity, which is, in any case, a country which occupies a relatively small geographical area. All these factors make Japan the ideal country where other types of organization than banks could move into the banking sector. We can, consequently, expect to see a great deal happening in this respect in the future.

In Europe the situation varies considerably from one country to the next. In Scandinavia, for example, where national identities are strong and national brandings are common, newcomers from other sectors have made considerable inroads into the banking industry. Elsewhere in Europe the situation is very much that of only gradual change compared to the burgeoning competition in the United Kingdom. For example, in France, the supermarket chain Carrefour – one of the biggest players in the market with 147 superstores around France – is the only retailer of any size involved in the banking market at present. It was also, interestingly, the *first* European retailer to get involved in financial services and banking in anything like an ambitious way: the foundations of Carrefour's Services Financiers (a separate division) dates back to 1980.

In most other continental European countries the general pattern is that one or two newcomers from other sectors are certainly launching initiatives to enter the banking industry, but there is nothing like the level of competitiveness prevailing which one sees in Britain. And there is another factor alluded to earlier. As Philip Springuel, Brussels-based principal market analyst of European research think-tank Organisation and Technology Research, pointed out to me: 'Some countries, like Belgium, are simply not candidates at present for retailers to move into banking because the banking market is regulated by laws which keep them out.'

Springuel was also a useful source of information about developments in the former eastern Europe. He has identified developments in Russia and the Czech Republic which suggest that retailers in these countries are taking an active interest in opportunities in the banking sector. This is in many respects what we would expect, as the market economy banking infrastructures of these and other eastern (or central) European countries are still fluid and the opportunities for well-funded and resourceful (in every sense) newcomers are immense.

Finally, retailers and financial services organizations are making some gradual headway in banking in Spain and Portugal; two countries where retailers and financial services organizations have traditionally been highly competitive.

Representative case studies

I call the following case studies 'representative' because they provide considerable general information about how newcomers are approaching the difficult business of competing with traditional banks. The case studies concern two types of organizations: retailers and financial services companies.

Rather than presenting merely the bare bones of what has been going on, I have written up the case studies in the form of business stories. The justification for doing this is that ultimately the move from one type of functionality into another type of functionality is for any corporate organization a cultural as well as procedural change and this needs to be reflected in the substance of the case study.

The organizations featured in these case studies are as follows:

■ Carrefour (France);

■ Direct Line (UK);

■ First Direct (UK);

■ Prudential Banking (UK);

■ Sainsbury's Bank (UK);

■ Virgin Direct (UK).

Case Study: Carrefour

Researching this particular case study was a great pleasure, as it provided a pretext to visit the Carrefour hypermarket closest to my home: the one at the Cité Europe shopping centre in Calais, France. This enormous shopping mall, which itself contains an only slightly less enormous Carrefour, is conveniently located close to the exit on the French side of 'Le Shuttle', the Channel Tunnel. However, inspired by my multiple viewings of the intensely romantic film *Titanic*, I decided to go by ferry. This turned out to be close to the least romantic experience possible: the ship was full of English tourists whose only objective was evidently to buy as much drink at their destination as they could and who managed the singular feat of being totally drunk even before they reached the vicinity of the shopping mall.

However, the journey was worth it merely for the experience of visiting a Carrefour hypermarket. There is a deep love of the extreme and the spectacular in the French soul, and Carrefour marries the two very well. Quite apart from appearing to sell just about everything it's possible to buy on earth, except perhaps for a tame elephant, the range of food and drink available at Carrefour defies belief. Nothing on display at any United Kingdom supermarket can even start to compete with the bakery counter, the in-store butcher, the fish counter which includes shark, octopus and oysters, or the vast number of aisles containing bottles of wine and cans of beer stacked inexplicably about 20 feet high.

The first Carrefour hypermarket in France opened in 1963, with 1966 seeing the opening of the biggest self-service store in Europe at that time. In 1969 Carrefour started its programme of expanding abroad, and went public in 1970. Since then it has grown to operate in 14 countries, with a continual programme of expansion being planned in other countries. There are now a total of 117 stores in France. The organization is also active in vertical supply and in a number of other retail activities.

Carrefour started to become involved with financial services in 1980, when it launched what was then known as the Societé des Paiements Pass. The purpose of this was itself to launch the Carrefour 'Pass' credit card.

Later in the decade, Societé des Paiements Pass diversified into other financial services, including personal loans – first offered in 1987, and savings facilities, which were launched in 1989.

The total range of services now offered by Carrefour's Services Financiers are as follows:

- 'pass' credit card;

- savings account for day-to-day deposit and withdrawal;

- term savings bond;

- life assurance with an investment element;

- car loan;

- personal loan.

The response to the financial services launched by Carrefour has been extremely impressive. There are currently about two million customers of the financial services division and customer research shows that about one-fifth of all Carrefour customers use at least one financial service supplied by Services Financiers.

Assessment

The initiative Carrefour launched to move into financial services has been a big success. As the first such initiative in the world, Services Financiers leads the way for what a retail chain can reasonably hope to achieve with financial services. The key to Carrefour's success in this respect has been to market its financial services heavily through the medium of its shops, and to introduce new services gradually to win customer acceptance.

Case Study: Direct Line

Introduction

Direct Line Insurance (referred to as Direct Line for the remainder of this case study) is one of the UK's largest motor insurers and one of the UK's top 10 insurers of homes and their contents. It employs more than 3500 people and has assets of £1.2 billion and a total of three million customers.

Direct Line also takes pride in its ability to improve its internal efficiency. Its current internal cost per in-force policy is £45, which is considerably lower than the industry average.

Peter Wood, founder and chief executive of Direct Line, summarized the company's commercial aims as 'excellent service delivered by enthusiastic, well-trained people and supported by effective systems and marketing'.

Independent research in July 1995 found high levels of satisfaction with Direct Line's new claims and repair services: 95 per cent of customers stated that they would recommend Direct Line's claims service to their friends. Judging from Direct Line's success since then, it has not faltered in providing customers with satisfaction.

Origins

Direct Line originated in the early 1990s when a group of businessmen, led by a marketing and computing expert called Peter Wood, started to look at the insurance business from a new perspective. Their idea, which seems obvious enough now (especially in view of Direct Line's much-feted success) but which was revolutionary at the time, was to create an insurance company focused entirely around customer needs, and which would deliver its services through that highly accessible and convenient remote delivery tool: the telephone.

Peter Wood and his colleagues came to Direct Line with many years' experience in the provision of insurance and other financial services. This experience had led them to believe that above all, customers wanted four things from an insurance company:

- simplicity;

- convenience of access;

- quality of service;

- value for money.

The insight which Wood and his colleagues had was to see that these four needs were in no way contingent upon the existence of a branch network. This perception, of course, is at the heart of the success of the virtual banking revolution in the most general sense.

Traditionally, insurance (like the banking business) was a staid, deadly serious, dull industry, not the business you wanted to be in if you were a charismatic, ambitious person. Viewed in hindsight, this dullness didn't stem from the insurance business itself but from the way in which the business had developed. There was doubtless a time when insurance *was* exciting; in the old days when the business was transacted in coffee-houses, but over the years the business had become institutionalized. In many respects, by bringing insurance directly to the customer, Peter Wood and his colleagues made insurance exciting again.

The solution they proposed was simple but radical: cut out the middlemen and their commission; establish direct contact with the customer over the telephone; advertise widely and make full use of technological resources to make the transactions quick and simple.

Yet the aim was to go even further than this. It was to make insurance seem like fun, even entertainment. Direct Line became the UK's first insurance company which sold its policies solely by telephone. It was also the UK's first virtual insurance company. The justification for granting it this distinction consists of the following reasons:

- the bricks-and-mortar offices of Direct line were not visible to the customers and did not matter to them;

- the service was delivered remotely;

- the company emphasized the idea of the service being delivered remotely in its branding (i.e. its name);

- a real effort was made to minimize the cost of the service delivery to the customer (and, as we saw above, to the company).

The Direct Line concept proved successful from the outset. The first Direct Line office opened for business in Croydon on 2 April 1985 with 63 staff selling motor insurance. The service included quotations over the phone (at the time an unusual service to provide), a 24-hour accident helpline and a windscreen replacement service. Note, incidentally, that Direct Line shared one feature with all virtual start-ups; it required a heavy – and inevitably speculative – initial investment.

Direct Line continued to innovate after its launch. In July 1988 it started the UK's first 'Teleclaims' service – a telephone-based way to settle customer claims, with claims forms filled in over the telephone and authorization to proceed with the repair being given almost at once.

Initially, Direct Line had only advertised in the print media: its advertising being based around the Enid Blyton characters Noddy and Big Ears, riding around in their little car.

In January 1990 the company advertised for the first time on British television. At this time the company was solely a motor insurance firm. The new advertising campaign centred around a friendly visual image of a little red telephone on wheels. This image emphasized the convenience, simplicity and remote nature of how the service was delivered, as well as the nature of the insurance the company was offering.

The advertising was successful and has made a considerable contribution to Direct Line's rapid growth. In 1990, when the TV advertising started, it was still unusual for a bank to offer a purely telephone-based service. This simple business proposition, coupled with a forceful and user-friendly advertising proved irresistible.

By March 1992 the number of motor policies in force reached 500,000, with 1 million policies attained by July the following year.

Ideas cannot be copyrighted, and the idea of creating an insurance company which operates using the telephone as its primary delivery mechanism soon spawned a succession of imitators providing a similar telephone-based service. The imitators did not, in most cases, however, have the complete courage of their convictions, for they tended to use their existing name, plus the word 'Direct' rather than create a completely new organization. It was as if they were, in a commercial sense, attempting to have their cake and eat it, too.

None of Direct Line's imitators has done as well as it has, and none has displayed such a resourceful approach to innovation.

The move to offering banking products

From the outset, Direct Line was envisaged as a financial institution that would offer banking products as well as simply insurance. The banking wing of Direct Line – Direct Line Financial Services (DLFS) – was established in 1993 to offer additional products to Direct Line Insurance customers. It was initially set up as a separate company.

DLFS kicked off with its move to providing banking-related services when it started offering unsecured personal loans in July 1993. The spur to inaugurating this new service was a flurry of enquiries from many Direct Line insurance customers who were buying new cars and asked whether a personal loan could be arranged as easily as the purchase of their insurance.

This confirms a theme running through this book: the fact that 'primary degree of desire' factors frequently drive the progress of organizations whose very nature limits them substantially to offering only fulfilment of the secondary degree of desire.

Since July 1993 Direct Line has made a continual and deliberate effort to broaden its product range and customer base. Today, it offers unsecured personal loans, mortgages, savings accounts featuring instant access, a Personalized Equity Plan (PEP) which tracks the stock exchange index, fixed-term bonds and life insurance. The company's mortgage and savings products are available nationwide, while personal loans are offered to Direct Line customers and also to customers who are fully comprehensive motor policyholders with any other insurance company.

One of the many positive attributes of Direct Line's organization is that it has a highly articulate and helpful press office, and while a researcher needs to take care not to be unduly swayed by this helpful fact, there is no denying that a communicative press office which has a genuinely interesting message to put across is always a huge asset for any organization. Direct Line's press office is unequivocal about the organization's objectives: 'all our products have been developed with the same aims in mind,' it comments, 'to provide the cast consumer with something better than what is already available. All our products are easy to understand, and offer excellent value with no hidden charges.'

In August 1996, DLFS merged formally with Direct Line Life Insurance Company, an organization originally established in February 1995 to offer a range of protection-only life insurance products (i.e. not contain any investment element). Following the successful development of products including mortgage protection cover and fixed term life insurance, plus the addition in 1996 of a Tracker PEP, Direct Line announced a joint venture with Scottish Widows in July 1997 to develop the sales and marketing of its life and PEP products' stock.

Direct Line's Instant Access account has been designed with some particularly interesting user-friendly features. Interest is calculated daily and customers can have it paid annually or monthly into their Direct Line account or another nominated account. The organization claims to 'calculate interest more fairly than most other banks and building societies by paying interest on withdrawals until funds reach their nominated external accounts.'

Another interesting idea is what Direct Line colourfully refers to as the Personal 'Jam Jar' Facility. This offers customers an easy-to-use money-organizing facility enabling customers to segment their savings in up to 20 sub-accounts to suit their requirements. For example, one account might be named 'holiday', another 'home improvements', another 'car'. Money, while held separately in these sub-accounts, will be pooled to maximize interest.

By the end of May 1997, Direct Line achieved a milestone of writing more than £1.6 billion worth of business comprising £1 billion of mortgages, £500 million of savings and £110 million of personal loans. Its success continues unabated today, as it continues to launch attractive new financial products.

Assessment

What is undoubtedly impressive about Direct Line both from an insurance and banking perspective is that its approach towards selling financial services has demonstrated a clearly conscious desire to bring these services closer to the public by using virtual delivery methods. There has been nothing accidental in Direct Line's technique; everything has been planned carefully from the outset.

Traditionally among the most monolithic of industries, the large stone buildings of the major insurance companies aptly symbolize the solidity, reliability and yet immovability of these organizations. Direct Line proved what should really have been clear anyway: that the solid buildings didn't matter in the least; that only the customers' needs mattered. In a perfectly literal sense, Direct Line has brought insurance and banking services into the twenty-first century.

In retrospect, the idea of supplying insurance services by telephone and cutting out the middleman seems obvious, but in the mid-1980s, when electronic delivery was still in its infancy, it by no means seemed such a straightforwardly good idea. Direct Line has proven a fundamental principle that lies at the heart of virtual financial services: that the days when the bricks-and-mortar infrastructure of an organization were what mattered have now, as a consequence of the impact of electronic delivery facilities and networks which the customer can access remotely, receded. Nowadays what matters is the fundamental nature of the service itself, and the speed, accuracy and cost-effectiveness with which the vendor can deliver it.

A source at Direct Line told me that the organization considers that it owes its success to important secondary factors, in particular:

■ the training and the enthusiasm of its staff;

■ its development of a clear corporate branding which explains the nature of the service;

■ its running of an advertising campaign which is clearly focused, has mass-market appeal and supports the branding;

■ its ability to communicate its message to the outside world generally.

The role of technology in Direct Line's growth

A newcomer as successful as Direct Line would naturally be expected to have a useful tale to tell regarding its attitude towards virtual technology consequently approached Direct Line on this subject.

The company emphasized that it was careful to keep the precise details of its technology to itself, as the way it used technology, and the type of technology it used, was an obvious aspect of its competitive advantage. However, it was happy to make a formal statement to us about its attitude to technology, which I append here. I present this interesting document substantially as supplied by Direct Line, as Exhibit 5.1. The only difference between their text and this version is that I have removed overly self-promotional text.

Exhibit 5.1 The role of information technology (IT) in the growth of Direct Line

When Direct Line entered the motor insurance market in 1985 it was led by an IT professional committed to the realization of an innovative idea. It was also derided. Laughter rang through the hallowed halls of the UK general insurance industry at the prospect of insurance being sold over the phone.

Yet in less than 10 years, Direct Line became the largest private motor insurer the UK has ever seen, breaking through the two million policyholder barrier in 1994 with profits that made the company the 'jewel in the crown' of its parents, the Royal Bank of Scotland, in the eyes of city analysts.

From day one, the use of IT enabled Direct Line to deal with its customers quickly, efficiently and economically. Using the telephone as its sole distribution channel the company cut out the middlemen of insurance – brokers and intermediaries – and their commissions putting consumer and provider in direct contact with one another.

Twelve years later it seems that no financial services company is complete without the word 'direct' grafted onto at least part of its operations. In many cases, the term is used synonymously with 'via the telephone' – a description which misses the point completely if it simply refers to a business where the telephone is used as a new front end for an old system.

When Direct Line was launched on 2 April 1985, 30 operators were linked to a small IBM mainframe running software designed and implemented by an in-house team in just six months. Each operator took calls from the ultimate in warm leads – members of the public who had taken the trouble to telephone for a quote. Details of their insurance requirements, including personal, cover, car and usage details, were entered on screen and the risk analysed through a systems-based underwriting protocol and rating structure.

The success of this system was not simply down to telephones but the IT systems behind those telephones. Ditching the paper-based approach to insurance administration, Direct Line opted for integrated data processing and storage which simultaneously boosted productivity, cut running costs and enhanced business information.

Between 1985 and 1990 the company grew steadily. Systems were enhanced as volumes grew and, as larger computers were needed, a conversion to MVS took place. At this stage Direct Line was a small to medium-sized insurer – but one with massive potential to improve its market position. The company had developed a business infrastructure with the capacity and cost profile to push prices down while service standards improved.

With the arrival in 1990 of the famous red phone on wheels with its chatty jingle, public awareness of Direct Line reached a critical mass at a period when most of the traditional composite insurers introduced rate rises. As a result, the premiums on offer at Direct Line were low enough to undercut the vast majority of insurers at just the right time.

More and more people started to cross the 'Direct' bridge and they in turn told their friends. Between 1991 and 1994 Direct Line increased its total market share from 2.1 per cent to 10.9 per cent, adding over 1.5 million customers. This represented an increase in premium income of £524 million in a three-year period – in other words over £500,000 for each working day. This exodus shocked the rest of the industry to the core and at this point the advantages of Direct Line's IT-based approach were thrown into sharp focus.

The company's lean infrastructure enabled it to respond speedily to any changes in the market incurring only minimal costs in doing so – there were no brokers to inform, no new rating manuals to circulate, no remote systems to update. The rating structure could be amended and changes implemented invisibly and seamlessly with no effect whatever on the telephone operators talking to customers.

From the beginning, Direct Line technology and the data it supported were closely guarded secrets. The company pioneered precise risk rating choosing, for instance, to rate cars in 99 different groups instead of the 20 used elsewhere in the market. It also aimed to bring the benefits of lower premiums to middle market motorists who had always borne higher premiums so that insurers could 'smooth' the cost of cover over a broad portfolio of risks.

As the number of policyholders increased, rating was further refined. Claims statistics were fed back into the underwriting criteria to enable even more accurate risk assessment. This process worked as a 'virtuous circle' making Direct Line's rating structure an increasingly precious commodity.

Like bodysnatchers in centuries past, competitors who sprang up aiming to duplicate Direct Line's success could piece together the hardware, but faced an uphill struggle to develop the all-important data and software that would breathe life into it.

In the past three years, the growth of Direct Line's business – and the need to bring its advantages to millions of customers each year – had sparked the need for ever faster data processing and greater handling capacity. Single annual upgrades became inadequate to cope with IT demands placed and in one year alone there were three major upgrades. By 1995 the company had one of the largest mainframes available at the time, and had built its own wide area network, linking all of its offices together.

In addition, new products and regional offices placed greater maintenance demands on systems which currently need to offer simultaneous access for thousands of operators, selling a wide range of financial services products from six locations around the UK.

Today, the company handles over 15 million telephone calls a year – yet it still employs less than 3500 full time staff. With the implementation of countrywide call-switching systems it continues to provide a reliable and an almost instantaneous service to callers even during peak periods.

At the start of 1996, a machine with the power and capacity to support the company's business objectives for years to come was introduced, with the purchase of the Hitachi Data System's Skyline 41. It has engines which are twice the power of the older top end mainframes, and can be expanded further to twice its current size – with the potential to continue with an expanded configuration through to the end of the decade.

Today, Direct Line is a case study for technology-based operations which have made the company the world's lowest running-cost insurance provider. With IT as the facilitator for its underwriting, marketing and claims handling, the company's productivity has created new benchmarks for an industry. And these systems – far from making it monolithic – enable Direct Line to be supremely flexible. The company enjoys the benefits of second by second information about every part of its business. Sales and claims statistics are updated each moment so that business decisions or rate changes can be made quickly and responsively given any changes in market conditions.

Information technology is hard wired into the culture of Direct Line. It is one of the key factors influencing any decision about the operations or future direction of the company. The other however is still the most important. It is the customer – but that is another story.

Source: Direct Line

Case Study: First Direct

Origins

First Direct, which has with some justification been called the UK's first virtual bank, grew out of the conviction of its parent company, the Midland Bank (which became part of the Hong Kong & Shanghai Banking Corporation in 1992) that the time was right for a complete change of direction in personal banking.

This conviction arose within the Midland Bank in the late 1980s. At this time, Midland Bank wanted to increase its market share among more prosperous customers: something it had not succeeded in doing by acquisition and which it was finding difficult to achieve through organic growth. Midland believed that the industry was oversupplied, and found that profits were hard to achieve due to the cost cutting which all banks had to undertake as they increasingly found themselves competing with the lower cost base of the building societies. Furthermore, customers were becoming more discerning and were demanding higher levels of service and a return to a more personal approach from their banks.

The Midland Bank suspected that radical thinking would be required to break free from these constraints. A development team – known as 'Project Raincloud' – was formed within the bank and charged with this task.

From the outset, the team suspected that there was a place for a completely new, completely different kind of banking service, but they did not at this stage know in which way it would be different, or how it would operate, or the kind of services it would offer.

For some time Midland Bank had been collecting evidence that a growing number of customers had a deep-rooted frustration with the traditional banking system. This was confirmed by research commissioned in 1989 by the Midland from the independent research organization MORI. This research revealed that customers were progressively making less use of their branch network. (The more recent research conducted by Girobank and quoted earlier in this book does of course provide evidence that this trend is continuing.)

According to MORI, one in five people said they had not visited their branch in the previous month, 51 per cent said they would rather visit their branch as rarely as possible, and 48 per cent said they had never yet met their branch manager. Encouragingly, 27 per cent said they wished they were able to conduct more business with the bank over the telephone.

This research was echoed by similar findings uncovered by the research organization the Henley Centre for Forecasting, which found that customer demand for better banking services was higher than in any other retail sector. Friendly and knowledgeable staff were considered most important, alongside convenient opening hours and quick and easy transactions.

The team came to the conclusion that the way forward appeared to be some form of direct banking – dealing with customers over the telephone – but the research emphasized that there had to be human contact. According to MORI, 75 per cent of those interested in a telephone banking service wanted a person on the other end of the line, not a computer. This particular finding was accorded a great deal of importance within the team's exploratory work.

Surveying the banking industry around the world, the Project Raincloud team found that a tremendous number of financial transactions were already being carried out by telephone. Many banks were already offering what were in effect embryonic telephone banking services that were extensions of the existing branch network. For example, customers might ring in to their branch to request details of account balances, fund transfers and so on.

The Project Raincloud team decided that merely adding telephone banking functionality to their existing branch network was not the way forward, while tacitly conceding that there was no stopping the general trend that customers would want increasing levels of telephone contact with their branches, and ultimately branches would have to cater for this. But if this was the case, why not set up a bank that would only provide services over the telephone: that would not have a physical branch structure at all?

This, in fact, was the overall conclusion of the Project Raincloud team. The result of this thinking was the Midland Bank's decision to launch the UK's first 24-hour telephone bank, First Direct. This was the first virtual bank in Britain.

First Direct came into being at midnight on 1 October 1989. By the end of January 1996, First Direct had more than 560,000 customers. According to First Direct, 85 per cent of customers have recommended the bank to at least one other person.

Facts about First Direct's service

■ First Direct is a virtual bank. Its customers have no reason to visit its physical premises, although they can if they wish make use of the facilities at its parent bank the Midland to undertake transactions.

■ First Direct deals with telephone customers by using only human operators to answer their calls: there is no voice recognition or automated response. First Direct says that the reason for this is that it is what customers want.

■ Telephone calls made to First Direct by customers cost the customer the price of a local call. First Direct therefore subsidizes customers' calls, although it will not reveal how much it spends annually on this subsidy.

■ The security of the telephone call (i.e. to ensure that the person who is making the call is a bona fide customer) is, obviously, a major concern for First Direct. Two security methods are used: First, the customer chooses a password when he joins the bank (the password will remain the same until such time as the customer decides to change it). Every time he makes a call to the bank, the operator asks him for two different specified letters of the password (e.g. the first and third letter, the second and fifth) with the specification changing every time he makes a call. This makes it impossible for someone who is overhearing the call (or who might be on a crossed line) to know what the password is.

   Second, when the customer joins the bank he is asked to supply five pieces of personal information which an impostor would be unlikely to know. For ethical reasons these are not stated in this report, but the type of information that would be useful in this respect would be, for example, the maiden name of the customer's mother. This is not information that an impostor would readily know. Each time the customer phones the bank, he is asked to supply one of the five pieces of information.

■ The telephones are answered by staff known as banking representatives (BRs), who are only permitted to speak to customers after having successfully completed an intensive seven-week training course, which includes four weeks spent looking in-depth at products and systems, communications and telephone techniques and, most importantly, the needs of the customer.

First Direct told me: 'All staff are coached to be more than just order takers – as well as recording what the customer has asked, their role is to ascertain that what the customer has asked for is what the customer really needs.' Incidentally, an important part of the training course is devoted to dealing with bad-tempered or abusive customers.

■ In total there are more than 1200 banking representatives at First Direct, although they will not all be on duty at the same time.

■ First Direct receives an average of 32,000 calls per day.

■ 10 per cent of customers call two to three times a week; 19 per cent call once a week; 18 per cent call once a month. The remaining 53 per cent call less frequently than once a month.

■ 49 per cent of customers are aged between 18 and 34; 40 per cent of customers between 35 and 54. Interestingly, there is a slight trend for the number of customers in the lower age-range to increase and the number in the higher age-range to decrease, as in 1994 47 per cent of customers were in the 18–34 age-range and 43 per cent in the 35–54 range. This suggests that the principal growth area for the virtual service is among younger people, although it must be conceded that older people are evidently only marginally less likely to use a virtual service than their younger counterparts.

- Throughout First Direct's history, the most usual reason for customers to make phone calls has been and is to obtain a balance enquiry. The second and third most usual reasons are, respectively, to use the automated bill payment service and to make a funds transfer between accounts.

- First Direct prides itself on its 24-hour all-year-round service. It is open all the time, day and night and on all public holidays. On Christmas Day 1997 First Direct dealt with 1,546 calls, and on New Year's Day 1998 with 11,644 calls.

Assessment

In order to test the First Direct service, I made three calls to the main First Direct number (0800 242424) without warning and asked various questions about the service. Two of the staff who answered were female and one male. All the calls were answered within three rings and in a helpful and positive way. I had a real sense that the staff members had been trained in a good telephone manner, and were sincere in their desire to help.

I found out the following points from my queries:

- That First Direct is first and foremost a telephone bank.

- That credit items can either be paid in by posting them to the bank, by paying them in over the counter of any branch of Midland Bank, or via a deposit terminal inside any Midland Bank branch.

- That an application form for a prospective customer can be completed on the phone during the first enquiry, and that after the questions have been asked the prospective customer will be told whether First Direct can offer him a banking service.

- That the banking service includes a cheque book, and a three-function plastic card that functions as a cheque guarantee card, an ATM card and a debit card.

- That the current account comes complete with a free £250 overdraft facility.

- That the customer can apply for a First Direct Visa card.

With more than half a million customers on its books, there is little doubt that First Direct has been a success. First Direct's overall business target when it started trading in 1989 was to win one million customers by the year 2001, and a source at First Direct said that the number of customers to date is what the bank expects in order to meet this target, although the bank has a policy of not revealing precise customer numbers.

First Direct has proven not only that a virtual bank can work, and work well, but also that customers are more than happy to transact most of their banking activities via the telephone. First Direct is therefore an important pioneer in virtual banking.

It is difficult not to be highly impressed with the care which First Direct has lavished on its staff training, and the way that products have been designed with the customer in mind. First Direct now sells loans and mortgages to customers who do not bank with it. This was not the case for the first few years of its operation, and can only reflect the increasing confidence of its operations.

What happens if a First Direct customer asks for a transaction or transfer to be made and then denies having asked for this? First Direct deals with this problem by recording all incoming calls (and the rare outgoing calls), and by keeping a careful log of all transactions. My First Direct source said that these kind of repudiated transactions were not a problem for the bank.

The only problem the source said the bank had faced during the time since it started to trade was the challenge of convincing people that a telephone bank could give them a full banking service. If this was ever a serious problem, it would have been so only in the first year or so of First Direct's operations. Throughout the 1990s, the principle that a telephone banking service cannot only be as good as a branch-based service but even better, seems to have been comprehensively accepted as much by customers as by banking professionals.

Finally, the most significant – and, perhaps, ironic – point to make about First Direct is that while it has gone on from strength to strength, its parent organization the Midland Bank experienced financial problems in the early 1990s and was taken over by the Hong Kong and Shanghai Bank in 1992.

Case Study: Prudential Banking

Introduction

The Prudential Assurance Company is one of the United Kingdom's oldest insurance companies. It was founded in 1848, primarily to offer working people a way to amass enough funds under a life insurance policy to pay for a decent burial. In the middle of the nineteenth century, one of the many fears which the impoverished working class had to face was that they would not have enough money to pay for their own funeral and would be forced to suffer the humiliation of being buried in a pauper's grave, where they might have no tombstone at all, or be commemorated by one of those hardly dignified tombstones sometimes seen in old churchyards, with the deceased person only being remembered by his or her initials.

To help its Victorian customers deal with this pressing but hardly financially ambitious problem, the Prudential offered famous 'penny policies'. The premiums for these were collected by local agents who over time became symbolized in the figurative notion of the 'Man from the Pru': a quaint idea that was successfully revived in a 1997 advertising campaign for the company. It was necessary to collect the premiums in person, and in cash, because at that time the Prudential's customers would be as unlikely to hold a bank account than they would to have worn a top hat.

The Prudential prospered in a business where quantities of customers were more important than individual customers' personal prosperity. As it grew, it provided a wide range of insurance facilities, but life assurance always remained its principal product base. Like all life insurance companies, it eventually diversified into life policies which contained an investment element, the level of which could be chosen by customers.

The modern Prudential

By the 1990s, the Prudential had about six million customers in the UK and was paying out around £1 billion to them annually in policy maturations. When one considers that this amounts to about £4 million per business day, the scale of the Prudential's activities can be better understood.

Business was booming, but there was one basic problem. 'The challenge we faced in the early 1990s was the same one we had faced for many years,' a source at the Prudential said. 'This was that once we had paid the maturation value over to a customer, we never saw that money again. The customer would simply put it in his or her bank or building society, or would spend it. Either way, usually we had no further involvement in the process.'

Until the late 1980s, the banking industry in the United Kingdom was regulated in such a way that it was difficult for newcomers to break in. However, once a succession of different Acts of Parliament had altered this position, the way was clear for organizations such as the Prudential to think about ways of moving into banking.

The Prudential was already providing one banking-type service. For many years it had been helping its customers to obtain mortgage finance by arranging mortgages through a panel of lenders with which it had forged contacts. By the early 1990s it was arranging about £700 million of mortgage finance for its customers every year. However, it was at that stage in no sense a bank.

The launch of Prudential Banking

All this changed in October 1996, when the Prudential made the historic decision to launch a separate division called Prudential Banking. From the outset the objective was to capitalize on the Prudential's existing customer base by offering customers its own range of mortgages and deposit accounts. These would be sold by the Prudential's 6000-strong regulated sales force, as well as by telephone and post, with the overall organization being based at the Prudential's state-of-the-art operations centre in the West Midlands. The new division would have no branches where customers could pay in cheques to the accounts: they would simply send credit items in to the bank by post.

The Prudential source I spoke to said:

> Before we launched the banking service we conducted extensive research among our customers to find out what they did and didn't like about the service they currently obtained from their bank. The consensus was that many customers felt that their banks let them down and didn't really deliver the goods when it came to service. We therefore decided it was important to start by offering a relatively narrow product portfolio and proving that we could really deliver a high quality of service through the virtual service we were setting up. Our overall strategy was to start small, do the job properly, and win over our existing customers to use our services, as well as customers who were not already with the Prudential.

Generally, the types of customer the Prudential was winning for its new banking division were the same working-class people who had been using its life insurance services, although affluent customers were also being attracted by the new products. Naturally, the days when its customers had no greater aspirations in life than to be able to pay for a decent funeral were long past. Its customers are by now reasonably prosperous and have the financial aspirations of providing the good things of life for themselves in this life rather than the next. Prudential's customer base as a whole is getting much broader in terms of social make-up. That said, the organization is confident of attracting wealthier customers in time to come. It feels that this basic policy of keeping the product range simple and giving a first-class service, coupled with the huge brand value of the Prudential name, is bound to guarantee the real success of the organization in due course.

To date four types of products are on offer: mortgages (there are currently about 100,000 of these with Prudential banking customers); 60-day access deposit account; instant access deposit account; and personal loans.

Prudential has already supplied loans to nearly 3000 customers as a consequence of having one of the most competitive rates in the marketplace, as well as the relatively unusual feature of having no early redemption penalties.

Prudential Banking and technology

The way in which Prudential Banking has made use of technology to facilitate this speedy implementation provides an object lesson in the mechanics of launching a new virtual banking service from scratch.

Prudential took the direct, virtual approach in order to maximize its chance of gaining the necessary volume of business in a relatively short period of time, as well as achieving a desired level of customer service to retain market share over the longer term. It was certainly the quickest and most cost-effective route to the banking marketplace, but it was one heavily reliant on the right technology to make it happen successfully.

After a careful and thoughtful procurement process, Prudential decided to base its banking software around the International Comprehensive Banking System (ICBS), supplied by the banking system vendor Fiserv. This is an integrated retail banking system capable of handling a large customer database and correspondingly high daily transaction volumes.

Given the level of competitor activity, once a decision had been made by Prudential to enter the banking marketplace as a direct participant, it was naturally important to establish a presence in the marketplace as quickly as possible. Richard Duvall, head of information technology at Prudential Banking, says he was aware that the implementation process of just nine months was extremely ambitious.

> Technology had a crucial role to play in enabling us to launch on time – October 1, 1996 – and within our budget. It was absolutely essential that the system met a number of demanding functional criteria. Firstly it had to be extremely flexible, and capable of rapid change. Secondly, it needed to be easy to implement and cost-effective to install and operate. We have found that Fiserv ICBS closely matched these requirements.

With an eye on the need to expand its product range in the near future, Prudential Banking recognized that what was needed provisionally was a 'front end' system to complement the 'back end' strength of ICBS by increasing its information management capability. Prudential decided to source another system from Fiserv, a customer relationship management product – known as Fiserv Alliant – to enable it to take advantage of cross-selling opportunities while still maintaining its ability to provide rapid, consistent and personal service.

'If cross-selling of products is to develop to its full potential,' Duvall says, 'Then simple access to in-depth data held for the customer is paramount. But there's another, less tangible benefit: we will be able to nurture the kind of personal relationship with a customer that has been absent in banking for some time now.'

The Alliant product allows all the information required to manage the customer relationship to be gathered on one system, avoiding duplication and wasted effort, and ensuring convenience and speed of response for the customer, as well as less cost for Prudential. Alliant provides instant access to a comprehensive contact history as well as enabling the outcome of each conversation to be measured. Workflow capabilities increase efficiency by scheduling and then tracking the progress of all tasks, thus enabling the setting and monitoring of performance standards.

'Fiserv's suite of products is enabling us to fulfil our promises to our customers: to provide them with better products and no hidden charges,' said Duvall. 'The systems we have bought enable us to test and implement new products quickly and cost-effectively, facilitating the rapid development of simple, tailor-made products that suit customers' requirements.'

Assessment

Like many newcomers to the banking markets from other sectors, Prudential Banking is experiencing gradual rather than explosive growth. In fairness to Prudential, however, this was what they intended from the outset. Beyond doubt the organization has the financial resources to maintain and support its presence in the banking industry for as long as is required to turn this presence into a complete success. Overall, there seems little doubt that Prudential Banking will be increasingly successful at winning new customers who have no existing relationship with Prudential, and also at converting more and more of the Prudential customer base into banking customers.

Case Study: Sainsbury's Bank

Introduction

The French writer Balzac once observed that all great fortunes begin with a crime. In the case of the illustrious food retailing family, Sainsbury, their fortune began with a shop. The emporium in question was founded in Drury Lane by John and Mary Sainsbury in 1869 to supply dairy products in the West End.

The small shop prospered. Strict attention to hygiene, a real awareness of what customers wanted and a wide variety of wholesome goods were all factors accounting for its success, but the innovative spirit of the couple also played a key role.

The way in which food was supplied in London during the mid-Victorian period was changing quickly due to the increased use of the railway. Today, when we take for granted that – to paraphrase Dr Johnson's famous remark – there is in London all the variety of food that life can afford, it's easy to forget that this was by no means always the case. In the eighteenth century, sheer physical problems of distribution meant that the diet of most Londoners was restricted to ale, salted meat, bread and the occasional vegetable.

By the 1860s, however, the use of the railway had greatly broadened the range of delicacies available to Londoners. The middle-class lady of the house could read Isabella Beeton's *Book of Household Management* (itself first published in 1861) and be confident that the often hugely ambitious recipes contained therein were perfectly feasible, given that she knew where to shop. The Sainsburys were perfectly placed to meet the new demand for superior provisions for middle-class households, and spared no effort to deliver top-quality goods.

For example, they saw that milk brought into London directly from farms in Somerset and Devon would be of much better quality than the sorry liquid produced by cows kept in cramped and dirty conditions in London. The couple used the railways to bring in milk from the West Country – their milk became renowned as 'Sainsbury's railway milk'. The fame of this white nectar made the Sainsbury's shop known throughout London and led to the middle-class – or at least their servants – flocking to it.

With popularity came expansion into other shops. By 1882 there were four Sainsbury emporia. That same year, John Sainsbury constructed his own bacon-smoking stoves. The bacon he smoked in these became the first Sainsbury brand product. He also decided to supply a superior range of products which he packaged more elaborately.

By 1900, the Sainsbury chain had increased to 48 shops. Every establishment was still run on traditional lines, with customers coming to a counter and asking for what they wanted, rather than using self-service.

Developing a corporate identity

Considering that Sainsbury's is now so large and, like all supermarket chains, has sometimes been subjected to complaints that it damages communities by preventing small local grocery shops from making a living, it is somewhat ironic that in 1900, John Sainsbury himself was faced with competition from large retailers who were moving in on the food market.

In order to assert the quality of his shops and to emphasize the 'Sainsbury' identity, he refitted his shops with carefully designed tiled walls, ceramic mosaic floors and marble-topped counters. A new rule book was drawn up to formalize methods of trading and working practices: an example of regulations for corporate identity standardization which are familiar today to anyone who has worked in a large retailing organization.

Sainsbury's now had a distinctive shop design, product packaging and a culture dedicated to maximizing the quality of the food on offer and overall customer service. Customers walking into any of the chain's shops would instantly recognize them as Sainsbury's.

Other innovations followed. During the First World War, the British Government's policy of slaughtering a large proportion of its young men on the field of Flanders naturally caused large shortages in the male workforce. John Sainsbury took a step which seems a matter of commonsense now but which was highly innovative at the time: he recruited women to work as shop assistants. Many of these new recruits stayed on after the war and progressed to become shop managers. The idea of a woman becoming a manager of any branch of a retail chain was virtually unheard of at the time, but it happened at Sainsbury's.

In the 1920s, Sainsbury's created its own transport fleet to meet the expansion out of London of its retail chain. This was a major innovation at the time.

The move to being a major food retailer

By January 1928, when John Sainsbury died, the chain he had started was one of the UK's major food retailers. It went on to greater strength under his eldest son, the number of branches reaching beyond 300 by the 1920s and extending from Kent to Nottinghamshire. The chain was controlled from the company's headquarters at Blackfriars, London, where the administrative staff were located. Also located in Blackfriars were the depot and a factory which produced sausages and other cooked meat products for the branches.

In the 1950s, Sainsbury's was one of the first in the UK to introduce the American idea of self-service shops. A new house style was devised with checkouts, trolleys, refrigerated cabinets, fluorescent lighting, as well as a new and simplified product packaging design. During the 1950s, all shops were converted to this new format.

In the 1970s, Sainsbury's responded to strikes, the oil crisis and rising inflation by looking at new and innovative ways of becoming more efficient. New stores were built, which were much bigger than supermarkets of the past. This new style of store, which was already in evidence in America, had ample parking facilities, and exciting, new in-store outlets such as bakeries and delicatessens. The new stores also started to sell non-food products such as hardware, cleaning materials and household utensils. They were better suited to the lifestyle of people who wanted to pick up as much of their week's shopping in one visit and from one shop as they could.

The 1980s and 1990s were also a time of innovation and further success for Sainsbury's. The retailer was among the first to introduce many new types of technology into shops, including scanning checkouts, EFTPoS, computerized stock control and sales-based ordering.

Problems in the 1990s

However, during the mid 1990s, Sainsbury's results were not as good as they had been. The organization also lost a great deal of its impetus as an innovator. It was perceived as launching its loyalty card, 'Reward', too late in the day. By the time Reward was available, its rivals Tesco and Safeway had already been highly successful with their own loyalty cards. In April 1997 Tesco announced record profits and attributed these to its loyalty card.

Sainsbury's, which had been to some extent left behind by its rivals in the matter of loyalty cards, was determined not to be left behind in the new race among large supermarkets to move into financial services. By April 1997, Safeway and Tesco had both announced the creation of a special new loyalty card, run in conjunction with a financial institution (Royal Bank of Scotland in the case of Tesco and Abbey National in the case of Safeway) which would effectively be a spearhead for eventually launching a range of financial services and using the loyalty card customer base as the basis for the new services.

Faced with this competition, Sainsbury's decided to move into financial services itself. Resurrecting the innovative spirit of John Sainsbury, Sainsbury's decided to go one step further than entering into a joint venture based on a new type of loyalty card. Instead, Sainsbury's resolved to create its own bank.

The creation of Sainsbury's Bank

Sainsbury's decision to create a bank stemmed from a conviction that a retailer with its customer base and customer loyalty could form a bank which would be well-suited to meeting the needs of its customers, as well as being profitable. The need for the bank to be profitable in its own right was identified at the outset. Sainsbury's Bank would be run as a commercial venture, not simply a promotional tool to win customers to use Sainsbury's as their grocer.

Certainly, as discussed earlier in this chapter, the basic rationale of a major retailer going in to banking makes sense. Obtaining money – or access to payment services – to buy food is a major primary use of funds which people hold at financial institutions. For many families, expenditure on food is their second highest monthly expenditure after their rent or mortgage payment, and their principal expenditure if they have no rent or mortgage payment. Today's supermarkets typically have under one roof a pharmacy, butcher's shop, bakery, delicatessen, fishmonger, dry cleaner, newsagent, clothes shop, hardware shop as well as general household goods shops and a food shop; it makes sense to include access to financial services, and even access to a bank, in the same premises. Furthermore, it seems a natural progression for a retailer to be in some direct way involved in facilitating customer expenditure, cutting out the middleman that the banks represent.

Another point to make is a social one. We have already seen that on the whole, people do not necessarily *like* to visit a branch of their financial institution: they make the visit because they need access to their funds. On the other hand, for most people – perhaps excluding mothers with two wailing toddlers in tow – a visit to a supermarket is a fairly pleasant experience. Certainly it is designed to be so, with wide aisles, helpful assistants, a considerable range of things to spend money on, and opportunities to sample produce and obtain recipes.

Indeed, the English-speaking worlds are, if anything, somewhat behind continental Europe in their acceptance of the notion of the supermarket visit as entertainment. In France and Spain, for example, supermarkets are designed to be enjoyable places to visit, with fast-food stalls, a wide range of other shops, and even children's funfairs all under one roof or in one area. Even in the UK, where supermarket shopping is not yet quite as total a shopping experience, people often rendezvous with their friends in supermarkets, and frequently bump into them by accident.

Advantages to customers of banking with a large retailer

The advantages to the customer of combining a supermarket visit with what is in effect a visit to their bank are as follows:

■ Convenience of location: the customer doesn't need to make a special trip to his or her branch but can combine the visit to the supermarket with one to the bank.

■ The customer has the confidence that the bank will be secure. Supermarkets rarely go out of business, and in fact as businesses they are usually particularly strong and creditworthy. Even customers who don't know that will be aware that funds deposited at a bank run by a retailer should be extremely secure.

■ Customers can enjoy special gifts and bonuses for spending money at the supermarket and using the retailer's bank. As with all retailer banks, Sainsbury's Bank allows the customer to use the loyalty card as the focal point of the customer's relationship with the bank and the retailer.

Advantages for a retailer of launching a bank

The principal advantage here is that customer information can be used as the basis for selling a wide range of financial services. This information will typically be obtained from customers when they apply for their loyalty card. Usually the information will be updated by the retailer on a regular basis.

The process of selling to customers who are already members of the loyalty card scheme is, however, not always clear-cut. For one thing, most retailers are still relatively unsophisticated in terms of the level of information they have obtained from their loyalty card holders. Furthermore, there are restrictions placed by the Data Protection Act on the extent to which cross-selling by a retailer's bank to the retailer's supermarket customers is possible. However, there is no doubt that a retailer's loyalty card customer base represents a tremendous market for financial services.

Senior directors at Sainsbury's started their investigation of the possibilities of launching a financial services resource by considering the notion of launching a Sainsbury's credit card. Thinking on this matter started seriously in 1994, but was shelved in favour of creating a loyalty bonus discount card, called 'Reward'. This was launched in June 1996. As we have seen, Sainsbury's was late in launching a loyalty card compared with its rivals. The Reward card initially allowed customers to collect British Airways air miles. This facility is still available, but the card has now expanded its features to enable customers to accumulate free phone calls through British Telecom, discounts at a major restaurant chain and the opportunity to make donations to the NSPCC charity. There is also a more straightforward system of incentives whereby expenditure held on the Reward card (which features a magnetic strip that is connected to a central database storing details of amounts spent) can be 'translated' into cash vouchers to be used when shopping (on the basis of £1 worth of vouchers for every £100 spent) or into gifts. Some lines of merchandise offer extra Reward points, thereby giving Sainsbury's the opportunity to encourage shoppers to buy certain products.

As of the time of writing there are now around nine million holders of the Reward card.

Launch of Sainsbury's Bank

Sainsbury's Bank was launched on February 19 1997. It was initially opened in Scotland, the North of England and the Midlands, with a roll-out geared at taking the bank nationwide by the summer of 1997. The Bank is the result of a joint venture between Sainsbury's, which owns 55 per cent, and the Bank of Scotland, which owns 45 per cent. It was approved as an institution under the Banking Act on January 30, 1997.

The principal elements of the Bank's services are as follows:

- An Instant Access savings account offering a gross annual interest rate of 6.5 per cent.

- A Christmas Saver account.

- A 'Classic' Visa credit card for customers with average income levels.

- A 'Gold' Visa credit card for customers with above-average income levels.

Note that both types of credit card enable cardholders to earn extra Reward Points wherever they shop – even in rival supermarkets. Furthermore, incentives will be paid in cash or points on the Reward card to customers who transfer from their existing credit cards to Sainsbury's Bank credit card.

- ATMs branded as Sainsbury's Bank machines are being introduced in selected stores. They connect with the link ATM system.

- Sainsbury's Bank operates a 24-hour free direct telephone banking facility.

- Sainsbury's Bank is currently rolling out a range of financial products, including personal loans, mortgages and insurance.

Richard Chadwick, deputy chief executive of Sainsbury's Bank, gave me some insights into the strategic attitudes and objectives which led to the creation of Sainsbury's Bank.

He emphasized the importance Sainsbury's placed on the tender which led to the bank of Scotland being chosen as the business partner in the venture. 'We invited around 40 institutions to tender for the joint venture,' he said. 'We were looking for a business partner which was a true cultural fit with our own organization: that is they had to be in tune with our need for a dynamic bank which would set a trend for innovation and developing attractive services.'

Chadwick is clearly ambitious for his baby.

Certainly, we see the Sainsbury's customer base as an essential resource in the success of the Bank. Throughout the UK, about 12 million people visit a Sainsbury's shop every week. Of these, around nine million are Reward card customers. We have detailed information on about around 4.5 million of these Reward customers: this being the number of customers who replied to a mailing we sent out requesting further information about them.

Sainsbury's Bank is most definitely a commercial venture separate from the supermarket retailing arm. It is not simply an extension of our loyalty scheme, but a profit centre in its own right. Frankly, we are not on the whole impressed with the success achieved by other retailers who have moved into financial services. I'd better not mention any by name, but many seem to have had lots of problems making their venture profitable and even when it is, the amount of money they are making is not impressive. We are extremely alive to the notions of profitable and unprofitable customers. We are aware that our Instant Access savings account will probably have some customers who keep a low balance on it and make lots of small transactions. We are aiming to make our principal profit from our lending products, our credit cards (not just in terms of interest, but also from interchange fees from retailers) and from our insurance products. In order to maximize the profits we gain from these services, we are taking every step to market them efficiently.

Chadwick added:

> Our aim is to use the Reward database as a means of creating a list of potential customers. We are looking at the areas where people live and grading them according to post code analysis. We are also keeping records of household income, expenditure patterns and any information we can gather about behaviour and lifestyles. We are able to use the Reward database in our own work but we are not allowed under the Data Protection Act to pass on certain types of information to the retailing arm of Sainsbury's. For example, credit card expenditure by our customers will reveal details of other shops and supermarkets where our customers shop, but we are not allowed to pass this on to the retail arm.
>
> Generally, our definition of the business aims of the bank seems to me to fit in with the general trend that is going on in the banking world. This is a definite decline in the influence of traditional financial institutions compared to those with retailer connections and a shake out of unprofitable financial institutions. *We firmly believe that conventional banks have fallen down in recognizing what customers really want and in presenting themselves to customers as user-friendly organizations. Supermarkets which act as bankers can gain a major edge here.* [my italics]
>
> Of course, unless we actually put this philosophy into practice, there's not much point in formulating it. However, we are putting it into practice. For one thing, we are keeping our customers informed up-front about changes to the way we run their accounts. We are also committed to a policy of complete transparency in our dealings with customers. This is particularly important for sensitive issues such as credit card applications. If we have to decline a credit card application we will give customers full information about why this has happened. In some cases, the customer may be able to take the step which will allow us to grant the credit, such as by the customer proving that a previous credit arrangement which our credit reference agency showed us as not yet settled had in fact been settled.

Current progress

The total number of accounts with Sainsbury's Bank is now 600,000, and new accounts continue to be acquired at a rate of more than 100,000 per week. The Bank currently had a total of £1.4 billion on deposit.

The most recently launched products were personal loans, which hit the market in June 1997, a flexible mortgage which was launched in July 1997 and a range of general insurance products which were launched in January 1998.

Richard Chadwick's comments for the medium-term future of the Bank and its prognosis were: 'Our intention is to offer a wide range of banking products across most product sectors. We will not try to be all things to all men. Products will be simple, easy to use and will offer good value for money, which we take to mean fair rates plus excellent service'.

He added that permanent marketing stands, including a freephone and marketing literature, were being rolled out into all of Sainsbury's 378 stores in the UK. He pointed out that these stores could be adapted to include a touch-screen kiosk. Finally, he pointed out that ATMs branded with Sainsbury's Bank are being installed at present in all new stores and existing stores where space becomes available. There are currently 20 Sainsbury's Bank branded ATMs in the United Kingdom, and all Sainsbury's Bank customers can use any of the machines operated by the UK national ATM network. Ultimately, the aim is to install a Sainsbury's Bank ATM in every Sainsbury's branch in the country.

Sainsbury's Bank and its use of technology to sell retail financial services

The principal use of technology at Sainsbury's Bank for this purpose is based around state-of-the-art relational database (RDB) technology to maximize its marketing opportunities, given the constraints of the Data Protection Act mentioned above. The purpose of the RDB technology is to identify customers who are likely to be purchasers of banking products as a result of their existing relationship with Sainsbury's. Other uses of technology to sell financial services to customers are similarly oriented around extrapolating the use of existing databases, such as the Reward Card database.

Finally, like other new financial institutions offering a direct, telephone-based service, Sainsbury's Bank makes full use of the latest call centre technology, to facilitate a maximum quality of customer service over the telephone.

Richard Chadwick commented: 'In broad terms, we will give serious consideration to any technology which helps us fulfil our three fundamental commercial objectives of flexibility of service, speed to market of new products and services, and low internal costs.'

Assessment

Sainsbury's Bank has certainly made a major impact on the UK banking industry and there is little doubt that it is destined to be a major player here. That said, looking at the losses which it has made since it started trading confirms that a newcomer from another sector needs to have substantial financial backing from a parent organization if it is to survive the first few years when the launch costs and cost of marketing mean that losses are almost inevitable. Sainsbury's Bank lost £6.5 million to February 1997, and losses for the year between March 1997 and February 1998 were even higher: currently estimated at between £15 and £20 million.

Regarding these losses, Richard Chadwick commented: 'These losses stem from the infrastructure cost of setting up the new bank, and also from the marketing costs associated with the launch. The costs are approximately what we were expecting. We will, all being well, move into profitability during the trading year 1998–1999.'

Case Study: Virgin Direct

Introduction

Few people in the UK or the United States can fail to have heard of the Virgin organization, run by the charismatic entrepreneur and adventurer Richard Branson. The name stems from Branson's perception of himself and his colleagues back in the 1960s, when they launched their Virgin record label: as untried in business. The label was phenomenally successful, partly because of Branson's ability to spot musical talent and bring it to a wider audience. Since then, he has become involved in other businesses which interest him, but his approach is not that of the dilettante, but rather that of the hard-headed businessman who sees a gap in the market and sets out to exploit it.

An example is his highly successful airline Virgin Atlantic, which has become a popular passenger-friendly airline by giving passengers more leg room, even in economy class, providing personalized videos with a wide range of choice and by offering first class passengers a widely-publicized service whereby they are picked up from their homes and set down at their actual destination by limousine, given certain distance constraints on where they live and where they are going in relation to the airport.

These twin concepts of spotting a hole in the market and designing products that are truly user-friendly inspired Branson in his most recent business venture: the launch of Virgin Direct Personal Financial Services in March 1995.

The launch of Virgin Direct

At the time of the launch, Branson himself appeared in advertisements regarding the new organization to tell customers why he wanted to become involved in this area. He said that he believed most existing financial service organizations did not pay much heed to what customers wanted and did not give them value for money because salesmen were used by the organization and a large part of initial premiums or contributions went to meeting salesmen's commission.

As Virgin Direct itself explains in its press material: 'Virgin moved into financial services because of the vast gulf between existing companies and the customers whose needs they were supposed to be meeting.'

Virgin Direct's aim is stated as simply being to offer straightforward, good quality products at the lowest price. The organization makes a great deal of its refusal to compromise on customer service and has nothing to do with salesmen. Everything is sold direct. As Rowan Gormley, Virgin Direct's managing director explained to me when we spoke about Virgin Direct in 1997: 'What we're doing is incredibly simple. *We've merely designed products from the customer's – and not the actuary's point of view.* This is an approach which, in just over two years of operation, has attracted more than 120,000 customers, who have placed £650 million of funds under management with us.' (my italics)

Virgin Direct is based around a telephone service. There is only one phone number, and calls to this are charged at local rates. Lines are open between 8 am and 10 pm, seven days a week, and every day of the year except Christmas Day. The company sets great store by the quality of its telephone staff and trains them rigorously in answering customer queries and selling to new customers. As a result, Virgin claims a track record of one in four new business enquiries being converted to a sale, where the industry average is closer to one in 10.

The range of Virgin products spans investment, life insurance, income protection and personal pensions. There are two Virgin Personal Equity Plans (PEPs): Virgin Growth PEP and Virgin Income PEP, with the principal difference between them being that the first is designed for long-term growth and the second for investors seeking income. There is also a Virgin Life Insurance policy which provides straightforward term insurance with no investment element. Another product is the Virgin Survival Plan, which is an income protection policy designed to help customers who suffer a serious illness or accident. It pays out in the case of an accident which affects the customer to a specified extent. It also pays out on formal medical diagnosis of 19 serious medical conditions. Finally, the Virgin Personal Pension is an index-linked pension fund which gives customers a straightforward way to save for their retirement and offers a simple charging basis focused around a £2 charge per contribution, but no bid–offer spread, policy fees or switching fees.

The following is a summary of major events at Virgin Direct since the organization was launched.

Details of major events since the launch

1995

March	Virgin Direct launched.
April	Virgin Growth PEP attracts £42 million in first four weeks.
June	Launch of regular saving payment option for Virgin Growth PEP.

September	Virgin Atlantic stewardess storms Fidelity Direct's boardroom to issue the Virgin Challenge (PEP performance/pricing challenge).
October	New style, corporate bond fund – Virgin Income PEP – launched.
November	Parts company with Norwich Union and forms joint venture with Australian Mutual Provident.

1996

March	Virgin Growth PEP ranked first out of 137 funds in the UK Growth and Income sector with return of 28.13 per cent.
	Virgin Direct's first ever TV advertising campaign broadcast, starring Richard Branson.
April	Virgin celebrates first birthday.
	Virgin's PEPs attract over £145 million in the 35 days running up to the end of the tax year end.
June	Enters the protection market, with the launch of Virgin Life Insurance and Survival Plan. Poaches former Scottish Widow, Debbie Moore, to promote the new products.
November	Enters the pension market with a clear and straightforward savings plan.
	Virgin Direct is recognized as the UK's fastest growing direct PEP company since its launch 18 months ago with over £400 million under management (Source: AUTIF based on net sales direct from the public January 1996 to October 1996).

1997

February	Virgin Direct announces 100,000 customers.
	Virgin hits the £ half billion mark in funds under management.
April	Virgin Growth PEP becomes the UK's best selling index tracking PEP, taking on more new customers than any other during the PEP season. Virgin Direct reaches 120,000 customers and £650 million of cash under management.
July	Virgin Growth PEP confirmed as being Britain's most popular PEP.
August	Virgin reaches the milestone of £1 billion of funds under management.
October	Virgin Direct and the Royal Bank of Scotland join forces to launch the enigmatically titled 'One': a revolutionary banking account set to turn personal banking on its head by breaking down what Virgin calls the 'artificial barrier between savings and borrowing'.

December   Virgin's personal pension information pack wins a Plain
              Language Award 1997 for outstandingly good documents.
              This award is presented by the Plain Language Commission
              and is becoming widely regarded as evidence of an
              organization's ability to communicate to its customers.

1998

January   The new bank account One becomes available to the public.

Some further comments about One are necessary. Launched with great
fanfare – Richard Branson is not known for keeping a low profile – One is a
personal current account which has just one statement and one phone
number and which integrates under one umbrella account featuring all the
customer's dealings with Virgin. The idea is that the customer will operate his
banking with Virgin and have various loan facilities as approved (such as
mortgage, credit card, personal loans and overdrafts) and deposit facilities in
the same account. All borrowings through the account are at mortgage rate.
Customers must be home-owners and will generally be expected to
undertake most of their banking through the account – they need to agree
to pay their salary into it. The idea is that customers decide how much money
they need to meet their financial needs, including their mortgage, credit
cards and other loans. Virgin then agrees a suitable overall credit limit with the
customer. This is known as the 'facility' and the minimum is £50,000.

A customer's facility needs to be enough to pay for all their
commitments and it must be secured on the customer's house. Clearly,
customer's can only use the account if they agree to switch their mortgage
to it. They are also required to pay their monthly income into the account.
The entire operation of the account is over the telephone, with telephones
being manned 24-hours a day.

The account is being targeted at people with mortgages beyond
£50,000. At the time of writing, it is too early to know whether One is
going to be a success, but Virgin reports an 'encouraging' response to the
account to date. What is clear is that the idea of a single integrated bank
account which contains all the customer's borrowings is precisely the kind
of idea which newcomers are generating in the bid to make a success of
their entry into the banking market. Traditional banks will need to keep
very much on their toes if they are not to be left behind. That said, Virgin
needed to team up with the Royal Bank of Scotland to bring the idea to a
practical fruition. It therefore seems that newcomers and traditional banks
need not necessarily be locked into competitive loggerheads but have
plenty of scope to work together to each other's clear benefit.

Assessment

Close investigation of Virgin Direct reveals that the business has certainly
been successful within its initial objectives, but that it would have been

difficult to keep it viable if the Virgin organization had not been prepared to bankroll it in its early days, which can be seen as continuing.

Virgin has sought to win customers solely from direct response advertising which induces customers to telephone the Virgin number and talk to a telephone assistant. Tony Wood, marketing director of Virgin Direct, emphasized that an increasing amount of business was coming from personal referrals from existing customers, who would make such recommendations to their friends and acquaintances purely because they wanted to share the idea of what Virgin was offering rather than because of any incentive.

Initially, Virgin targeted customers in the 'respectable and secure middle life' age range of 45 to 55; the idea being that these people were more likely to have funds available for investment. Note, incidentally, that none of the initial Virgin products involve Virgin being exposed to any credit risk, although clearly this is no longer the case. Tony Wood explained that after the initial launch, the more recent trend has been for younger customers to opt to use Virgin's services. However, Virgin does not use its retail outlets to sell its financial services.

As far as handling the fundamental challenge of taking in investors' money – the need to manage the money in a regulated and secure way so that it performs at a high level – Virgin regards itself as too virginal in this business to handle the management itself, but contracts it out to the Norwich Union: one of the largest insurance companies and fund management organizations in the business. Fund performance results have generally been good enough for Virgin to claim itself as offering consistently good performance. Virgin also contracts out a considerable part of its administration resources.

Tony Wood concedes, however, that financial services is not a business to be in unless you have good funding from the outset.

> In order to make a financial services organization profitable you need a large number of customers and extensive funds under management. You probably aren't going to get that in the early years because you are still building up both the customer base and the range of funds under management. Ironically, the more successful you are, the deeper your pockets need to be, because you need to have an organization which can provide all levels of sales and administrative support from the outset without the standard being compromised.

For its investment management products, Virgin makes its revenue from annual management fees and from small administration fees. Clearly, these are not yet going to be at such a level that they can even fully cover the salaries of the 300 people Virgin direct employs, let alone the technological infrastructure, advertising and administrative costs (which are of course payable even though much of this is contracted out). At present, therefore, Virgin Direct is still consuming its parent company's money. However, the branding process seems to have worked, and Tony Wood is confident that by 1999 the organization will be a profit centre for Virgin in its own right. The lesson here seems to be that when seeking to exploit the new opportunities to deliver financial services remotely to customers who appreciate an organization which is geared around being customer-friendly, the new financial services organization needs to have extensive financial backing.

Virgin Direct and its use of technology to sell retail financial services

Virgin Direct, like Direct Line and First Direct, has an almost messianic belief in basing the telephone-based telephone sales process around a system that only requires the customer to provide details once, with those details being passed to other departments as required.

All customer information is stored in a database which used the customer's name as the central criterion of the filing system. As with Direct Line, this methodology emphasizes the focus on customer service, and actually facilitates the process.

Strategic guidelines: how banks can fight back

Finally, how can banks – traditional banks, that is – fight back against the onslaught of competition from newcomers who come from other sectors?

At the start of Chapter 2 of this book I suggested three principal ways for banks to fight against the new competition stemming from newcomers to their industry.

First, I proposed that banks create their own retailer network, such as by purchasing an existing network. This is already happening, but more as a way of a bank capturing business within certain niche retail sectors – such as selling cars – rather than as a way for banks to move into retailing on a large scale.

Second, I suggested that banks consider entering joint ventures with existing retailers in order to, in effect, beat the gatecrashers at their own game. This is certainly happening, such as in the case of the Abbey National and the UK food retailer Safeway (which is now independent of its former US counterpart), which have joined forces to launch a Visa debit card together which gives shoppers the opportunity to save on a store loyalty card.

Third, there is the radical option for the bank to move its entire focus to selling retail products and services in the widest sense and no longer simply being seen as a bank selling banking services. There is no reason why the current banking services could not be part of the new retail mix, but the main idea would be for the bank to metamorphosize into a completely different type of organization.

It is interesting that while retailers have been more than happy to move in on banking services, and in many respects changing the entire public profile as a result, banks have not been willing to go the other way, at least not to date. This is no doubt because banks feel that ultimately they are better off sticking at what they do best and living with the problem of newcomers as well as they can. Certainly, diversifying on a substantial scale into other retail activities would be definitely risky for any bank.

Ultimately, the best way for banks to fight back seems to me for them to create a truly effective and well marketed virtual resource which they should seriously consider launching as a new division of new branch rather than simply adding the virtualization to their existing operations. Establishing it as a new brand is likely to maximize its innovativeness under general customer appeal.

An analogy can be drawn in this respect with how the traditional banks treated ATMs from the marketing perspective and how smaller, more intensively competitive institutions treated them. Traditional banks simply saw ATMs as an appendix of their existing services, and incorporated the ATM functionality into the range of features associated with the traditional products.

On the other hand, smaller, more competitively aggressive organizations institutions tended to launch new types of account based around these the ATMs, thereby drawing attention to the ATM functionality in the most effective way and ensuring that customers were extremely aware of the benefits of the ATMs when they became involved with a new banking product.

The result was that these smaller institutions generally scored a big success with ATMs and were able to attract many customers of traditional banks to their new-style ATMs-related accounts. The traditional banks, on the other hand, won no compulsive competitive advantage and even now, at least in the United Kingdom, tend to view their ATMs simply as external resources for the processing of routine transactions rather than as powerful ways to attract customers in their own right.

The only real exception to this in the United Kingdom is the Midland Bank, which has redesigned its branches to make them substantially focused around automated machines and which has been very successful in de-emphasizing the counter in favour of encouraging customers to use the automatic machines and to regard the bank very much as a facility for making automatic transactions.

That said, the Midland Bank has also been careful to ensure that during banking hours there are courteous and capable staff in the banking hall to assist customers who need advice on how to use the machines. Furthermore, there are also counter facilities for customers who prefer to do business that way.

I myself have noticed that, as a Midland customer, I am happy to use the automated facilities to obtain cash and pay in small cheques or obtain an updated statement, but when I have a fairly substantial cheque to pay in (this does happen, even to writers) I prefer to use the counter cashier as I vaguely feel that a large cheque is more secure if paid in over the counter rather than through an automatic deposit machine. Furthermore, there are banks (though not the Midland) where a cheque paid in through an ATM is credited to the account a day later than would have been the case if it had been paid in over a counter. In any event, it seems likely that there will always be a place for bank branches and that the need for some human interaction in a branch will never disappear completely. This may be an optimistic thought as far as traditional banks are concerned, and it is certainly an appropriate note on which to end this chapter.

6 The cash machine comes of age

Introduction

The cash machine – or the automated teller machine (ATM) as it is more formally known – is the most visible, and perhaps most revolutionary, element of the virtual banking revolution.

That it has changed our lives is incontestable. Every day, millions of people around the world in thousands of walks of life rely on the speed and convenience of cash machines to get access to the money they need and then get on with their daily business with the minimum of delay. Like the microwave oven, convenience foods, dual cyclone vacuum cleaners, personal computers, and all the host of time-saving devices which the technological revolution of the past 25 years has given us, the cash machine provides us with more time to do the things we want to do by enabling us to do the things we don't want to do as rapidly as possible.

And this is the point. Banks and other financial institutions may promote their cash machines by showing an attractive model withdrawing funds and smiling as she does so, but the truth of the matter is that nobody much wants to use a cash machine at all. We would much rather be with our friends, or making money, or fishing, or even shopping.

Not only has the cash machine brought a level of convenience to our lives that was not there before, but it has enabled people in all types of social class and job specifications to obtain banking facilities when this would otherwise have been impossible. In my discussion of cash machines earlier in this book I have already pointed out how the banks which first deployed them had to learn that the people who could obtain the greatest utility from these machines were blue-collar workers who would not have time to go to their bank branch during week. Clearly, people working in jobs where they have no access to a town centre during the day can gain great benefits from cash machines, and there are hundreds of professions whose smooth functioning would be difficult without these machines. How many movies have been completed within budget and been created more efficiently? How many important meetings have been completed and the task accomplished because the participants knew that they could obtain funds after hours? How many surgical operations have been more successful because the surgeon was not distracted, even for a moment, by wondering how he would be able to get hold of some money later on?

And that is only to talk about cash machines' use in the customer's own country. International ATM sharing has created a scenario where a customer can literally travel the world and withdraw funds in dozens of countries in local currency, given that his account back home will stand the transaction. International ATM sharing has made a significant contribution towards mobility around the world, and as more people become aware of the opportunities they have to withdraw funds internationally, the mobility will surely increase even further.

Traveller's cheques have always been among the more unsatisfactory financial instruments: you pay a commission charge to buy them, you often pay a commission charge to cash them, they are not especially secure, anyone can forge your signature because they can see it on the cheque, and many cheque-encashment places don't require the customer to present his or her passport when cashing the cheque.

Traveller's cheques are horribly easy to lose, and no amount of efficiency at replacing them on the part of the bank issuing them can mitigate the enormous inconvenience of losing them. As for the situation when the issuing bank does *not* display efficiency and speed of replacement, in such cases the traveller's predicament rapidly becomes a nightmare. When, at the age of 20, I set off to spend six months or so in Europe in 1977, I lost my traveller's cheques in Marseilles a week or so into the jaunt. Because they were drawn on a bank that was not well known in France, I was forced to come back to England to receive reimbursement. I only did so after about one month, by which time I had rather lost my wanderlust.

International ATM sharing does away with all the horrors of traveller's cheques, and with the even greater horror of taking foreign currency abroad (or your own currency and aiming to change it) and finding that you've lost it, or that you can't remember where in your vast array of baggage you put the money. International cash machine sharing is simple, easy, and ultra-secure, as you don't have to worry about any cash until the moment you want to withdraw it. If you spend the cash soon afterwards, it's been in your wallet for the very shortest time.

I have already looked at the origins of the cash machine and some of the principal staging posts in its development. This chapter now examines cash machines from a more strategic perspective, in order to suggest how banks can make the greatest use for them, as far as the bank's own commercial objectives are concerned. The chapter concludes, as the previous one did, with specific strategic guidelines on how to make the most of ATMs.

The technical nature of the ATM

Viewed from a purely technical perspective, an ATM is simply a safe with an electro-mechanical input and output system which is itself controlled by a (usually) fully electronic user interface.

Organizations that manufacture ATMs – these include Fujitsu, IBM, NCR and Siemens-Nixdorf – have expended great effort on the user interface itself; taking considerable care to maximize the speed of the entire customer interaction and keeping the language used for the interaction process as clear and straightforward as feasible. Most ATMs nowadays use a cathode-ray tube (CRT) for the visual interface, although some ATMs of an older design make use of a system whereby the different interface pages are scrolled mechanically behind a glass screen. Incidentally, one reason why colour ATM screens have not taken off is because no one has yet developed a reliable colour screen which is easily visible in exterior daylight. Inside lobbies the problem of daylight (and the light itself) is less acute, and some lobby ATMs do feature a colour display.

It is important that an ATM's user interface should not only be easy to use and clearly understandable but should be designed so as to minimize the likelihood of the customer leaving without taking from the machine all the things he needs to take. These are: the cash (if any has been dispensed), the paper receipt (if one has been requested) and, above all, the card. There is no doubt that the card is the most likely item to be forgotten by a customer, who sees the purpose of the interactive process being to obtain cash. Consequently, ATMs usually have some kind of sound alarm which only ceases when the customer has removed his card from the slot. Some machines also provide visual messages to remind the customer to retrieve the card, especially if the function is one where the customer is not going to be lingering by the machine until the cash has been dispensed.

In order to prevent security problems if the customer nevertheless forgets to retrieve the card, the machine will 'swallow' the card after a short period: normally about 30 seconds. The customer will then usually need to apply centrally to get the card returned, although if the ATM is situated in the lobby or through the wall of a branch where he is known, he can sometimes get the card back from the ATM by asking for the branch to extract it.

ATMs and security

The overriding need facing ATM operators is that their machines dispense requested functionality to a bona fide holder of a card which operates the ATM, and to prevent an unauthorized user of the card from gaining access to the machine's functions. This dual functionality needs to be extremely easy for a genuine customer to use and, ideally, impossible for an illicit card user, and is met in the vast majority of ATMs by the use of a four-digit number which the bona fide customer is asked to remember and not write down. Four digits seem from experience to represent an appropriate balance between the need for the number to be easy to remember, and the need for the number to have sufficient permutations so that the chance of an illicit user guessing the number is negligible. In the case of a four-digit number, there are $9 \times 9 \times 9 \times 9$ permutations altogether (i.e. 6561) if zero is not permitted as an option, and 10,000 if it is.

The PIN

This four-digit number is known as the personal identification number (PIN). It is often, tautologically, called the PIN number. Whether or not tautology is used in its nomenclature, it remains the most effective, and simplest, way to authorize an ATM transaction.

PINs are so secret that even staff who operate the bank's computer systems do not have access to them. As soon as a customer inputs the PIN into the system it will be encrypted and will therefore never occur 'in the clear' – that is, in its decrypted form – anywhere in the system. Furthermore, PINs are generated within the system by an automatic process; they are printed inside the PIN-issuing envelope.

The most obvious security hazard associated with any PIN occurs at the point at which it is issued to customers. For this reason, plastic cards and the PINS relating to them are never posted together to a customer. Instead, what happens is that the plastic card is posted to a customer and the PIN then posted a few days later, sometimes only after the customer has returned an acknowledgement slip to confirm that he received the card. This prevents the illicit use of the card and the PIN by someone who intercepts the customer's mail. Of course, theoretically there is nothing to stop such an unauthorized person forging the customer's signature and returning the acknowledgement slip. Consequently, to deal with this problem, some banks only issue PINs in person to customers who come in with the card and some identification.

The next most obvious security hazards associated with a PIN occur if a customer discloses the PIN to a third party. Unfortunately, many customers see one benefit of using ATMs being that they can deliver the card to a friend or relative, tell them the PIN, and get the friend or relative to withdraw funds for them or make some other transaction. Admittedly, one can hardly blame some customers for thinking like this: it isn't difficult to imagine a scenario where somebody is ill, infirm, or just too busy to visit the ATM themselves and find it useful to ask somebody else to do this. However, people who give somebody else their PIN are in every case breaking the terms under which the card and the PIN were issued. Furthermore, experience shows that it is often this kind of behaviour which leads to a customer finding transactions on his statement which he did not believe he made. Friends or relatives sometimes turn dishonest when given such an obvious opportunity to do so, or may make mistakes.

In any event, a large proportion of so-called 'phantom withdrawals' are made at ATMs local to where the customer lives, thereby suggesting that an abuse of the security of the card and PIN is the reason for the problem, unless of course the customer simply forgot about a transaction.

Police reports about ATM card fraud (or, indeed, EFTPoS card fraud) frequently focus on the almost unbelievable ineptitude of many customers when it comes to how they handle their PIN. It appears that, although usually only four digits long, many people do not find it easy to remember and frequently write it down somewhere in their wallet, often on a slip of paper kept very close to the card itself. There are also many people who actually write the PIN on the card, the folly of which should be more than obvious.

In fairness to customers, a four-digit PIN is not as easy to remember as many banks seem to think. The reader will doubtless have his or her own experience of forgetting a PIN, often at a critical moment. This is especially likely to happen if you have not used your PIN for some time. It is also a problem if you have several cards, each with a different PIN, although most banks nowadays allow customers to change their PIN to a number they can either readily remember, or else a number which, as it covers all their cards, is more difficult to forget. Incidentally, many people still persist in choosing an obvious number such as 1111 for their PIN, while others often choose their birthday (for example, 5957 if, like me, you were born on September 5 1957). The security hazards of choosing one's birthday, when there are very likely other documents in one's wallet which would reveal this, should be obvious. Since I have raised this personal note, I ought to explain that I myself use the same PIN for all my bank cards, but that I don't trust to my memory but instead write my PIN down in my wallet on a piece of card. However, I write the numbers out in full as words in Finnish, a language which for various unimportant reasons I happen to speak. I have always known that I am breaking general instructions never to write down one's PIN in one's wallet, but I've never believed that the chances of a Finnish-speaking mugger stealing my wallet were very high. That said, if I ever return to Finland on a business trip, I am going to have to rethink my PIN mnemonic procedure, or I might find that some lucky pickpocket in Helsinki had an agreeable evening at my expense, and found international ATM sharing an extremely pleasurable development.

A plastic card without a PIN should not present a security problem. All ATMs are programmed to set a definite limit on the number of attempts that can be made to key in the PIN before the card is captured by the machine: most set the limit at three such attempts, the idea being that if the customer makes more than three mistakes with keying in the PIN, maybe the customer who is using the card is not the person who should be using it.

Biometrics

Are there better ways to authorize ATM transactions than the use of a PIN? Logically, any authorization system which involves some kind of token being presented or an authorization code being remembered suffers from the basic problem that a customer who presents the token or remembers the code will gain access. The most effective authorization systems of all depend on a biological attribute of the bona fide person being used to verify that the person attempting access is the right one. Such authorization systems are known within the security industry as *biometrics*. There are a variety of these, ranging from systems which digitize a thumbprint and compare a proffered sample against a stored true record, to systems which scan an entire hand-print, make use of a voice-print, or scan the subject's retina in one or both eyes.

All these systems suffer from the basic problem that they are not really suitable for use with an ATM because of their great expense, the susceptibility of the components to damage, and the intrusiveness of the authorization process. In particular, retina scanning seems to me an entirely unsatisfactory authorization method for any ATM transaction. Would it mean the subject having to take off his glasses and therefore being less able to see a mugger approaching? Would the subject not fear that the process might damage his eyes? Besides, anyone who has seen the Sylvester Stallone film *Demolition Man*, where a criminal escapes from prison by the simple but effective expedient of removing one of the prison governor's eyes and holding it up on the end of a pen to a retina scanner, is unlikely ever to be able to think of retina scanning in quite the same way again.

In the medium to long term, it is likely that thumbprint or fingerprint authorization will become inexpensive and reliable, when it would be an ideal authorisation system for an ATM. In the meantime banks, and the customers, are stuck with the PIN system.

On- and off-line operation

The final point to make about ATM security concerns the way in which the computerized connection across a data communications line is made between the ATM and the bank's central computer.

The nature of this connection has important implications for ATM security. In the early ATMs, and even today in many ATM networks operated by banks in developing countries, the link between the ATM and the bank's own computer is not maintained all the time, but is only made at certain times of the day or night. Frequently, either in order to save money on data communications by avoiding peak periods, or because the night is the most logical time to update the central computer on transactions that occurred during the day, the connection is made at night, with all the day's transactions being sent via a proprietary telephone line or a standard telephone line to the central computer.

Early ATMs in developed countries also adopted this way of doing things, which is known as off-line operation. Technical limitations of many early ATM networks in developed countries meant that off-line operation was the norm. Naturally, where there is no immediate connection between the ATM and the central computer, the central computer cannot be used for the authorization process. As a result, the only way to authorize the transaction in this case is for the PIN to be stored on the customer's card, almost always in an encrypted form.

Furthermore, as the central computer is not involved in the process in the case of off-line operation, the ATM has no way of 'knowing' whether the customer's account can bear the transaction. Consequently, all that can be done is for the card to have a daily withdrawal limit and for some electronic means to be used for the ATM to 'know' when the customer's limit for a particular date has been reached.

This is all very well, but by the time ATM networks were starting to proliferate, electronic means were readily available to copy the magnetic stripe on a plastic card as many times as the counterfeit wished. It was consequently possible for a stolen ATM card to be used on many occasions during the same day to withdraw funds to the daily limit, given that of course the person illicitly doing this would need the customer's PIN. There were even cases of customers duplicating their own cards in the knowledge that by the time the bank found out about it, the customer would have withdrawn more than enough funds to make the exercise worthwhile.

By the late 1970s there was a clear trend for off-line operation to be abandoned, at least in developed countries, in favour of systems which featured a direct and simultaneous link between the ATM and the host computer. These systems were known as on-line systems. They carried with them the enormous advantages that the PIN would no longer need to be stored on the card's magnetic stripe, albeit in encrypted form, but could be stored within the entire network. Furthermore, an on-line system ensured that, as well as complying with the daily cash withdrawal limit (which has been retained, partly for general security reasons and also to prevent an ATM being emptied of cash too quickly), the customer had sufficient cleared funds in his account to bear the transaction, or, where there were insufficient cleared funds, a borrowing facility existed which would cover the withdrawal.

Beyond these principal advantages of on-line operation, on-line connection also enables the bank to offer a much wider range of functionality than is possible when operation is in off-line mode.

For these reasons, on-line operation has become the norm for ATM networks in developed countries, and is rapidly becoming the target objective for ATMs in developed countries. For the purpose of this book, it should be assumed that all ATM networks discussed operate in on-line mode unless it is made clear that this is not the case.

ATM functionality

World-wide, the range of functionality provided by ATMs is fairly broad and varies a good deal between the different cultural requirements of the countries where ATMs are deployed.

Overall, as we have seen, ATMs fall into two categories: *lobby ATMs*, installed in branch lobbies, and *through-the-wall ATMs*, which are installed in walls at an increasingly wide range of locations – not only branches of banks but also in shopping malls, alongside department stores and supermarkets, and in small, 'kiosk-type' mini-branches which are being seen more and more in areas where people congregate, ranging from railway stations to shopping malls, airports and even on board ship, with the link between the ATM and the host computer being maintained by radio telephone.

Some through-the-wall (TTW) ATMs are installed in entrance lobbies of branches to which customer's gain access by swiping the card through a card-swipe located outside. Once the card is verified, the lobby doors open. These entrance lobbies are particularly useful for security reasons as they let the customer complete the transaction without any potential mugger or thief being in the immediate vicinity. Entrance lobbies are also obviously useful in cold countries such as Canada and in Scandinavia: indeed, most ATMs in these countries are in fact located in these lobbies.

The actual functions which ATMs provide can be separated into two types: *core functionality*, provided by most ATMs in most countries, and *additional functionality*, provided by some ATMs in some countries and often varying considerably between countries.

Core functionality

This usually consists of:

■ cash withdrawal;

■ balance enquiry (whether displayed on screen or printed out);

■ statement ordering facility.

Additional functionality

This will typically include one or more of the following:

■ cheque book request facility;

■ deposit (but for practical reasons, the deposit facility is usually confined to customers of the financial institutions running the ATM in question; it isn't usually available via a shared ATM network);

■ funds transfer facility: this would usually involve a customer-initiated transfer of funds to a pre-arranged destination, such as a utilities company account to pay a bill or to another customer account;

■ mini-statement facility: this is usually available as a print-out, and typically covers the last 10 transactions or movements on the accounts;

■ PIN change facility;

- pass book update facility: this feature is found in many lobby ATMs, and also in some TTW ATMs in countries where pass books are popular;

- traveller's cheque dispensing: this is a fairly uncommon facility, but some ATMs offer it at international airports.

The strategic direction of the ATM

It may seem somewhat ironic to talk of the strategic direction of something so rooted to its spot in the wall or the branch lobby, but while the ATM might be literally stationary, it is certainly not static as far as its role in a bank's virtual delivery strategy is concerned.

The importance of the ATM as the world's first virtual banking delivery mechanism and as an electronic banking tool which has proved extremely popular with customers around the world, means that for most banks the ATM is always going to be at the core of their commercial strategy. Even banks which are committed to maintaining a branch presence on a greater or lesser extent rely heavily on ATMs to provide a means for their customers to carry out routine transactions. It is doubtful whether the banking industry as we know it today could continue in its present form without ATMs, as there would simply be too much pressure on branches for routine transactions and the cost equation would no longer make sense. We would, in effect, be back in the dark ages of banking when to have a bank account was a privilege and banks treated their customers with considerable condescension.

Furthermore, even virtual banks which have set up primarily telephone-based organizations naturally need some way of delivering cash to their customers, and the ATM is the only virtual means available for doing this.

There is a distinct trend towards banks broadening the range of functions provided by their ATMs. There is no particular reason why a customer should not be able to carry out pretty well all banking functions via ATMs, although certainly some functions would only be capable of being carried out via ATMs in a lobby. For example, many people are not keen to make deposits via an external ATM because there is a clear risk of theft while the deposit is being made and also psychologically people often feel less 'comfortable' about making a deposit into an external slot than one inside a lobby. There is also a trend towards the deployment of specialized machines which only offer one or two functions, such as deposit and/or statement ordering. The obvious advantage of a bank deploying specialized machines is that the queue for the machine will be confined to those who actually want that particular function and consequently should be shorter than a general queue.

ATMs also will continue to provide smaller banks with the opportunity to offer a national service by linking up with a shared cash machine network.

As far as shared networks themselves are concerned, there is a trend towards regional ATM networks in large countries to merge and for the gradual emergence of a relatively small number of national networks in a large country, and for the creation of just one or two national networks in smaller countries. For example, mergers between regional ATM networks in the United States have shrunk the overall number of networks from 46 in 1996 to 41 in 1997.

The nature of shared ATM networks varies between countries. Some networks are only for ATMs – such as LINK in the United Kingdom. Others include both ATMs and EFTPoS: this is generally the case, for example, among the networks in the United States. Whatever the function of the shared network, the benefits of sharing are so great that it is certain to be a permanent fixture in the virtual banking world.

I have often thought that ATMs have the potential to provide far more functions than are currently available on them: that they could be used for a wide range of communications purposes – even as emergency measures to alert police, ambulance or fire services. There is also no reason at all why sharing in the future between banks and suppliers of other important services – such as airlines – couldn't lead to ATMs which allowed customers to pay for a wide range of services via the automatic facility and even to obtain tickets and other important documents via ATM. No doubt the increasing proliferation of smart cards (discussed in detail in Chapter 9 of this book) will create more opportunities for such link-ups and developments which benefit all participating parties as well as the customer.

Strategically, therefore, the importance of the ATM in the virtual banking revolution is assured. It would be no exaggeration to say that the revolution could hardly proceed without it, any more than a railway train could proceed without an engine.

ATMs around the world

There are no particularly great insights to be gained from providing a detailed analysis of the number of ATMs in different countries around the world. All that needs to be said, in addition to my comments earlier in this chapter, is that the ATM has established a dominating presence in the world's banking industries and, indeed, in the social infrastructures of our towns and cities. People are as likely to queue for their ATM as they are to queue to enter their favourite shop during a busy Saturday morning: the difference is that *nobody* enjoys queuing for the ATM. To an extent the increasing tendency for networks (and even banks) operating ATMs to merge in order to save overall costs is a great benefit to the consumer, as it means that many high streets today accommodate several or even numerous ATMs, which all run on the same network and which are therefore accessible by the customer.

World-wide, the highest concentrations of ATMs per capita, as we might expect, occur in countries where the payment culture is primarily cash-based. This is especially true of the Far East, and it is therefore not surprising that

Japan has the greatest number of ATMs per capita, with the total currently running at about 128,000 for a population of about 110 million, compared to 165,000 in the United States for a population of about 250 million. Incidentally, in Europe, the country with the highest density of ATMs in relation to population is Spain, with 765 machines per million people. Note, also that, great as the total of ATMs in Japan is, many of these are located inside bank branches and are often inaccessible outside banking hours.

The country with the largest number of regional cash ATM networks is the United States. This is primarily for historical reasons: United States banks have always been to some extent restricted to the geographical areas where they are permitted to operate, and as a result shared ATM networks in the United States for a long time tended to be substantially state-based. Today, however, the largest regional networks in the United States span several states, normally within a particular part of the United States. For example, Star System, which comprises a grand total of 959 financial institutions, mainly operates on the West Coast and the states adjacent to them. In total, the network operates 30,804 ATMs located in the walls of branches and 10,081 ATMs located away from branches, plus 498,300 EFTPoS terminals. These ATMs and terminals can be accessed by a total of 34,490,631 issued cards, and are located in 12 states. These, in order of the number of ATMs in each one are: California, Nevada, Arizona, Oregon, Hawaii, Utah, Washington, Idaho, Colorado, New Mexico, Wyoming, and Montana.

Figure 6.1. provides details of the four largest shared regional networks in the US.

Case studies

In these two case studies my aim is to focus on useful strategic insights into how ATMs work, and what makes a shared network successful. I believe that the stories of the UK national shared ATM network, LINK, and the story of Atos Payment Services, admirably meet this requirement.

Case Study: LINK

LINK is the brand name of LINK Interchange Network Limited, the UK's only shared, branded ATM network. It operates its own computer systems which provide a switching service to member institutions. LINK was established in 1986. The network operates 24 hours a day, 365 days a year. It currently (as of February 1998) has 26 member institutions, which operate a total of 8091 ATMs. As ATMs operated by the TSB, National Westminster and the Royal Bank of Scotland also provide access to LINK cardholders, the total number of LINK-accessible ATMs is 14,731.

FIGURE 6.1 *The four largest shared regional networks in the US*

1. Star System

401 West A Street, Suite 600, San Diego, CA 92101   619-234-4774   **Fax:** 619-234-3208
Director: Ronald Congemi, President and CEO

STAR.

Network Name: Star System Inc.
Ownership: 18 Member Institutions

Organization: Star System Inc.
Market: CA, NV, AZ, OR, HI, UT, WA, ID, CO, NM, WY, MT

MONTHLY TRANSACTIONS		TRANSACTION ANALYSIS		
1997:	217,885,820	ATMS:	187,685,820	
1996:	189,871,720	POS:	30,200,000	
		Switch:	62,708,622	
		Interchange:	28%	
		Per ATM:	6,093	

TERMINALS ON-LINE		MEMBERSHIP MAKEUP		NETWORK CARDS
Total ATMs:	30,804 (23,668 in 1996)	Banks: 391		34,490,631
Off-Premise:	10,081	S&Ls: 69		
POS Devices:	498,300	CUs: 499		DATE ORGANIZED
All Terminals:	529,104	Total: 959		September 1984

Note: Deluxe Electronic Payment Systems switches transactions. New Star logo introduced in July 1997 represents both POS and ATM services, phasing out Explore mark.

2. Honor

2600 Lake Lucien Drive, Suite 180, Maitland, FL 32751   407-875-2500   **Fax:** 407-875-2501

HONOR

Network Name: Honor
Ownership: 45 Member Institutions

Organization: Honor Technologies Inc.
Market: FL, GA, NC, SC, TN, MD, VA, AL, MS, WV, DE, NJ, PA, DC

MONTHLY TRANSACTIONS		TRANSACTION ANALYSIS		
1997:	164,742,368	ATMS:	145,346,259	
1996:	105,388,244	POS:	19,396,109	
		Switch:	81,375,331	
		Interchange:	22%	
		Per ATM:	5,191	

TERMINALS ON-LINE		MEMBERSHIP MAKEUP		NETWORK CARDS
Total ATMs:	28,000 (11,939 in 1996)	Banks: 1,270		40,000,000
Off-Premise:	8,400	S&Ls: 156		
POS Devices:	350,000	CUs: 444		DATE ORGANIZED
All Terminals:	378,000	Total: 1,870		October 1990

Note: The network switches its transactions. Honor Technologies was established in January 1997 following Honor's merger with Most and Alert.

3. NYCE

300 Tice Boulevard, Woodcliff Lake NJ 07675   201-930-9400   **Fax:** 201-930-0432
Director: Dennis F. Lynch, President and CEO

NYCE

Network Name: NYCE
Ownership: 118 Financial Institutions

Organization: NYCE Corporation
Market: NY, NJ, PA, MA, ME, NH, VT, CT, RI, DE and Puerto Rico

MONTHLY TRANSACTIONS		TRANSACTION ANALYSIS		
1997:	145,267,000	ATMS:	137,067,000	
1996:	136,787,000	POS:	8,200,000	
		Switch:	40,200,000	
		Interchange:	25%	
		Per ATM:	7,336	

TERMINALS ON-LINE		MEMBERSHIP MAKEUP		NETWORK CARDS
Total ATMs:	18,684 (17,874 in 1996)	Banks: 616		30,900,000
Off-Premise:	5,245	S&Ls: 149		
POS Devices:	256,000	CUs: 552		DATE ORGANIZED
All Terminals:	274,684	Total: 1,317		October 1984

Note: The network switches its transactions, and supports electronic benefits transfer transactions for the Northeast Coalition of States.

4. MAC

1100 Carr Road, Wilmington, DE 19809   302-791-8000   *Fax: 302-791-8700*
Director: Philip A. Valvardi III, President

Network Name: MAC
Ownership: Electronic Payment Services Inc.

Organization: Money Access Service Inc.
Market: DE, IN, KY, MI, NH, NJ, NY, OH, PA, WV and 35 other states

MONTHLY TRANSACTIONS	
1997:	138,500,000
1996:	125,176,000

TRANSACTION ANALYSIS	
ATMS:	129,000,000
POS:	9,500,000
Switch:	105,000,000
Interchange:	40%
Per ATM:	5,059

TERMINALS ON-LINE	
Total ATMs:	25,500 (22,500 in 1996)
Off-Premise:	8,300
POS Devices:	400,164
All Terminals:	425,664

Note: Switching is performed by EPS.

MEMBERSHIP MAKEUP	
Banks:	1,084
S&Ls:	331
CUs:	681
Total:	2,096

NETWORK CARDS
36,500,000

DATE ORGANIZED
September 1979

LINK members have 22.7 million cards in circulation (39.5 million including TSB, National Westminster Bank, Royal Bank of Scotland, Sainsbury's Bank and Tesco Personal Finance).

The major UK clearing banks operate what are in effect two shared ATM networks: MINT (the Midland Bank, National Westminster Bank and TSB) and 'Four Bank' (Bank of Scotland, Barclays, Lloyds and Royal Bank of Scotland). The crucial differences between these networks and LINK are:

- the brandings of the banks' networks are not actively promoted, whereas the LINK branding is

- the banks which participate in MINT and Four Bank do so merely to offer their customers extra convenience. LINK members, on the other hand, fully support the branding;

- the MINT and Four Bank networks have no independent function, but LINK acts to develop new types of ATM sharing arrangements (e.g. international arrangements).

The specific role of LINK is to act as the agency that handles the 'switch' of an ATM transaction from one member to another. What this means is that LINK only handles 'disloyal' or 'not on us' transactions, i.e. transactions which an individual customer initiates at an ATM that is not owned by the institution that issued the card. Conversely, loyal transactions (i.e. those initiated by a customer at an ATM which *is* owned by the institution that issued the card) are not handled by LINK but by the member itself.

As a consortium organization, LINK is owned by its members. Some are connected to LINK via Atos UK, a certified LINK service provider based in Welwyn Garden City (Atos UK is profiled below). These members are indicated below by an 'A' after their name. As of the end of February 1998 the members of LINK were as follows:

- Abbey National plc
- Airdrie Savings Bank
- Alliance & Leicester Group
- American Express Europe (A)
- Bank of Scotland
- Birmingham Midshires Building Society (A)
- Bradford and Bingley Building Society
- Bristol and West plc
- Britannia Building Society (A)
- Chelsea Building Society (A)
- Citibank Savings (Diners Club Europe)
- Clydesdale Bank
- Co-operative Bank

- Coventry Building Society
- Cumberland Building Society
- Derbyshire Building Society (A)
- Dunfermline Building Society (A)
- Halifax plc
- HFC Bank
- Nationwide Building Society
- Northern Rock Building Society
- Norwich and Peterborough Building Society (A)
- Portman Building Society (A)
- Woolwich plc
- Western Trust & Savings (A)
- Yorkshire Bank
- Yorkshire Building Society

In addition, through a reciprocity agreement, LINK cardholders can use TSB Bank, National Westminster Bank, and Royal Bank of Scotland ATMs, and TSB, National Westminster Bank, Sainsbury's Bank and Tesco Personal Finance cardholders can use LINK branded ATMs.

Origins of UK ATM networks

The most interesting insights into LINK's growth and success are obtained by looking at LINK in the context of the entire growth of ATM networks in the UK.

The UK's first cash dispensers, branded 'Barclaycash', were installed by Barclays Bank in 1967. They were not strictly speaking ATMs, as their function was restricted to providing cash. They were only open for limited periods in the day and were off-line (i.e. not connected to the central computer in real time). Still, they were obviously an important new resource for banks, and other major banks – showing that unerring ability to follow the crowd for which banks are, generally, famous – were quick to follow suit. In particular, the Midland, National Westminster (which was formed from the District Bank, National Provincial and Westminster Banks in 1970), Clydesdale, Williams & Glyns Bank and the Bank of Scotland all took to implementing cash machines with some enthusiasm. By 1972 there were nearly 900 machines in the UK, most of them owned by the Midland and National Westminster.

The first implementation in the UK of a machine which was recognizably an automated teller machine (ATM) rather than simply a cash dispenser is regarded as having taken place on 30 June 1975, when Barclays Bank installed a machine outside its High Street, Oxford branch. This machine could provide balances and offered a statement ordering facility, as well as dispensing cash.

These early ATMs, though, like the cash dispensers, were off-line. As I explain above, off-line ATMs carry security problems (cards can be copied and each copy used to withdraw cash to the maximum daily limit) as well as having severely limited usefulness to the customer, as up-to-date balances cannot be retrieved.

In 1977 the number of off-line cash machines and ATMs in the UK peaked at just over 1300. From then on, off-line terminals began to disappear in favour of a new generation of on-line machines: where real-time contact with the institution's central computer is maintained at all times when the machine is switched on.

In addition to the change of attitude which led to the majority of the machines being on-line, there was – from the late 1970s onwards – the view that ATMs ought ideally to be operational round the clock. Previously, many ATMs were only open when the bank branch itself was open: which was often only from about 9.30am to 3.30pm every day. The machines were originally seen as supplementary resources to the branches' daily operation: it took some time for institutions to realize that the whole point of ATMs was that they could be used at all times of the day and night – and particularly by people who were not able to get to their branch during the day. Now, in the mid-1990s, when bank branches are typically open until 5.30pm most days and on Saturday morning, and when institutions make concerted efforts to present themselves as customer-friendly organizations, it is easy to forget that only about 20 years ago, banks still behaved rather like government offices which see themselves almost as doing customers a favour by being open. Furthermore, people who worked long hours in a factory or offices well away from the town centre would literally never be able to visit their branch during opening hours, except on days off or holidays.

In fairness to the UK's institutions, a similar mistake had been made in the early days of ATMs in the US, where banks not only kept their ATMs open for strictly limited periods of the day, but confined the issue of ATM cards to their wealthiest customers. The less wealthy customers – such as the blue-collar workers who could rarely visit their banks and who were therefore the very people who could best benefit from an ATM's services – were at first not given access to ATMs at all.

There is no specific date which marks the dawn in the UK (or the US, for that matter) of the notion that far from being mere mechanical supplements to a branch's resources, ATMs had the potential to be exciting, dynamic delivery systems which could greatly extend an institution's operating base and give it a real competitive edge over its rivals. All that can really be said is that by the early 1980s institutions were finally cottoning on to this idea, and had started to realize that their ATMs ought to be open for the longest possible part of the day (which, in practice, meant all the time) and that cards ought to be as freely available to customers as was compatible with the institution protecting itself against potential loss and dishonesty.

In 1982 an agreement was reached between the Midland and National Westminster Banks and their subsidiaries for the provision of reciprocal cash withdrawal facilities. The Clydesdale and Northern Banks (previously subsidiaries of the Midland) have remained as sharing partners since their sale to the National Australia Bank in 1987. In 1989 this agreement was expanded to include the TSB.

In response to the initial Midland/National Westminster agreement, the remaining major clearing banks – Barclays, Lloyds, Bank of Scotland and the Royal Bank of Scotland – came to an agreement to share their ATMs. Technical considerations, however, meant that the network did not become operational until 1987.

Despite the UK banks' efforts to share their ATM networks, they never adopted the same competitive attitude to ATMs that the building societies did. It was the building societies that led the way towards the recognition of the true role that ATMs play in virtual financial services, namely:

■ specifically, to enable customers to obtain cash round-the-clock;

■ generally, to provide a dynamic, on-line, round-the-clock tool for delivering the institution's services to its customers;

■ to give customers levels of speed and convenience with which a visit to the branch cannot compare;

■ to give customers the benefit (often not fully understood by institutions) of being able to find out information about his account which it might be embarrassing to ascertain from a human cashier. If, for example, a customer is unsure whether he has sufficient funds in his account to allow a withdrawal of £50, he will usually prefer to find this out from a dispassionate, non-human machine rather than from a human cashier – who may, incidentally, not always speak quietly.

Why did the building societies steal a march on the banks in the development and creative conceptualization of the possibilities of ATMs, and especially of shared ATM networks?

The most important reason is the sheer scale of the competitive benefits ATMs could offer the societies. The building societies tended to draw their customer base from specific cities or regions, where the societies had originated in the nineteenth century as providers of savings schemes whereby artisans could purchase their own homes. Even in the 1980s – by which time the largest societies tended to have nationwide customer bases – many societies were still essentially regional in their operations. The prospect of participating in shared ATM networks gave them the chance not only of dramatically extending the geographical domain of their activities, but of also being able to offer existing customers a nationwide banking service. Even if a society was only small and could only afford to install (say) about a dozen ATMs of its own, by taking part in a shared national ATM network it could none the less offer a genuinely nationwide service. ATMs, therefore, had the potential to wipe out all that portion of the national clearing banks' competitive advantage that stemmed from their national presence.

There were other reasons, too. ATMs appealed greatly to the new, dynamic, go-getting generation of financial institution executives – executives who saw more opportunities to make a mark at building societies than at clearing banks – and who were fascinated by the opportunities technology offered for changing the face of financial services. Many of these executives accurately perceived that the clearing banks' monolithic structures and traditional approach to the provision of financial services 'represented an obstacle to the clearing banks' ability to compete effectively with small and more dynamic financial institutions. Furthermore, in the early 1980s the clearing banks, despite their efforts to form shared networks, were not exploiting the functional possibilities of ATMs to their fullest extent, whether in terms of keeping the ATMs open for the maximum periods or in terms of the actual facilities offered by the ATM. Many banks' ATMs were shut late at night and on Sundays, and the facilities offered tended to be limited to cash withdrawals, balance enquiries and statement ordering.

The Halifax Building Society's 'Cardcash' account

There was, clearly, a hole in the market, and in July 1983 the Halifax Building Society – which, at the time, was the largest UK building society (it became a bank in 1997) – set out to fill this hole by creating the UK's first-ever retail banking account specifically designed to be orientated around the ATM rather than the branch.

The rapid growth in the Cardcash customer base during the mid 1980s illustrates just how receptive the UK public were to the notion of a personal bank account based on a plastic card and an ATM. Cardcash account holders were not debarred from entering the branch, which they might want to do if they wished to make a complex transaction or had a problem, but in principle the idea of the account was that the customer could operate it solely through the ATM.

The Halifax's principal reason for launching Cardcash was to steal a march on its competitors and dramatically increase the number of retail account holders who used its services. It did, however, have three operational reasons for the launch. These were:

■ to offer a banking service that was as far as possible paperless and which therefore operated at minimum cost;

■ to reduce the growing volume of over-the-counter transactions and thereby to reduce costs of branch operation (especially costs of employing staff);

■ to provide its customers with banking facilities when the branches were closed and therefore win and retain customer loyalty.

The creation of the Cardcash account – which in hindsight seems such a good idea and a remarkable anticipation of the virtual scenarios of the late 1990s – was at the time an act of real courage and resourcefulness. The Halifax had no way of knowing whether the idea of an ATM-based account would work. But it did, and it is to the credit of the Halifax Building Society that it could foresee at such a relatively early date the appeal of such an account. The implicit question which the launch of the new account posed was: *will customers accept the idea of a bank account which embodies a new kind of perception of what a retail financial institution is? The answer was, unequivocally, yes,* and the reverberations of that answer are still ringing loud and clear around the virtual scenarios of today.

From the outset, Cardcash allowed customers a much wider range of facilities from the ATM than had ever been previously available, namely:

■ cash withdrawal;

■ deposit-making (cash or cheques);

■ statement ordering;

■ mini-statement facility;

■ balance enquiry;

■ funds transfer to another Halifax account;

■ PIN selection facility.

In 1985, the Halifax added to this list by offering customers the facility to use the ATM to make payments to third parties (typically utility companies, credit card organizations and so on), once the customer had asked the Halifax to set up a funds transfer facility in advance.

By 1985, then, Halifax ATMs were offering Cardcash customers a remarkable range of functions. Indeed, even now, more than 10 years later, no bank or building society offers more functionality than this, although many building societies have now boosted the range of functionality offered to match that which the Halifax provided in 1985.

One facility not available from the Halifax's ATMs – nor indeed, from the ATMs of other building societies – is the opportunity to purchase traveller's cheques, which can be obtained, for example, through ATMs operated by American Express. On the whole, though, the Halifax – and other large building societies – continue to offer through their ATMs most of the facilities that a customer could reasonably want.

The number of Cardcash account holders reached 1 million in January 1986. The Halifax points out that the number of actual Cardcash cards issued is about 140 per cent of the total number of accounts, since many are joint accounts.

In 1989 the Halifax launched its 'Maxim' account, which, in addition to giving customers an ATM card that would give them access to the same variety of ATM-delivered facilities as Cardcash, also gave customers a cheque book. Maxim was targeted directly at Cardcash account holders who wanted a cheque book as well as an ATM card.

The launch of Maxim has meant that Cardcash is now in effect targeted at the Society's younger customers, who want the powerful ATM facility but do not yet want a cheque book, or who do not qualify for one according to the Halifax's criteria.

Cardcash was so successful that for several years in the mid 1980s – at a time when all other building societies were busy concluding arrangements to share their ATMs with each other – the Halifax deliberately held out against sharing its ATMs. When, in 1987, the author met a senior executive at the Halifax and asked him why this was the case, he said that the Halifax would only share with other ATM networks when the society was certain that Cardcash had given it all the competitive advantage that could be extracted from it.

Clearly, opening the Halifax's ATMs to non-Halifax customers was only going to make sense when the benefits of giving Halifax customers access to non-Halifax machines on a shared network was perceived by the Halifax as outweighing the competitive advantage of making Halifax machines exclusive to the society's customers. One factor which made the decision easier at the time was that the size, nationwide operation and financial muscle of the Halifax had enabled it to create its own proprietary ATM network which was around 900 machines strong at the time and therefore itself very much a national ATM network.

The competitive benefit question was finally resolved in 1989, when the Halifax's directors decided that enough competitive advantage had been extracted and that it was now time to go with the flow and join LINK. The story of Cardcash consequently became LINK's. Cardcash is, however, very much alive as an account, as shown by the current tally of 3.26 million account holders for Cardcash and the Halifax Current Account (which Maxim was renamed in June 1997). Note that the Halifax does not provide separate figures for account holders for these two accounts, but the numbers of holders of each type of account are probably approximately similar. Today, the Cardcash account holder base is regarded by the Halifax as something of a pool of potential Halifax Current Accounts, and also as the way into the Halifax for young people opening their first bank account. This particular aspect of the role of Cardcash was emphasized in the late 1980s when the account was advertised on television by a comic version of Dracula – a figure presumably designed to appeal to young people – being depicted using his Cardcash card to fetch cash from a Halifax ATM at night. Thus was marketing appeal merged with the usefulness of the Dracula character for emphasizing that the account could be used at night.

MATRIX

LINK was not the first shared network to be opened in the UK. It went live in November 1986, but a rival network went live earlier. This was MATRIX, which had started operations in January of the same year. MATRIX had been born out of a 1982 initiative taken by the Building Societies Association (BSA). The BSA had recognized that ATMs could give societies more opportunities to compete with their arch-rivals, the banks. A feasibility study was prepared, which supported the idea of some kind of shared building society network, although it was seen from the outset that running the network would require sensitive management of membership issues, as high start-up costs would inevitably be involved, and it would be necessary for the larger societies, rather than the smaller ones, to bear the brunt of those costs.

MATRIX differed from LINK in that MATRIX was intended from the outset to be a building societies-only network, whereas LINK – while certainly targeted mainly at building societies – had no such limitation. Otherwise, both networks were run by people intensely committed to the benefits and synergy arising from the notion of the shared ATM network; people who had in many cases been to the US and seen how successfully shared ATMs were working over there. There is no doubt that the success of the Halifax Building Society's Cardcash account was also an inspirational force to these pioneers of shared networks. In 1986, I was working as assistant PR adviser to the organization Funds Transfer Sharing (FTS), the consortium which acted as a gateway to LINK for various institutions and which, after various metamorphoses, has become Atos UK, the next case study in this chapter.

I well recall the atmosphere of energy and excitement which infused the creation of FTS and LINK, and the good-natured but earnest competition which prevailed between LINK and MATRIX. Electronic delivery of financial services, while requiring a disciplined approach to numerous key factors that are discussed in detail later in this report, should never be allowed to become mundane and routine. Virtual financial services are exciting, and if the institutions which are behind them implement them with energy, vigour and inspiration, it is likely that implementations will be created that give customers the kind of benefits that make them come back for more.

Following the establishment of MATRIX and LINK, the two networks entered a period of fierce competition, combined with extensive efforts taken by both organizations to win the British public over to the notion that an ATM was as serious and important a part of a bank's infrastructure as the traditional bricks-and-mortar branch. It was still to be some years before institutions and networks alike would start to realize that ATMs – and all the other kinds of system for delivering a virtual financial service – might actually be *more* serious and important a part of a bank's infrastructure than the bricks-and-mortar branch.

In 1988 this somewhat wasteful competition ended in what was, after all, a fairly predictable fashion: the two networks merged, with LINK being chosen as the name of the new network. The same managers who formerly competed so vigorously now work alongside one another at LINK's headquarters in Harrogate, North Yorkshire.

LINK's technological resources

The LINK central computer uses a six-processor Tandem K2000 system, with the back-up site also using a six-processor Tandem K2000 system. The system is open all the time, with a two or three person team of operators on site at all times.

The central system has 58 gigabytes of mass storage and is capable of processing 4080 transactions a minute (i.e. 68 per second). Note that this capacity, while certainly adequate for LINK's purposes, is by no means as powerful as that required by other major operators of private financial networks. Visa International's VisaNet ATM, debit card and credit card system, for example, must be able to cope with many hundreds of transactions per second, and frequently far more than this. For example, in the run-up to Christmas, VisaNet frequently processes up to 2000 transactions per second from cardholders around the world.

LINK has a 'back up' or disaster recovery site located about 20 miles from the main centre at Harrogate. All its members are permanently connected to this site. The disaster recovery site – which is intended for use if a major incident cripples the main computer centre – can be brought into full use within an hour of a disaster happening. LINK runs the disaster recovery site live about twice a year in order to test it.

The LINK computer centre itself is protected by back-up generators and uninterruptible power supplies.

LINK's overall benefits to customers

LINK summarizes its overall benefits to cardholders as:

- a strong, clear, national identity which is widely recognized, providing a clear customer right of way;

- a consistent, known set of services, namely: cash withdrawal up to a maximum of £250, a fast cash option, balance enquiries, and (dependent upon the type of machine) a transaction receipt with a balance;

- service available round the clock;

- a high level of redundancy within the network as there are usually several LINK ATMs within any High Street;

- a fully on-line service with high levels of protection and security.

Benefits to LINK members

These are listed as:

- the ability to offer customers a countrywide ATM network with minimal investment and running costs;

- the opportunity to earn income by supplying ATM usage to customers of other institutions;

- mutual reinforcement of each member's advertising and marketing;

- membership of a mutual interest group which enables members to compete more effectively with other institutions.

Membership fees

A joining fee is payable on entry to the network. If the new member's system is being connected directly to the LINK central switch (i.e. rather than coming through a certified service bureau such as Atos UK) a connection fee is payable.

A fixed monthly membership fee is also payable; with this varying slightly according to the size of the institution concerned. A monthly processor fee is payable by those members whose system is connected directly to the LINK central switch.

A transaction switching fee (known as the switch fee) is payable to LINK for every transaction which crosses the switch. (Note: Some institutions pass this charge on to customers every time customers make a switched transaction: others do not.)

Branding requirements

There is a LINK logo which must be reproduced on all cards issued by members to their customers. Most institutions put this logo on the front of their cards, but some (e.g. the Abbey National, formerly the UK's number two building society and now a publicly owned bank) put it on the back.

LINK's basic operating rule is that any LINK card must be accepted in any ATM showing the LINK logo.

LINK gateways

LINK is a system which is closed in the sense that it only provides services to member companies and their customers. By definition, all LINK members participate in the core ATM sharing services.

However, some members wish to use LINK's additional service of acting as a 'gateway' to other ATM and electronic payment systems. Such access points are called 'gateways'. LINK is currently operating or developing three of these:

■ a gateway to PLUS via the Royal Bank of Canada;

■ a gateway to Mastercard/Europay;

■ a gateway to Visa.

PLUS is an international ATM and debit card system which operates world-wide. It originated as a national system in the US and through ownership by Visa International has gradually been extended around the world. Most ATMs which participate in PLUS are part of a more local network. About 50 per cent of the ATMs within LINK are connected to the PLUS system and can therefore accept PLUS card transactions from visitors to the UK.

Mastercard/Europay operates a world-wide network of ATMs. Europay operates the Mastercard network within Europe from a service centre in Brussels. LINK connected to the Europay network can, therefore, offer members a connection for the issuing and acquiring of Cirrus, eurocheque, Eurocard and Mastercard transactions with minimum development costs.

LINK has developed a further gateway to Visa International. This is used to enable LINK members to connect to and to then issue Visa debit cards with the absolute minimum development costs. Cards issued may then include both Delta and Electron cards.

LINK offers a Single Message service and a Basc 1/Base 2 service. Each of these services is available to any LINK member upon payment of additional fees. Members will usually need to join the appropriate card scheme in order to participate.

Assessment

LINK is, and continues to be, an unequivocal success. The reasons for its success are:

■ its clear and concise business objective;

■ its management from the outset by enthusiastic, committed and creative staff;

- its foundations were laid at a time when customers wanted the widest access to ATMs, whatever particular institution they banked with;

- customers were offered a wide range of functions through the ATM (often more functions than banks were offering through their ATMs);

- members were committed to the principle of sharing, and understood that the creation of a truly nationwide shared ATM network would give them the chance to compete directly with the major clearing banks;

- unlike the clearing bank networks, LINK exploited to the full its branded status and projected this branding to members and the public alike;

- LINK was always reliable from a technical perspective;

- LINK's decision from the outset to be an on-line, real-time system minimized the security problems faced by members and customers, and maximized the benefits members could offer customers in terms of functionality delivered through the ATM.

ATMs in the UK today

Finally, it is useful to look at the current situation in the UK as regards ATMs. Note that this includes all ATMs, not just those which are operated by LINK members.

Today, all ATMs in Britain offer cash withdrawals, balance enquiries and will produce a receipt either on demand or automatically.

The most popular services in the UK, apart from cash withdrawal and balance enquiries are chequebook ordering, PIN change and account to account transfer. In the UK, there are currently 326 machines per million of population and 96 ATMs per 100 bank and building society branches. Ninety-four per cent of machines in the UK are full-function ATMs: six per cent are simple cash dispensers. The volume of cash withdrawals made at ATMs and cash dispensers in the UK exceeded 1.4 billion during 1996, an increase of three per cent over the previous year.

The average value of an ATM cash withdrawal in the UK is £51. Ninety-six per cent of all UK ATMs are shared: only four per cent are not shared and virtually all of these are lobby machines. The most popular brand of ATM in the UK is NCR which accounts for over 60 per cent of the market. Most ATMs are installed in the walls of banks or building societies, with a much smaller proportion inside the branches. Machines in other sites such as retailers, railway stations and so on account for only a small proportion of the total.

More than 67 per cent of the cash in the UK is issued via ATMs; this proportion increases nearly every year.

Case Study: Atos UK

Introduction

The final case study examined in this chapter is that of the UK arm of Atos. Atos is now the fifth largest information technology services company in Europe. It provides services for a number of blue-chip organizations in banking and finance as well as in the retail and supply chain market.

Atos is a French-based company and has operations in France, Germany, Italy, Spain, Portugal, Switzerland as well as the United Kingdom. The company was created in summer 1997 following the merger of Sligos and Axime, two leading European information technology service companies. It has more than 8700 employees and sales of FF6.2 billion in Europe.

The headquarters of the Atos Group are in Paris and it has offices in the UK at Welwyn Garden City, Walton-on-Thames, Solihull and Manchester. Atos is expanding its UK operations at present and in December 1997 signed a letter of intent with Co-operative Retail Services to outsource its entire information technology division in Rochdale.

The services currently offered by Atos demonstrate how the supply of ATM services is increasingly one that can be delegated to a service provider, and that indeed there are often very good financial reasons for doing so.

Altogether, the four core types of service offered to clients are:

- *Outsourcing*. Atos provides a variety of outsourcing services which range from developing network management applications to managing all of a customer's information technology system.

- *Electronic banking services*. Atos processes more than 1.5 billion electronic transactions each year, including card, cheque and ATM transactions. Traditionally it also manages call centres for its clients on a 24-hours a day, seven days a week basis.

- *Multimedia*. Atos provides customers with a full range of videotex, audiotex, fax and Internet technologies as well as Internet Access Provider services.

- *Professional services/systems integration*. Atos offers customers a service based around the design, development, installation and maintenance of information systems in order to meet the demands of a single European currency, the year 2000 and the integration of new technologies such as the Internet.

Origins

So much for the corporate statement; now on to the more interesting matter of the story of the man who founded the organization which would one day become the UK arm of Atos.

This man was Rob Farbrother, a former operations director of Citibank. In 1985, Farbrother helped form an organization known as Funds Transfer Sharing (FTS): a consortium of financial institutions that wished to benefit from participating in a shared ATM network. In 1989 FTS underwent a management buy-out to become Nexus Payment Systems International, which established a successful track record in marketing a wide range of electronic payment services to customers world-wide. In 1991 Nexus announced a 'strategic alliance' with Sligos which made Sligos a majority shareholder of Nexus. This move was followed on 14 June 1993 by an announcement that Nexus had changed its name to Sligos Payment Services and had increased its stake in the organization to 89 per cent. Nexus was subsequently bought out completely by Sligos. The sale of his equity in Nexus made Farbrother (and some of the other directors who had participated in the management buy-out) a rich man. However, he simply went on working. The attitude which Farbrother brought to creating FTS is extremely revealing of the role of ATMs in a strategic sense.

Farbrother's first key appointment in electronic banking was at the Abbey National Building Society (now the Abbey National), where he played a lead role in automating the institution's cashiers' desks. In a revealing interview with me, Farbrother discussed some of the formative influences on his thinking as an electronic banking specialist. One of these was George Orwell's *Nineteen Eighty-Four,* about which Farbrother comments:

> The book had an effect on me I am sure Orwell did not intend his readers to feel. I saw in it a vision of a society where automation played a crucial role. *I decided then that I wanted to become a part of that automation, rather than a victim of it.* But I did not want the automation to be oppressive. I felt strongly that if the right people were in charge of the automation process, that process might be a benefit to mankind, rather than something oppressive. (my italics).

One's first impression is that this is a curious response to *Nineteen Eighty-Four;* further reflection reveals, however, that it is a profound one. Orwell is a pessimist, at least as far as the effect advanced technology could have on mankind was concerned, while Farbrother is an optimist. Of course, what is remarkable about *Nineteen Eighty-Four* in the context of a report such as this is that Orwell's book is remarkably *devoid* of technology: apart from the all-seeing and all-hearing telescreen. Computers, for example, are not mentioned once in the book. Yet Farbrother instinctively felt that the depiction of the future in Orwell's famous novel *had* to be a technological one: it was as if his own views regarding how technology would develop in future were overwhelming Orwell's bleaker vision.

What is unquestionable is that when 1984 actually arrived, the world – or at least the world of the developed industrialized West – fitted in much more closely with the blueprint of what Farbrother instinctively expected than what Orwell's gloomy broodings appeared to have foretold. Technology generally was making people's lives easier across a wide range of human activity.

More specifically, by 1984 virtual banking was already well on the way to being established as an easy and convenient means for people to gain access to banking services, and – ironically, perhaps, in view of Orwell's message of future society composed of three rigid class differences represented by the Inner Party, the Outer Party, and the 'proles' – was a significant force for the creation of a more egalitarian society. People no longer went to their banks cap in hand, hoping for the chance to be allowed to open an account; the banks had to compete actively for customers and knew that customers were likely to move their business and their funds to another institution if they became disillusioned with their existing one.

Indeed, by 1984 technology had shown itself to be at least as much of a beneficial force as a malign one: the party ideologues of *Nineteen Eighty-Four* had, in effect, found that they could enjoy richer pickings by finding out what the public wanted from technology and implementing this to the benefit of the public rather than by adhering to a repressive and soulless ideology. As for the 'telescreen', there was one in almost every living-room – and frequently one elsewhere in the home, too – but it was merely providing entertainment (and would in time provide a home-based remote banking information resource), and it operated on a strictly one-way basis.

Comparison of the world of *Nineteen Eighty-Four* with that of the actual 1984 is probably unfair. Anyone reading Orwell's book will realize that it is more an exaggerated depiction of the war years in Britain – and a warning of what life could become like if such a climate persisted indefinitely – than an account of what is really likely to happen in the future. Orwell himself was subsequently strenuously to deny that his book represented what he really thought was going to happen in the future: that the novel was instead essentially a warning.

What really matters here, though, is the fundamentally optimistic approach to technology adopted by Farbrother (who, incidentally, was born in 1948, the year *Nineteen Eighty-Four* was written) and his commitment throughout his career to the principle that technology can and should be delivering benefits, not problems. Where better to put those beliefs into action than in the banking sector, which deals with that most emotive and important of human needs: money?

Farbrother left school in 1965 after taking his O Levels, and went into computing, rising to senior programmer status at food giant Tesco. He entered the financial technology business in 1969, when he joined the Abbey National Building Society. He stayed there until 1983, when he was recruited by Citibank as operations director with a special developmental responsibility.

It was during Farbrother's time at Citibank that the process began which led to his participation in the early days of the national shared ATM network LINK (profiled in detail above) and to the foundation of the independent consortium FTS. In 1984, Citibank, seeing the considerable lead the major UK clearing banks had established over it in providing retail financial services, made a policy decision to help organize a network of retail financial institutions which were also anxious to gain the maximum competitive impetus over the largest clearers. Citibank's aim was to be an integral part of a network of institutions that would take advantage of the latest developments in electronic payment systems (i.e. virtual banking) in order to compete with the established clearers.

Farbrother, who in 1984 was appointed chairman of the FTS ATM evaluation team, now comments:

> In the early 1980s there was a real fear at Citibank – and in many other institutions which were not major clearers – that if action was not taken quickly to redress the competitive balance, they ran the risk of being swamped by the large banks who were denying them access to the banking industry's umbrella organizations.

In particular, the large clearers enjoyed what was in essence a 'built-in' advantage over their second-rung rivals.

For one thing, if customers had their salaries paid into their accounts at a clearing bank from their employers' account at another clearing bank, the money would be in the employees' accounts on payday. If, on the other hand, the salaries were paid into a building society from employers' clearing bank accounts it would not be in the employees' accounts for another two days. The reason was that at this time building societies (and other institutions which were not major clearers) were not allowed to join the Bankers Automated Clearing System (BACS) and therefore did not receive the same rapid clearing privileges which the major clearers enjoyed.

Another serious competitive problem under which the non-clearers laboured was the simple point that – as we have seen – by the early 1980s the clearing banks had deployed ATMs extensively throughout the UK, thereby in effect extending their branches' opening hours – an extension which was increasingly tending to be round-the-clock.

One of the most fundamental points to be made about technology is that it is available to everybody. Farbrother and several of his Citibank colleagues came enthusiastically to believe that payment systems technology offered a huge potential for smaller financial institutions – including even the smallest ones – to compete with their larger rivals (note: worldwide, Citibank was of course in no sense a small institution, but in the UK it was and has remained so, mainly because it does not have a major presence on the UK high streets).

As Farbrother puts it:

If these small institutions could join forces and set up technological infrastructures which they could share with one another, there was every reason to believe that they could offer their own customers a comparable – and perhaps even superior – level of service to that provided by the large clearers.

It is worth pointing out that in 1984 the political and regulatory climate in the UK was also right for the development of new, technology-based networks within the retail banking sector. Political and regulatory factors are not necessary prerequisites for the development of such networks, but they certainly help.

In the 1983 General Election the ruling Conservative government had been given one of the strongest mandates ever given by a UK electorate. High on the new government's priorities was the reform of the financial sector: a sector which was felt to be based far too much on outdated trade practices, some of which appeared to restrict new entry and inhibit trade.

This thinking was to have its most dynamic expression in the 1986 'Big Bang' – in which the operation of the Stock Exchange was radically deregulated and automated – and the passage into law of the 1986 Financial Services Act in the same year, which specified a new regulatory framework for the investment business. However, the retail financial industry was also coming under government scrutiny. In particular, the UK building societies – which had always had the greatest aggregate share of the UK savings cake, but which had always been encumbered by regulations that essentially confined them to a role as savings institutions and mortgage lenders – were clearly regarded by the government as representing a considerable reserve of institution strength.

In 1985 the Childs Report was published, which recommended sweeping measures to give the UK building societies the opportunity to run accounts offering a full range of banking services. This year also saw the intensification of the ideas of Farbrother and his colleagues and the planning for the launch of LINK and FTS, with the latter operating as an entry gateway into LINK for institutions which – either for internal political reasons or for reasons of cost – did not wish to become full LINK members. FTS offered institutions a deal which had to be regarded as giving value for money: an initial membership fee of £50,000, and a written commitment to installing a minimum of 10 ATMs during the first year of membership. With ATMs costing about £25,000 each in the mid-1980s, this meant that an institution would be able to offer its customers access to the nationwide LINK network for about £300,000: not big money by the standards of the financial sector, although the costs of issuing cards, and developing and marketing accounts would, of course, be in addition to this.

Farbrother played a key role in the final planning of the two new organizations: so much so that, with the blessing of Citibank, he was invited to work for FTS full-time. From a conceptual standpoint, one of his most important contributions as chairman of the ATM evaluation team was to lead the team to the conclusion that the route to the most productive and profitable deployment of ATMs would stem from deploying them as consumer-orientated facilities and not as technological innovations as such.

Farbrother says:

> The team arrived at this conclusion from its own instinctive beliefs, and also from observations such as that the first ATM deployed in the US which achieved real success during the 1970s in terms of attracting consumer transactions was known as 'Tilly the Teller'.

He adds:

> The point is that in the US, once ATM networks of any size started to be created they were 'humanized', with the result that many of the shared ATM networks in the US had and have user-friendly brand names: 'Magic Line' is one that springs to mind. In the UK, however, the need to orientate ATM networks around customers was recognized later than in the US. For example, the UK clearers which began deploying ATMs in the late 1960s and 1970s made no comparable effort to humanize their networks, but branded them rather unimaginatively with the name of the relevant bank, perhaps with the word 'cash' added. One has the impression that the idea that ATMs were a completely new delivery service offering hugely exciting marketing possibilities and the potential to provide what could be a seven-days-a-week, 24-hour service, hardly appears to have occurred to the banks at all in those days.

And he concludes:

> The reasons for this lack of insight into what ATMs really meant to financial institutions are not difficult to find. The big clearers were sure they were the leading providers of retail financial services in the UK, and regarded themselves as having an unassailable position in this respect. This being so, they did not see any reason to explore in depth the potential ATMs and ATM networks offered as competitive weapons. Looking back, I realize that one reason why FTS was able to move ahead so rapidly on the electronic banking front, and why – by 1986 – we were already well on the way to deploying electronic banking systems that represented a formidable competitive challenge to the status quo in the UK banking scene, was that we had understood that electronic banking systems *were as much marketing tools as service delivery tools,* and above all had to be directed around winning acceptance among customers. In specific terms, this meant that, from the outset, our ATMs were open for more hours in the day, and for more days in the week, than the big clearers' ATMs, and offered a wider range of services through the ATM than theirs did.

The creators of LINK and FTS shared the vision of founding a network and electronic banking infrastructure that would allow member institutions and their account holders to access the benefits offered by electronic banking systems (initially solely through a comprehensive and multi-function shared ATM facility, later through other types of virtual financial service), while simultaneously keeping the expense of deploying the technology reasonable and proportional to the institution's ability to pay. The financial benefits would stem directly from the fact that the network would be shared by numerous institutions which would reap the benefits offered by economies of scale.

Above all, the beneficiaries of the new system would be members of the public, who would gain access to an increasingly extensive shared national ATM network via financial institutions which had not been able to provide this service before the creation of FTS or LINK because the institutions did not, alone, have a sufficiently large share of the market to justify the high capital costs of setting up their own, dedicated, ATM network.

Between 1986 and 1989, FTS changed from being purely a consortium organization which acted as an ATM manager and a gateway for LINK, and became what was in effect a virtual banking facilitator: offering a wide range of services to retail institutions which wished to extract the maximum competitive edge from virtual banking. Throughout this business development process, the role of FTS as a gateway to LINK continued to remain central to its activities.

Early in 1996, having spearheaded what can reasonably be described as a revolution in the British banking industry, Farbrother moved to pastures new. He set up an organization which was originally called CashStop! and later, following a comment from a customer that this name did not precisely describe the function of the service, PayPoint. This is a new free national bill payment network for providing payment facilities so that customers can pay the bills of leading UK utility and service companies. The need for the organization arose partly from a general belief that utility companies' bills should be capable of being paid at many locations, and also because many utility organizations were moving offices out of town and city centres to showrooms located in business parks and shopping centres and consequently it was becoming difficult for people to pay their bills other than by visiting their post office or by posting their payment. With typical foresight, Farbrother focused on the need of the customer. To date, PayPoint has done very well and looks like being another success for him.

> My overall philosophy throughout my business career has been to create structured networks which benefit not only the member organizations but also the customers, and which provide ample scope for member organizations to compete like crazy behind the

common branding. This seems to me the right way for things to happen, facilitating competition but bringing everybody the benefit of shared networks, whatever the basic function of the network might be.

This comment says a very great deal indeed about how banks should compete with one another by means of operating ATM via shared networks.

Strategic guidelines: making the most of ATMs

How can banks make the most of ATMs? I propose the following guidelines:

1 Ensure that your ATMs operate round the clock and on every day of the year, and take every step to minimize periods when the network is out of service.

2 Operate on-line as much as you can: ideally all the time.

3 Take active steps to research what particular functions your customers need from the ATMs you operate and provide those functions.

4 Avoid charging customers for using ATMs: it is in your financial interests to get customers out of your branches and using your cash machines.

5 Ideally avoid charging your customers for transactions that take place over an ATM operated by an organization with which you share within a network. If you are insistent on making a charge for this, keep it low.

6 If you are a small bank, take every opportunity to compete with larger banks by offering a regional or national service via a regional or national shared ATM network.

7 Remember that many of your competitors may not yet realize how useful international ATM sharing is for their customers. You may be able to win an edge over them by offering such an international facility.

8 Be constantly vigilant about seeking out opportunities to offer services via your ATMs which rival banks will not be offering.

9 Make maximum use of lobby ATMs, including ATMs with specialized functions. They are popular with customers because they speed the transaction time in the bank and they relieve the burden on your cashiers.

10 Do your utmost to create new types of account that make the most of virtual banking services such as your ATM network. One clever way of promoting these new accounts is to offer people who join a free cheque for a few pounds (or equivalent) and inviting them to deposit it into one of your ATMs. When they've deposited it there, it's their money.

11 Support a shared ATM branding in which you participate and compete vigorously behind it.

7 Debit at the point of sale

Introduction

Debit at the point of sale – known more formally as Electronic Funds Transfer at Point of Sale (EFTPoS) – is, from the perspectives of functionality and operation, the most straightforward element of the virtual banking revolution. The enormous success it has enjoyed over the past 10 years is more unexpected than many bankers would have the frankness to admit.

When the idea of EFTPoS was first seriously suggested as a new banking technique in the early 1980s, it was not immediately clear why customers would want to use such a system. If the debit was going to happen on the same day when they made their transaction they would not enjoy the three-day float they would get from cheque payments. Furthermore, the use of a debit system would – it was thought – probably involve yet another plastic card in the customer's wallet. Besides, how would customers feel if the transaction was denied at the point of sale? Would that not be an extremely embarrassing and unwelcome incursion into what should be a pleasant experience: going shopping?

After all, say what you like about cash, it is at least a way to guarantee that a purchase can always be made. In addition, cheque guarantee cards meant that a cheque was as certain to be accepted as cash up to the threshold of the limit on the card. Would not customers have a simple resistance to making use of EFTPoS facilities, even if they were already familiar with taking money out of ATMs?

All these objections seemed reasonable at the time, but circumstances, and industry developments, have shown them to be largely irrelevant.

For one thing, banks quickly realized that they could easily integrate ATMs and EFTPoS functionality into the same card: there would be no need to carry an additional card to make debit transactions.

As for the possibility of a customer being embarrassed or discounted by having a transaction denied at the point of sale, the early EFTPoS systems – and many systems still operational today – do not require every transaction to be authorized directly in real-time but operate what is called a floor or house limit, with transactions beneath this limit being authorized automatically unless they involve what is known as Cashback (see below for more information about this) or are subject to random checks.

For all practical purposes, therefore, cardholders making routine, relatively small transactions can be confident that these will be permitted by the retailer. That said, there is a distinct trend for EFTPoS systems to move towards a procedure of real-time authorization for every transaction. Such systems naturally carry a greater likelihood of refused transactions. The fact that these real-time authorization systems have not met with customer rejection suggests that the whole idea of possible transaction refusal being a disincentive to customers to use debit is something of a red herring.

The truth of the matter appears to be that, as with ATMs, customers simply enjoy the benefits of being able to do away with cash and not having to fish out their cheque books and cheque guarantee cards. Handing over a plastic card to pay for a purchase has become a natural way to pay.

Debit at the point of sale, like ATMs, has swept the world. How do we do justice to it in a book such as this?

I see no particular strategic benefits to be gained from providing details of debit schemes world-wide with attached numbers of cardholders and transaction volumes. Even if this research were feasible for one author to complete, which it isn't, it would only tell us what I can set down simply here: that EFTPoS is a great success and that more and more retail transactions globally, at least in developed countries, make use of it. Readers who *do* seek detailed research about the scope of EFTPoS schemes around the world can obtain this, at a high but fair price, from professional research bodies such as London-based Retail Banking Research.

The following discussion of EFTPoS makes use of two terms which may not be familiar to all readers. These are the *card issuer* (or simply 'issuer'): that is, the financial institution which issues the debit card to the customer and runs the account, and the *acquirer*: the financial institution responsible for providing the retailer with card acceptance facilities. The issuer and acquirer are sometimes the same bank, but frequently they are not, and even when they are, different divisions will be involved in reconciling and settling the transaction.

Another term which needs to be explained at this early stage is 'Cashback'. This facility has undoubtedly played a major role in making EFTPoS as popular as it is among customers and retailers.

Cashback is a facility offered by debit card EFTPoS issuer banks (though not usually by credit and charge card issuers) which allows the customer to add some cash to the total value of an EFTPoS debit transaction.

In effect, the Cashback facility transforms a visit to a retail outlet into something resembling a visit to a branch of the customer's bank. As the debit card transaction involves a direct debit against a current or savings account, there is no reason why the retailer should not offer the customer some cash, as this simply increases the overall size of the debit. As long as the debit transaction is secure there is no possible risk of loss to the retailer.

The amount of cash which a customer can obtain in this way varies from one retailer to the next; it is around £50 in the United Kingdom. Cashback is usually only available when the transaction can be debited immediately in real-time against the customer's account: the obvious security hazards if this rule was not applied are clear.

For customers, Cashback allows them to integrate the process of paying for a purchase with the withdrawal of cash from their account. Usually only large retail chains offer Cashback, and it is true that many of these big chains have ATMs set into the walls of their stores or other retail complex, or even in the lobby. The customer is therefore unlikely to be far from an ATM at locations where he can obtain Cashback. Even so, customers appreciate the chance to get cash when they pay for their goods, and during the same transaction.

The benefits of Cashback to retailers are in many respects even greater. To reiterate a point I have often made in this book, handling cash is not only troublesome and costly for retailers, but also creates security problems. Offering Cashback is a perfect way to transform physical cash into reliable electronic data which cannot be stolen and which is not cumbersome to handle. What happens is that the cash taken by the retail outlet becomes a kind of float which, given that it is properly accounted for, can be taken in from one transaction and paid out to another customer, with the retailer being paid for the cash by the acquirer bank. It is a perfect, and highly compelling, example of the virtual banking revolution at work, because the acquirer bank or issuer bank is nowhere to be seen in relation to the transaction.

The three main types of debit

There are three types of EFTPoS transaction: one involving a debit being made against a current account or savings account, one involving a debit being made against a credit card facility, and one being made against a charge card facility.

All these types of transaction are equally valid forms of EFTPoS, but note that the term 'debit card' has come to mean a card used for an EFTPoS transaction against a current or savings account. The familiar terms 'credit card' and 'charge card' are still used for cards which activate a debit against, respectively, a credit card and charge card facility.

The justification for interpreting the phrase 'debit' as meaning a card which activates a debit against a current or savings account is that increasingly the trend is for these kind of debits to be conducted entirely by electronic means.

Where this procedure applies, the transaction is authorized electronically by reference to the customer's account held at the issuer bank (with the authorization happening whether or not the transaction exceeds the house limit), and with the details of the transaction either being sent by the retailer to the acquirer, and then on to the issuer, by purely electronic means. The signature verification process is only used to keep an audit trail of the procedure, and to verify the customer's identity.

On the other hand, many credit card and charge card transactions are not fully electronic. Typically what happens in their case is that the transaction is authorized electronically by reference to the cardholder's account, but the payment procedure is initiated by a paper voucher which the customer signs. At the end of the day these vouchers are collected by the retailer and forwarded to the organization which issues the credit or charge card.

Even within these three types of EFTPoS there are variations in how things are done. If the debit is not below the house limit, the transaction amount may not be taken off the customer's account until the next day, or even two or three days later. It is impossible to generalize about how EFTPoS takes place on a global basis: the procedures vary between systems and between countries, with some international systems doing things differently in different countries. However, these variations need not concern us unduly: all we need to be concerned about are the relationships between the four parties involved: that is, the customer, the retailer, the issuer and the acquirer.

Advantages of EFTPoS to each of the four parties

The advantages of debit at point of sale to these four parties are as follows:

- *The customer.* Faster and more convenient transactions, no need to carry cash (or can carry less cash), statement provided of all purchases, possible increased status.

- *The retailer.* Improved customer service (but only because customers like using debit), reduced problems associated with using cash, acquirer and issuer bank bear the burden of fraud, more rapid throughput of sales transactions.

- *The issuer.* Improved customer appeal, capability of attracting more customers and greater deposits = more revenue = more profitability, some EFTPoS systems oblige the acquirer to pay the issuer for guaranteeing payment.

- *The acquirer.* Opportunities for substantial commission revenue gained from retailer.

Who pays for EFTPoS?

One of the many attractions of EFTPoS for banks is that they can obtain a revenue stream from it by imposing a commission charge on transactions. This commission is paid not by the customer but by the retailer. In practice the commission is simply deducted by the acquirer from the payment made to the retailer.

The amount of commission varies considerably between different types of EFTPoS suppliers. Credit and charge card operators have historically always charged more for transactions than debit card operators: this appears to derive from the point that today, as in the past, credit and charge cards confer status on cardholders and consequently they are likely to be held by wealthier people whose custom a retailer might be expected to have a special incentive for wishing to cultivate. That said, many retailers are more hard-headed about this than they were formerly and most are highly selective about what cards they do and don't accept precisely because of the level of commission they must pay. This selectivity is especially noticeable in the restaurant business, where relatively low profit margins makes it essential for even the highest-profile restaurant to exercise a tough policy over what cards they accept. Many readers will themselves have doubtless experienced the fact that even very good restaurants often expect payment in cash or by cheque, and will only take one or two debit cards and often no credit or charge cards at all.

Commission rates for EFTPoS transactions tend to vary between about one per cent and five per cent, with rates even among particular operators depending on the business throughput of individual retailers. Naturally, small retailers with fairly low throughputs on a particular card are likely to have to charge more than larger retailers with high transaction volumes on the card in question.

If the EFTPoS system is operated by a central organization which handles the cost-issuing over network, this commission will go to the organization. If, on the other hand, the network consists essentially of communications facilities between issuer and acquirer banks, the commission will go to the acquirer bank.

Issuer banks do not make revenue directly from issuing EFTPoS cards, but they will have an indirect revenue from winning more customers to use their services as a result of customers enjoying the EFTPoS, and wanting, the EFTPoS facility. In any event, experience has shown that issuer banks are always highly motivated to issue EFTPoS cards and that the increases in customers deriving from a bank offering this facility are substantial.

Where a central network organization acts as a branding for the EFTPoS system and as a facilitator for the environment, this organization will not receive commissions from transactions but will be funded by the issuer and acquirer banks which participate in the shared venture. Sometimes, as might be expected, the amount of funding provided by a particular issuer or acquirer bank will in some way depend on the number of cards featuring the branding issued by the issuer bank or on the number of transactions handled during a certain period by the acquirer.

A final point to make about charging for EFTPoS is that some debit card issuer banks make a small handling charge for Cashback. However, this is normally not the case.

Shared EFTPoS schemes

EFTPoS offers the same kind of incentives to banks and other financial institutions to concentrate in shared schemes as ATMs do. The same fundamental principle applies: the infrastructure is extremely expensive to set up and it makes perfect sense for all participants to contribute a share of the set up costs and/or running costs. Besides, the infrastructure is only going to be truly useful if issuer banks and acquirer banks are all taking part in it. This point is, therefore, a reinforcing argument for a shared network, just as the fact that the greater the number of banks participating in an ATM network the more useful it is, is a reinforcing argument in favour of ATM sharing.

Today, around the world, the only countries which do not have financial sectors featuring EFTPoS sharing are those with relatively primitive economies where one or two banks have a monopoly of the retail financial sector. Even in this case, there is almost always a justification for sharing EFTPoS resources if more than one bank is involved with it.

The two types of shared EFTPoS scheme

There are two principal types of shared EFTPoS network.

The first type features a central (or 'host') computer which acts as a giant switch and powers all the shared transactions. This is, for example, how Amex operates. Amex actually sends bills to its cardholders as well as operates the system. Most credit card and charge card EFTPoS systems operate in a similar way. For example, Visa also operates the central switch for the Visa network.

However, not all central switch providers manage their commercial activities in the same way. For example, while Amex operates very much as a profit-making venture and both handles its own central switch and the actual card-billing to merchants and to cardholders (or 'card members' as Amex prefers to put it), Visa is – and this may surprise some readers – actually a non-profit-making organization. It handles its own switch, but its members are the ones who bill merchants and customers. Visa is a consortium organization and funded by its members.

As one might expect, the burden of performance which falls on the central switch is enormous. Organizations such as Amex and Visa need to be able to deploy computers which can handle peak volumes of up to 2000 transactions per second and sometimes even higher levels.

Clearly there is no margin for error: the computer systems have to be absolutely fault-tolerant, meaning that transactions must be capable of being switched to a substitute computer system with no loss of integrity and ideally with no lost data. Furthermore, the system has got to be truly global. An American Express cardholder in Britain must, for example, be able to use his Amex card around the world whenever he wishes. Needless to say, the technology allowing him to, for example, pay for a restaurant meal in Sydney,

Australia, using an Amex card which is debited against his account back in Britain is formidable.

This first type of EFTPoS is more popular for credit and charge types of EFTPoS than for debit EFTPoS. Amex is strictly a charge and credit facility. Visa is usually a credit facility, but many Visa members use the brand for debit cards. Note that Visa has also originated a branding – Visa Electron – which is strictly a debit facility featuring real-time authorization.

The second type of system tends to be more popular for shared networks involving current account or deposit accounts. In this type of network, the shared network provides a card branding and orchestrates the collaborative process between participants, but does not provide a central switch. The actual transactions are not handled by the shared network at all but rather by the issuer and acquirer banks.

The highly successful UK shared EFTPoS networks Switch and Solo (both operated by Switch Card Services) are examples of this type of network. Paradoxically, perhaps, Switch does not have a switch.

A detailed case study of Switch Card Services is presented below.

International EFTPoS sharing

There is as much scope and general motivation for international EFTPoS sharing as there is for international ATM sharing.

International EFTPoS sharing involving such credit and charge card brands as Amex and Visa is well developed; indeed, in the case of Amex it was one of the reasons for launching the cards in the first place. Originally the transactions were not strictly speaking EFTPoS, as only the authorization took place electronically – assuming it was in excess of the house limit – and the actual transactions process was initiated by a paper voucher. However, nowadays the transaction is usually initiated electronically as well as authorized by this means if it exceeds the house limit. The paper voucher is increasingly simply a record-keeping system.

International EFTPoS sharing involving debit has not yet caught on to any great extent, probably because the banks involved are currently much more concerned with maximizing the market share in their domestic markets. However, the technology is very much in place and there is no reason at all why international debit sharing should not become much more widespread. In years to come it is almost certain to do so.

The security of the EFTPoS transaction

The situation here is very straightforward.

Where PIN authorization is used in conjunction with EFTPoS, the security of the transaction is high because there is no way that someone who has found a lost card or stolen it can know the customer's PIN, unless the customer has been careless in keeping the PIN secret. In the case of EFTPoS systems using a PIN, the security situation is very similar to that for an ATM network.

On the other hand, where the only security authorization procedure is the cardholder's signature, the overall system is, naturally, much less secure. If real-time authorization of transactions is involved, there will be some limit on the extent to which the fraudster can use the card, but this limit will only depend on the condition of the bona fide cardholders accounts, it will not be anything that could reasonably be described as a security system.

Otherwise, as long as a fraudster is the same sex as the cardholder, and can forge the cardholder's signature adequately, there is no reason why he should not be able to use the card until it is reported lost or stolen by the cardholder. Unfortunately, as we see in the case study, there is often a chronological discrepancy between when an issuer bank posts details of lost or stolen cards on its computer system and when a card network does this. Furthermore, it is up to the cardholder to notify the issuer bank about details of a card that has been lost or stolen. If the cardholder is not aware of this having happened, he is likely to face some liability for transactions enacted by a fraudster and not spotted with reasonable vigilance by the retailer.

Altogether, EFTPoS systems which do not use a PIN must be regarded as fundamentally unsatisfactory from a security perspective.

Case Study: Switch Card Services

Overview

In the mid 1980s, with the costs of processing cheques continuing to rise, three major UK banks saw the opportunity to create a fully electronic payment system. The system they decided to create was one that could be administered efficiently, would be easier and safer for retailers to handle and more convenient for consumers.

The idea behind the system was that the customer would be able to pay by means of a plastic card which would initiate a debit at the point of sale against the customer's bank account. The transaction would be authorized by means of a signature that would need to tally with the signature on the card.

The amount to be debited would typically be taken from the customer's account within the same period after the transaction as the usual clearance period for a cheque. The system would be fully electronic, in that details of the transaction would be 'acquired' (to use the industry term) by whichever bank the retailer was using and would then be relayed across an electronic data communications network to the bank which had issued the particular card used to make the payment (this bank was known as the 'issuer').

The three banks which joined forces were the Midland Bank, the National Westminster Bank and The Royal Bank of Scotland. The scheme they launched was called the Switch Card Scheme. After a preliminary period when the scheme was administered by these founder members, Switch Card Services was created to manage and market the scheme on behalf of a growing membership.

Since the first Switch transactions in October 1988, the scheme has grown to include other banks and building societies and now has more than 30 financial institution members, who together issue about 17.5 million cards in the UK. As about 80 per cent of the UK adult population is banked, this means that a substantial portion of the UK adult population holds a Switch card.

In 1997 the Switch card was joined by another fully electronic debit card programme, known as Solo. Using the same network infrastructure as Switch, Solo caters to the needs of what Switch Card Services somewhat euphemistically describes as 'a new group of shoppers.' What this actually means is that, as Solo requires transactions to be authorized in real-time, there is no risk of default because the customer has to have the funds in his account (or the transaction has to be within an agreed overdraft facility), if the transaction is to go ahead. Solo customers are therefore conceived to be those with whom the issuer bank does not have a long relationship or knows to have a less than perfect credit record. Solo is targeted at younger customers and also at new customers, or those who have blips on their credit record.

Solo has proved a success. It went live in July 1997, and by March 1998 had 1.5 million cardholders.

It will readily be seen that the principle behind Switch is very similar to that behind the shared ATM network. The participants join together in order to make use of an expensive infrastructure which they need and the cost of which can be shared out among participants, with new members paying a fee that contributes towards the cost of an infrastructure already in place. Given that there is a clear mutual incentive to use the infrastructure, the different participants can then compete with each other to persuade customers to make use of *their* Switch-branded card rather than another institution's.

One difference between the infrastructure of the Switch scheme and that of many other shared debit schemes has already been touched upon. This is that whereas many shared debit schemes make use of a central switch for all transactions, the Switch scheme makes use of network connections between issuer and acquirer banks, with Switch managing these connections. In practice the difference is principally a question of technical organization: the net effect, that a bank participates in a common branding and competes vigorously with other members of the same branding, is identical to that of the shared ATM network.

Like all successful electronic payment schemes, Switch Card Services likes to publicize the statistics relating to its own popularity. These are certainly impressive. Switch cardholders now make more than 60 million purchases every month: a figure that works out at around two million a day, just under 1400 a minute and about 23 per second around the clock. As with all payment network statistics, they are, however, only averages. In reality the proportion of transactions during busy shopping times such as lunchtime and Saturday mornings would be much higher, while the transaction volumes during the night – and especially during the 'dead' period between around midnight and five o'clock in the morning when very few retail outlets are open – would be much smaller.

Switch Card Services is also regarded internationally as something of a pioneer in debit card success. Even though the Switch system only operates in the UK, it has come to be seen as a world leader. As a source at Switch told me: 'Overseas banks from five continents have come to see us to learn how Switch has changed payment habits in Britain.'

Security

As we have seen, debit card schemes face obvious security problems, especially where a PIN system is not used. Switch does not make use of a PIN system, and other debit card schemes in Britain follow suit by relying on signature authorization.

The approach which Switch has adopted towards cad security is to develop what it refers to as a 'robust security system'. This, Switch says, offers 'stringent, effective control without losing the advantages of fast, convenient transactions'.

Switch makes the following additional points about its security procedures:

As a domestic card scheme, Switch is not open to international fraud or misuse. It is three times more successful in preventing fraud and misuse than rival card schemes.

Every retailer's terminal is linked to the Switch Hot Card System, so that every transaction can be checked quickly to identify stolen or lost cards being used fraudulently. All Solo transactions and any Switch transactions above the floor limits agreed by acquiring and retailer are also checked by the issuer before being authorized. As a further measure, Switch transactions below the floor limit are subject to routine and random checks.

Switch has put in place the Switch Risk Identification System to help acquirers pin-point stores with high fraud levels and work with retailers to introduce preventive measures.

All these controls result in the retrieval of thousands of lost, stolen and misused cards every month. To stay one step ahead of the fraudsters, we're also working on new security technologies, such as smart cards, to reduce fraud even further.

Of course, none of these measures can avoid the basic problem that anyone who finds a Switch card can use it if they are the same sex as the cardholder (whose name will of course be on the front of the card in embossed plastic letters) and if they can forge the cardholder's signature with enough accuracy to deceive the assistant at the point of sale. Such assistants, especially in high-volume retail outlets such as supermarkets, are frequently under great pressure of work and do not usually check signatures with particular care. They are also often young people, who may be working full- or part-time and whose motivation to stop their employer becoming a victim of fraud is not, it must be said, especially high.

The Switch Card Service guards against such card fraud by ensuring that details of all lost and stolen cards are fed into a security system which contains details of cards reported lost or stolen. However – and readers should pay particular attention to this point, as it is much less well known than it ought to be – in the case of Switch (and in the case of most debit card systems around the world), *this list of lost or stolen cards is not updated in real-time but only every 24 hours.*

The issuer bank, however, *will* update its system immediately the card is reported lost or stolen, *but this particular updating will only come into play if Cashback is involved or if the transaction is above the 'house limit': that is, the retailer's own limit above which transactions need to be authorized with the issuer bank.*

For most non-real-time systems – such as Switch – a house limit is fixed for convenience in order to avoid the delays which would be involved if every transaction had to be authorized against the cardholder's account. Switch house limits vary from one retail outlet to another: they are usually in the region of £100. Unfortunately, if a transaction is below the house limit and the system is not a real-time system, the transaction does not need to be authorized against the cardholder's account and therefore the retailer will not be able to pick up the fact that the card has been reported lost or stolen until the debit card system is loaded with this information: that is, the following day. If, however, the transaction exceeds the house limit, the transaction will need to be authorized against the issuer bank bank's records, and as these will be updated immediately the card is reported lost or stolen, the transaction will not be permitted.

Note that the transaction will also be checked in real-time against the issuer bank (even if the system is not a real-time system), if the transaction is subjected to one of the random tests that Switch conducts regularly as an added security precaution.

What all this boils down to is that a fraudster who uses a lost or stolen card below the house limit, and *doesn't* request Cashback and *isn't* subject to a random check, is likely to be 'safe' for 24 hours, but will be caught – or, at least, the transaction won't be allowed – if the transaction is above the house limit.

However, remember that all this only applies to debit card schemes which are not operating in real-time *for all transactions*. Schemes which do operate in real-time for all transactions, such as (in the United Kingdom) Electron, Solo and an increasing proportion of credit card schemes world-wide, are much more secure as the transaction will always be checked against the issuer bank. Assuming that the issuer bank has had time to update its system (which should happen as soon as the card is reported lost or stolen) the transaction will not be permitted. Incidentally, from a consumer point of view, customers are not liable for transactions once they have reported a card lost or stolen.

Naturally, cardholders who become aware that their cards have been lost or stolen are urged by the issuer bank to report the loss or theft immediately and warned that until they do so they may be liable for a proportion, or for all of the cost, of transactions made using the card. There is not much else that can be done from a security perspective as long as a magnetic stripe card is used, unless the issuer brings in a PIN authorization system, for which there is no standard infrastructure in the United Kingdom.

Why have PIN authorization systems not caught on for debit cards in the UK as they have, for example, in the US? The reason unquestionably stems from the fact that by the time that EFTPoS debit was starting to be established in Britain, credit and charge card transactions made using paper vouchers were so thoroughly ingrained as the way of doing things that there was no room for a new infrastructure. This is often the case with infrastructures that have been established at a time when the technology was less advanced than it is today: changing the infrastructure is too costly and difficult.

On the other hand, countries which have come to electronic banking much more recently can set up infrastructures featuring PIN authorization. (In Chapter 9, when I look at smart cards, we shall see this principle in operation again.)

A secondary reason why PIN authorization for EFTPoS has not caught on in Britain is probably due to the strange notion in the UK that providing any kind of service puts one in a highly subservient position in relation to the customer, especially in the retail industry. This being the case, retailers have little optimism that customers are going to like subjecting themselves to what is often a relatively lengthy transaction – that is, where PIN authorization is used – compared to simply giving the assistant the debit card to swipe through a terminal.

Besides, there *is* indeed something a little demeaning about having routinely to key in a PIN at point of sale. Even if the reader does not agree with my views here, it certainly cannot be denied that electronic payment facilities must always fit in with what is seen as acceptable within national cultures. Indeed, this point is one of the themes of this book.

Switch authorization

Switch cards are authorized in the following way:

1   The card is swiped through the retailer's terminal. This is an electronic card-reading device which has access to the Hot Card File – a list of lost and stolen cards which is updated daily. If the card is on the file, reference is made to the issuer via the acquirer for further instructions.

2   If expenditure is above the house limit agreed between retailer and acquirer, involves Cashback or is subject to a random check, the transaction is passed to the issuer via the acquirer for authorization. The issuer checks if the card is lost or stolen and whether the account has sufficient funds (including overdraft facilities) to cover the transaction.

3   If the transaction is authorized, the whole process will take less than five seconds. If, however, the card is lost or stolen, the issuer will send a referral message to the retailer's terminal. The retailer will then telephone the acquirer for further instructions. The card will not be returned to the fraudster. Needless to say, any fraudster who finds that there is a problem with an attempted transaction is unlikely to have any desire to stay in the retail pocket a moment longer.

4   If there are insufficient funds in the customer's account to cover the transaction, the transaction will be – as Switch puts it – 'politely declined.'

5   If the expenditure is below the agreed limit and the card is not recorded on the Hot Card File System, the transaction will be accepted, subject to the retailer's standard checks, such as signature verification.

Solo authorization

Solo card authorization is simpler than Switch authorization. As we have seen, each and every Solo transaction is referred for authorization to the issuer, to check for lost and stolen cards as well as to ensure there are sufficient funds in the cardholder's account.

This strict authorization process ensures credit control is fully maintained as well as guaranteeing the most stringent fraud control measures. The speed of updating of lost or stolen cards is greater among the issuer bank than the debit card system itself. Consequently, in the case of Solo authorization (and in the case of any other real-time authorization systems) any problems with the card will be immediately spotted and no transaction – either above or below the house limit – will be permitted.

Clearing and settlement

During the day Switch and Solo transactions are electronically gathered from retailer terminals by the acquirer. On the following day the acquirer passes the transactions to the appropriate issuer via Switch.

On the third day the issuer is required to settle for transactions with the acquirer.

The timing of retailer crediting and cardholder editing is at the members' discretion.

Payment guarantee

The card issuer provides a guarantee of payment to the acquirer for all authorized transactions, subject to the retailer complying with the rules of the Switch scheme.

Allocation of the benefits of Switch and Solo

Switch Card Services makes the following points about the benefits of Switch and Solo to the three parties involved, respectively: cardholders, retailers and banks and building societies.

Cardholders appreciate the speed and convenience which Switch and Solo offer: levels of speed and convenience which cheques and cash can never supply. Using these systems, there is no need to carry large amounts of cash or bulky cheque books, and it only takes seconds to pay. Statements itemize not just how much is spent, but where and when the purchase was made. Both cards offer freedom from restrictive cheque guarantee limits, but still provide the reassurance of spending control. Solo cardholders enjoy the additional comfort of knowing that each and every transaction will be checked against the available funds in their account. Increasingly, cardholders are also using their card to take advantage of mail and telephone ordering, as well as convenient Cashback facilities.

Retailers have been quick to see the benefits of all-electronic debit cards: less cashing-up time, less bookkeeping, quicker transactions at the point of sale, and reduced exposure to forged banknotes, bouncing cheques and stolen cards. Combined, all these elements mean that retailers can offer their customers Switch and Solo, safe in the knowledge that they have an efficient, robust and secure system behind them.

Supermarket groups and petrol companies were among the first to offer their customers the convenience of Switch. Today, with the introduction of modestly priced stand-alone terminals, even the most cost-conscious independent corner shop can share the same sophisticated payment system as the largest retail multiples.

Banks and building societies have also benefited from Switch's efficient system, allowing them to replace costly cheque-processing with a modern, streamlined and fully electronic payment procedure which has proved highly cost-effective.

Switch is particularly attractive to new members. SwitchNet, the dedicated data transmission network, has been designed to enable them to integrate their own information technology equipment without the need for significant investment and reprogramming.

In addition to offering their customers a convenient and appealing service, Switch Scheme members can, if they wish, add ATM and international point-of-sale facilities to their Switch and Solo card programmes. The current move from magnetic stripe to microchip technology will give card issuers even more options to add value to their card products in the future.

Extract from Switch Card Services' brochure for retailers

The following extract illustrates the advantages which Switch Card Services considers the Switch and Solo cards to have for retailers. The remainder of the material in this particular section is quoted verbatim from Switch and is not, therefore, as objective as the other material in this book.

1   *Offer your customers a convenient way to pay.* Switch and Solo debit cards give a quick, easy and convenient method of payment to cardholders and retailers alike. Switch is the UK's leading electronic debit card. Now joined by Solo, these cards are designed to appeal to every type of customer. Whether you run a shop, a mail order or telephone order business, both cards give your customers direct access to their accounts without the restraints of cheque guarantee limits.

2   *Simple to operate. In retail outlets.* Switch and Solo cards are swiped through an in-store terminal. This checks the card, records details of the transaction and obtains any necessary authorization. Your customer signs the receipt, and the stored transaction is then collected by your acquiring bank (the bank which processes your Switch/Solo transactions) and passed to the cardholder's bank via our own secure network.

3   *Speed at the till.* Switch and Solo transactions are fully electronic. It takes you just a few moments to print a receipt and check your customer's signature with that on the card. The result is less time spent queuing by your customers, and less time spent by you examining cheques and counting change. You can spend that time dealing with your next customer.

4   *Reducing fraud.* Every terminal accesses an automatically updated 'Hot Card File' which helps to prevent the use of lost or stolen cards. These and other controls result in the retrieval of thousands of lost, stolen or misused cards every year. Switch and Solo also offer you the security of holding less cash and cheques on your premises. And, of course, Switch and Solo reduce exposure to the problems of bounced cheques and forged bank notes.

5   *Less cashing-up and better cashflow.* With Switch and Solo, you spend less time cashing-up, less time banking and less time bookkeeping. A simple procedure at close of business will total your Switch and Solo transactions for that day. So rather than paying in your takings and waiting for cheques to clear, transactions are automatically credited to your business within a few days.

6   *Millions of customers.* With our two distinctive, well-marketed cards, we have become the largest debit card scheme in the UK. Put Switch and Solo logos in your window, and millions of customers can see that you value their custom enough to offer them a fast, convenient way to pay.

7   *Fast and secure.* Being fully electronic, Switch and Solo transactions can register in your account faster than payments made by cheque. As long as you have followed the procedures issued by your bank and have obtained the customer's signature, payment is guaranteed.

8   *A choice of equipment.* Terminals that accept Switch and Solo are also able to take a full range of plastic cards. Modestly priced stand-alone terminals mean even the most cost-conscious independent retailer can share the same sophisticated payment system as the largest retail multiples. You can choose to rent, lease or buy your terminal. Which terminal you choose will depend on your own particular requirements.

9   *Competitive pricing.* There is no across-the-board price for Switch and Solo. Charges are negotiated individually between you and the bank of your choice, ensuring competition amongst the Scheme's acquiring members (i.e. the banks offering Switch and Solo services).

10 *Signing up.* Securing the benefits of electronic payments for your business is easy. Major banks are able to give you details about joining thousands of retailers nationwide who are already benefiting from the Scheme. You will find a list of all of the acquiring banks for Switch and Solo on the back of this leaflet. Call any of them today for further details, and get Switch and Solo working for your business.

List of Switch Card Services Members, Nominated Group Companies and Card Issuer Associates

1   List of Members and Nominated Group Companies

The following is a list of current Members and current participating Nominated Group Companies. Nominated Group Companies are shown, indented, under their sponsoring Members.

a.   Alliance & Leicester plc
  i.   Girobank plc
b.   The Governor and Company of the Bank of Scotland
  i.   Capital Bank plc
  ii.   Bank of Wales plc
c.   Barclays Bank plc
d.   Clydesdale Bank plc
  i.   Northern Bank Limited
  ii.   Yorkshire Bank plc
e.   Halifax plc
f.   Lloyds Bank plc
g.   Midland Bank plc
  i.   Samuel Montagu & Co Limited
  ii.   The British Bank of the Middle East
  iii.   HSBC Investment Bank plc
h.   National Westminster Bank plc
  i.   Isle of Man Bank Limited
  ii.   Coutts & Co
  iii.   Ulster Bank Limited
i.   The Royal Bank of Scotland plc
  i.   The Royal Bank of Scotland (I.O.M.) Limited
  ii.   The Royal Bank of Scotland International Limited
  iii.   Adam & Company plc

2   List of Card Issuer Associates

The following is a list of current participating Card Issuer Associates. Card Issuer Associates are shown under their sponsoring Members.

a.   The Governor and Company of the Bank of Scotland
  Sainsbury's Bank plc
b.   Midland Bank plc
  Allied Irish Banks plc
  Bank of Ireland
  Britannia Building Society
  Chelsea Building Society
  Cumberland Building Society
  Derbyshire Building Society
  Norwich and Peterborough Building Society
  Yorkshire Building Society
c.   The Royal Bank of Scotland plc
  Whiteaway Laidlaw Bank Limited

Strategic guidelines: making the most of debit

The following strategic guidelines should be followed to extract the maximum benefit from EFTPoS:

1 Ensure that an EFTPoS debit facility is attached to all the new accounts you launch and explore ways of attaching such a facility to existing accounts.

2 Explore to the full the obvious advantages you can enjoy from becoming part of a shared EFTPoS network rather than trying to operate your own EFTPoS infrastructure.

3 Remember that EFTPoS schemes which feature real-time authorization for all transactions protect you and may also be highly acceptable to customers who know that no EFTPoS debit is likely to make their accounts overdrawn. Explore the opportunities which such real-time authorization systems can offer you.

4 International EFTPoS offers clear opportunities for an enterprising bank to gain an edge over its rivals which may not be implementing this and offering it with sufficient energy. Customers are likely to appreciate any initiative you take in this respect.

5 Where possible, make use of PIN authorization for EFTPoS transactions.

6 If you are acting as an acquirer for EFTPoS transactions, balance your very reasonable desire to maximize your commission revenue with the need to create goodwill among retailers. Remember that many EFTPoS brands have been discarded by retailers who are unwilling to pay what they perceive as unacceptable commission rates. Bear in mind that once a retailer has discarded your EFTPoS brand, bringing them back to it will be extremely difficult.

Banking on the telephone

Introduction

The first thing to say about telephone banking services is that even though they are designed to be used in the customer's home, they are almost as likely to end up being accessed from the customer's office. Indeed, research by leading UK telephone bank First Direct, suggests that about half the phone calls it receives are made during conventional office hours. Furthermore, First Direct has found that about 75 per cent of its customers are in full-time employment. Clearly, not everybody in full-time employment works during conventional office hours, but it is clear that a significant proportion of calls received by First Direct are made by customers from their work places.

Virtual banks do not like to draw this last conclusion, for the very good reason that it is strictly speaking illegal for a customer to call a bank from work, as the cost of the telephone call is in effect being stolen from the employer. Even where no charge is made for accessing the telephone banking service, there is still the point that paid work-time is being used by the customer. In any event, virtual banks do not circulate information about the proportion of calls likely to be made from the workplace, but the two statistics released by First Direct and quoted above strongly suggest that a significant proportion of such calls are made from the office rather than from home.

Telephone banking has not yet caught on to anything like the same extent as ATMs and EFTPoS. As an avid user of telephone banking services myself, I have often wondered why precisely its appeal is not yet widespread, despite superb technology being readily available for around five years, and reasonably acceptable technology being available for longer. Probably the truth of the matter is that the idea of using the telephone to conduct banking transactions is more alien to many people than a freelance writer such as myself might imagine. People might feel – doubtless on many occasions with justification – that the likelihood of them making a telephone call without being overheard or interrupted is low and that while such a call may be fine for phoning friends, it isn't for talking to one's bank, whether the bank is personified by a real person or an automated voice response system.

People might also feel nervous about conducting a banking transaction over the telephone. It is certainly true that most telephone banking services let the customer conduct major transfers of funds between, say, one account and another, and also enable the customer to pay for a third-party service such as a utility by means of the telephone service. However, the transaction is always reversible unless one is paying a third party.

Another problem is that most telephone banking services require a relatively lengthy number to be keyed in as an identification of the customer and then a four-digit quasi-PIN to be keyed in to authenticate the transaction. This, at least, is how things usually work when the telephone banking service makes use of an automated voice response system. Clearly, many people may not wish to be involved with such a process, although it is in fact possible to key ones personal numbers, and even one's PIN, into a memory button on one's telephone and to press this when the system requests identification and authentication. Note, however, that of course where a customer does this, the telephone banking system could be accessed by anybody using that memory button so this practice is only advisable if the telephone is genuinely secure.

Another problem with telephone banking services is that there is often surprising customer reluctance to talk to a real person on the telephone about banking matters. Most telephone banking services use some kind of voice response system for routine transactions and give the customer the opportunity to use a human operator for more complex transactions. Some systems, notably First Direct's, make use only of human operators and avoid automatic voice response altogether. Naturally, where human operators are used, there can be no use of a PIN as an authentication system as this would mean the operator knowing what the PIN was. Instead, what usually happens is that the operator asks the customer for a particular letter of a pre-arranged code word. The operator's computer will 'ask' the operator to request, say, the second or third letter of the code word, and this will allow the authentication process to happen without the operator needing to know what the code word is.

Finally, it should be noted that where automatic voice response is used, this will almost always require a customer to have a tone phone installed. Where this is not the case, the customer will often be unable to access the system.

Despite the restriction of the popularity of telephone banking stemming from customer resistance or technological factors, there is no doubt that telephone banking has found a high level of acceptability among professional people for whom the use of a telephone as a communications medium is absolutely second nature, and who are only too pleased to have a chance to access their bank accounts round the clock and enact transactions whenever they wish rather than having to go to an ATM, let alone visit a branch. Even if the proportion of such professional people within a bank remains static – and in fact there is evidence that it is growing – younger, computer literate people will be attaining their position in this class of professionals within the next five to 10 years and are likely to themselves find telephone banking extremely acceptable. We can confidently expect that in the future the benefits of these systems are likely to appeal to a wider range of people.

Types of banking service available via the telephone

The beauty of telephone banking is that every major banking service can be delivered via it apart from cash withdrawal. Even this last service can be included in a real sense in stored value card (SVC) schemes which permit the 'loading' of cards over the telephone. More details of this are in the following chapter, which looks at smart cards.

In summary, the typical range of services available via the telephone are as follows:

■ balance enquiry;

■ statement ordering;

■ chequebook request facility;

■ funds transfer between different accounts held by the customer at the bank (but note that these accounts usually have for security reasons to be 'linked' by the customer in advance by a visit to the branch);

■ funds transfer (i.e. payment) to third parties (e.g. payment of utility bills);

■ general account queries and advice (this would typically be supplied by a human operator even if the system used automated voice response technology;

■ ordering traveller's cheques from the bank, with these typically being available for collection from a physical branch or else supplied to the customer by registered post.

Types of telephone banking system

The range of telephone banking systems is surprisingly broad. Rather than describing every possible configuration of system, I propose to summarize the situation by making the following points.

There are in general three principal types of telephone banking service.

The first makes use of automated voice response technology. This involves the customer using his tone-phone to send what are in effect digitized data messages to the system in order to activate a particular service. The customer will always be 'prompted' by the service to provide one or more type of instruction.

Alternatively, some automated voice response systems require the customer to say one of a number of particular words down the telephone, with the system containing software which recognizes the word. The system works on a similar principle to those using tone commands.

The second type of service makes use of human operators entirely and doesn't use automated voice response at all. As we have seen, even systems which do use automated voice response will use human operators for other than routine transactions.

Finally, some telephone banking services are PC-based: that is, they use a personal computer which interfaces with the system via a data communications process delivered by the telephone. Some PC-based services use the customer's standard desktop PC, while others make use of a special dedicated terminal which is typically either supplied gratis to the customer or leased to the customer by the bank for a nominal charge.

The cost of telephone banking

Telephone banking offers banks such substantial opportunities to save money by transferring expensive branch-based transactions to automated, relatively inexpensive telephone-based systems, that most banks find more than sufficient financial reward from offering telephone banking services in having the opportunity to facilitate this transfer. For this reason, banks seek to give customers an attractive deal so as to make them want to use the system.

The practical outworking of this sentiment is that most banks are happy to subsidize much of the cost of making a call to the telephone system. Some banks actually offer free telephone calls, but the more usual system is to provide a special telephone number which is only charged at the local rate, and which will be subsidized by the bank. Where the bank is providing a special PC to the customer for use when accessing the system, the bank will usually make the terms of supply of this PC, and the cost of making a 'call' by means of it, extremely favourable to the customer, in order to encourage the customer to want to obtain the PC in the first place and to use it.

Customer attitudes towards PC banking

In Chapter 1 of this book I quoted at length from a useful customer survey conducted by the research organization PSI Global. This survey canvassed a sample of what were described as 'on-line' households in the United States. For the purposes of the survey, an on-line household is defined as one which makes use of an on-line banking service (which might include a standard telephone banking service) and/or the Internet.

The survey included some findings relating to PC banking and I have preferred to include these here, in this chapter, where they are clearly more relevant than they were in Chapter 1.

Obviously the nature of the sample (the satisfactoriness of which I have already questioned) means that the households surveyed are bound to have a slant in terms of their awareness of PC banking and use of it. The reader should certainly bear this point in mind. Even so, the findings of the survey are useful. The principal findings are as follows:

■ Whereas only six per cent of the sample made use of PC banking in 1996, this percentage had doubled by 1997 to 12 per cent. Between this period the availability of PC banking among the on-line consumer households questioned increased by 25 per cent, so the increase in usage is substantial.

■ Eight per cent of all on-line consumer households use personal financial management software to access PC banking services. Seven per cent use commercial on-line services or the Internet, while four per cent use a combination of these.

■ The average monthly fee for those in the sample who used PC banking services is $6.68. The median is $6.00.

■ As we might expect, awareness of PC banking functionality is near universal among on-line households. Nevertheless, the offering of such services by financial service providers is limited to just slightly more than one-third of all on-line consumer households.

■ Generally, PC banking users rate their PC banking product high in terms of ease of use, with little difference between the type of access methods utilized (i.e. personal financial management software, commercial on-line service/ Internet).

■ Despite the fact that the majority of PC banking users indicate that their PC banking product offers all the capabilities they desire, one-third to one-half have indicated a high level of interest in using PC banking for expanded functions such as loan payments, loan applications, obtaining product information, placing stopped payments (on cheques), requesting copies of cleared cheques, re-ordering cheques, and requesting copies of statements.

■ Currently, just three per cent of all United States households (12 per cent of on-line households) conduct financial account transactions using a PC and modem. Clearly, on-line consumer households are the ideal target market for expanding the PC banking user base.

Table 8.1. shows the different usage rates of various PC banking functions among households which use PC banking. (For example, 64 per cent of households using PC banking use the service to check their account balance, and so on).

TABLE 8.1 *PC banking by type of function (among on-line consumer households which use PC banking)*

Type of PC Banking Function	% Who Use It
Check account balance	64
Review cleared cheques	59
Download account statements	48
Transfer funds	45
Pay bills	31
Request copies of statements	19
Make loan payments	16
Obtain/download product information	15
Re-order cheques	11
Transfer copies of cleared cheques	7
Buy/sell investments	6
Apply for Visa/Mastercard credit card	5
Open account	4
Place stop payment on cheque	4
Apply for loan	3

(Source: PSI Global)

The primacy of the call centre in a telephone banking system

Central to the successful functioning of any telephone banking service is the *call centre*. This is the management and operational location to which customer calls are relayed and where operator technology and human operators are situated.

The past few years have seen considerable advances in the organization and automation of call centres, as well as a realization among banks that a good call centre can be a superb competitive weapon. Without doubt, call centres are an integral element of the virtual banking revolution.

Note, incidentally, that even where a human operator is handling the call, there are abundant opportunities for the operator to be made much more effective and efficient by making use of screen-based software which gives the operator access to a wide variety of information about the customer. One bank's use of this type of technology is detailed below.

So great is the importance of the call centre in today's financial services industry that some software organizations and consultancies are thriving merely from providing services relating to call centres to financial banks. One of these consultancies is known as the Customer Contact Centre. Based in

Bristol, it specializes in providing assistance with all aspects of running and operating a call centre.

Its managing director, Tony Collins, is a forthright commentator on the role of the call centre in today's retail financial industry. I asked him to expand on what he sees this role as being. His comments are as follows:

> I regard the role of the call centre as being to help a financial bank build a high value relationship between itself and its customers. The days of the old fashioned bank manager who would have a personal relationship with most of his customers are over, partly because of the sheer number of customers banks nowadays have and also because delivering banking services remotely is more cost-effective. Even though the 'bank manager as delivery mechanism' days are over for all but the most wealthy customers, a bank is still obliged to offer a similarly personal level of service.
>
> My conception of the role of the call centre is to act as the location where telephone operators are based who represent the bank in every respect: that is, the contact the customer has with them will in many cases amount to the bank's projection of itself to its customer base. People operating the service must therefore have real personality because their voice is representing the bank. Furthermore, it follows from this that the potential a particular bank has to differentiate itself from its rivals is substantially limited to how the operator differentiates himself or herself from other banks' operators.
>
> With the role of the operator being so crucial, it's difficult to see how any bank which only offers a facility for a customer to talk to an automated service can really obtain a great deal of edge in this respect. Of course, most banks which use automated facilities do offer customers the opportunity to talk to a real person as an alternative, but generally I think the use of a human operator most or all of the time is much more satisfactory.
>
> At the Customer Contact Centre we have undertaken a wide range of projects for banks around the world which want to create call centre facilities. What all these projects have in common is that we facilitate the opening of a dialogue between the bank and its customers. In many cases, we are helping banks *re-open* a dialogue with customers, because the customers will in many cases have got used to no longer having a bank manager with whom they can regularly discuss their financial affairs and will have been in a kind of limbo, without any easy access to staff.
>
> In a nutshell, banks want to talk to their customers and enable their customers to talk to them. This is what we facilitate.

Case Study: Bristol & West plc

This case study shows the results of a successful collaboration between Bristol & West plc (until July 1997 – when it became a bank – one of the

UK's leading building societies) and AIT plc, an ambitious and successful bespoke system house based in Henley-on-Thames.

How does an aggressive bank which is hungry for market share deploy an efficient and sophisticated computer system to support the implementation of a direct delivery service?

Often, where there is no existing system, the process is easier because the bank can work with a blank slate. In the case of the Bristol & West, the bank decided it wanted to develop a system that would allow it to sell a variety of personal financial services to customers outside its traditional catchment area in the south and west of England. To do this it decided it would develop a new kind of account – initially branded 'Asset' and rebranded 'Direct Savings' – which made extensive use of the telephone, offering a high level of customer service 24 hours a day, all year around. The account was a savings account open to customers with at least £5,000 to invest. Although the product has now closed to new account holders, existing account holders are still looked after very effectively and the product is regarded as a great success.

For Bristol & West, the solution to actually making the new account work as a telephone banking product was to run it on a telephone banking system called Teledirect, and developed and supplied by an Oxfordshire-based systems developer called AIT. Teledirect enabled the new account to be run by operators with access to software in which all details of a customer's accounts are visible to the operator as soon as a call comes in, with documents being scanned in and appearing on the screen, instead of having to be laboriously retrieved from filing cabinets.

Bristol & West already had core systems running on mainframe computers, but according to group services director Kevin Flanagan, the new system, and the account which it was designed to operate, needed to be orientated differently. 'It's customer driven, not core-driven,' he explained. 'On the core system, the screens cover one account at a time. Asset starts with the customer first, and we would expect that thinking to filter through to other areas of our business, too.'

This means that the operator using the Direct Saving 486-based workstation – one of about 30, each with a large 20-inch colour screen and 16 megabytes of memory – can see all the accounts a customer has with the Bristol & West, and offer guidance and advice to maximize their investments. Direct Savings also incorporates workflow management, but instead of merely tracking a job through the organization, it operates as a pooled system where costs can be allocated to any available operator of the appropriate level.

'A lot of our work can be done by several people; we're working 24 hours a day, 365 days a year, so you can't have a single personal account manager,' explains Ian Kennedy, group operations director. 'The personal touch is delivered by the system, not by the individual operator. We can note the customer's style on his or her file, as well as a satisfaction rating,' says Flanagan.

'There is room for notes designed to help the operator. For example, these notes would focus on the correct way to pronounce a customer's name, details of the customer's interest, information about whether they like to chat, and so on.' 'But', Flanagan stresses, 'the human side remains important: there is no use of voice response technology; all calls are answered by a person.'

Flanagan comments that when developing a system, merely starting with a blank sheet of paper is not enough. 'You have to be very clear and work through what you're going to achieve, for example the service levels expected by the customer,' he says. 'We have a choice – either the low risk option of tailoring existing systems, or a higher risk bespoke option, choosing the latter because it was more innovative and adaptable. It took a year to develop and we launched the system in January 1994; since then it has been a process of continuous refinement.'

As a result of the success of Direct Saving (which had 30,000 customers when it closed to new account holders), Flanagan has become convinced of the value of a software development method called prototyping. Traditionally, a specification is created for a program, teams of programmers set to work, and months or years later the users are presented with a working system and the question 'is this what you wanted?'. Using prototyping, uses are brought in right from the beginning to help decide how the system should look and work, with prototypes being created and discussed as the process goes on.

'We did a lot of prototyping of screen flows and so on, using a team selected for the conceptualizing skills, and carried out exercises involving people at different levels in the bank,' he says. 'We had a mixture of people familiar with other areas of Bristol & West and newcomers to the bank, since it was difficult for the former to step back and accept the Greenfield approach.'

The difficulty is in accepting that just because something has always been done a particular way, it does not need to be done that way in the future.

Hardware for the system was recommended by AIT and along with the workstations it incorporates a fault-tolerant Novell Netware local area network with six servers and a total of 10 gigabytes of on-line hard disk storage. A further 11 gigabytes is available on an optical disk jukebox; this is used for storing scanned documents on non-erasable 'write once, read-many' disks.

'The incoming post is scanned and all transactions passed through Asset,' Kennedy continues. 'The scanning process is quite sensitive – you need to get the density and contrast right, which takes trial and error. We have been going a year now and have 300,000 documents imaged.' Original paper copies are archived after scanning, initially for a year but the aim is to reduce this to six months.

The fault-tolerant hard disk subsystem stores all the correspondence that has been accessed in the last two weeks, although this may include older letters if an operator has specifically requested them. After this, a letter is moved onto the optical disk jukebox, and as the jukebox fills, the oldest disk is periodically archived and replaced with a blank one.

Tasks are assigned priorities, with older pending tasks being re-prioritized to ensure that they are done; on average, the system has 2000 jobs on general workflow. A free operator can either request the highest priority task from the pool, or specify a task. A scanned form or letter then appears on the screen and the operator can look up the account details, compare the signature with the sample stored on the system, input the details from the form, and approve whichever actions are required, such as sending out a letter or cheque. 'For the first couple of months, people didn't trust the workload system and chose to specify jobs,' said Kennedy. 'Now they do trust it.'

The telephone system is also linked in to the workstations. 'We have full computer-integrated telephoning,' boasts Kennedy. 'It routes calls to operators by type – we use an 0800 number for recruiting new customers and an 0345 number for existing customers.

One function that is not yet used is caller line identification (CLI), the system that allows a caller's telephone number to be identified before the call is answered. As Kennedy points out, not all telephone companies transfer the information across, so BT users will not receive the number of a Mercury user, say. In addition, he says experience in the US has shown a negative response to CLI – some see it as intrusive – and it may be a bit too technical for Direct Saving's older customer base.

All the signs are that customers are most impressed by the speed with which Asset can retrieve their details and respond to queries, and that operators are happy, too. The system has been through a testing first year – it was particularly stretched when all of a certain bond issue matured on the same day, the daily incoming call rate briefly jumping from the usual several hundred to over 2000 – and there is a file of requests from account managers for things that would improve service.

Kevin Flanagan says that Bristol & West will use both prototyping and workflow management again, and is looking to implement something similar to Direct Savings when it next replaces its less flexible account-driven branch computing systems. Anything to help give it that lever so vital in the increasingly competitive financial sector.

Figures 8.1, 8.2, 8.3 and 8.4 show illustrations from typical screens used in the Bristol & West's new system. Note how the user interface is designed to maximize the effectiveness of the customer service process.

For example, in Figure 8.2, the use of a 'PR Note' enables the operator to inject a level of personal service into the process. Interestingly, the use of such little notes in the customer service interaction dates back a long way. In the eighteenth century, tellers at the Bank of England would make little notes in

FIGURE 8.1 *Sample screen from Bristol & West's new system – I*

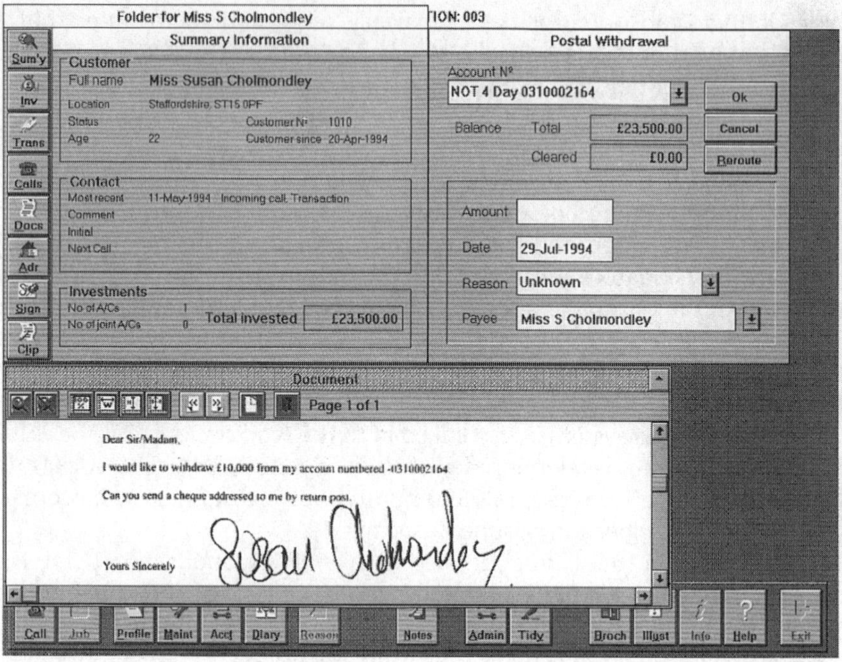

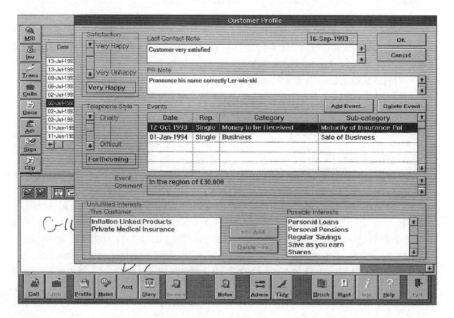

FIGURE 8.2 *Sample screen from Bristol & West's new system – II*

FIGURE 8.3 *Sample screen from Bristol & West's new system – III*

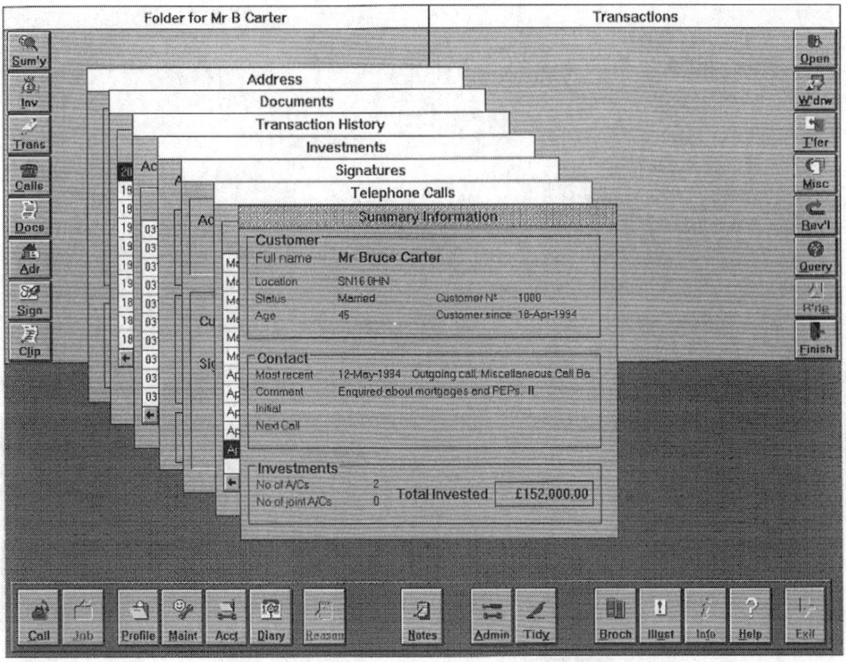

the margins of their account books to remind themselves which figures related to which customers. These notes were often considerably less flattering than in Figure 8.2. For example, one customer in the bank of England's ledger records was described as a 'little pug-faced woman with a squeaky voice'.

The age of technology, for all its inhuman horrors, at least seems to be in certain respects more polite than the past.

Case Study: Types of technological assistance in the call centre

Introduction

As we have seen on many occasions in this book, the effectiveness of the customer service banks deliver remotely is in many respects *the* key issue of the late 1990s for the banking industry, and is bound to be a central issue well into the new century.

FIGURE 8.4 *Sample screen from Bristol & West's new system – IV*

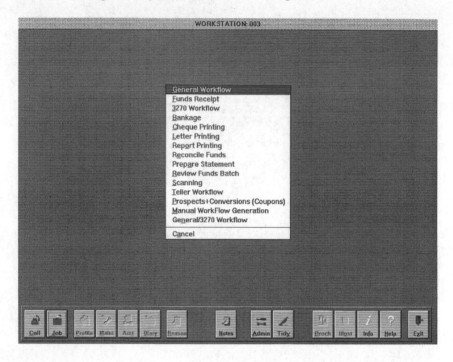

As an increasingly important element in the remote delivery mix, the future of telephone banking is particularly exciting. By enabling customers to transact their banking business from their homes rather than in the bank's physical branches – telephone banking will surely help to win higher proportions of customers over to remote delivery.

While telephone banking hasn't yet achieved anything like the level of penetration among customers that ATMs and EFTPoS have achieved, it has already demonstrated its potential to enable customers to carry out a range of banking functions by telephone. And let's bear in mind that the Mondex scheme – featured as a case study in the next chapter – has shown how remote loading of a stored value card (SVC) in a specially adapted telephone terminal is not only possible but also popular: not surprisingly, as such remote loading is really a form of cash withdrawal by phone.

These developments are all extremely important for the banking industry; yet in their race to lead the way in the provision of remote banking facilities in general and telephone banking in particular, banks need to ensure that they don't neglect the importance of paying attention to another important use of the telephone: providing an efficient, telephone-based facility for handling customer queries and customer complaints.

For the purposes of this case study, customer contact which fits into these categories can conveniently be summarized as that which *can't* be handled by automated telephone banking services.

Typical examples of such services would include: queries about financial service products such as credit cards, insurance, loans, mortgages; queries about the features of different accounts; requests for transactions which go beyond the parameters of standard telephone banking facilities; complaints; and dealing with all the other types of customer queries which being a retail bank involves. These aren't the type of queries which can be handled by an automated system: you need to have a real person there.

There are, generally, two schools of thought on how telephone customer enquiries and complaints should be dealt with by banks.

On the one hand, there are those who favour a branch-based approach. This certainly makes sense in terms of cementing the customer's relationship with the branch, but it's difficult to standardize levels of professionalism in dealing with customer enquiries across all the bank's branches.

The other approach is to handle customer queries and complaints on a national basis rather than on a branch basis. This tends to make standardization of the overall levels of professionalism and customer service much easier, and also tends to bring inevitable economies of scale and advantages of specialization.

My object here isn't to argue in favour of one of the two alternatives or the other, but rather to point out that, whichever option a bank chooses, the bank should make sure its staff dealing with the query or complaint have access to the right kind of technology to handle it.

What technology is available? In essence, we can identify two types: which might conveniently be described as *standard* customer service technology and *advanced* customer service technology.

By these terms 'standard' and 'advanced' I don't mean to imply that the standard technology is what everyone already has. This is far from being the case, and many bankers would enjoy significant improvements in the quality of their customer service if they were to ensure that this standard level of customer service technology was in place within their organization.

To do this, they should implement a customer service package running on a stand-alone PC or server networked to workstations, which can be used by the member of customer service staff while the telephone-based dialogue with the customer is taking place. The staff member will therefore be interacting visually with the computer screen during the dialogue.

The standard features provided by this screen-based customer service package typically include:

- A resource to enable all telephone-based customer contacts the staff member has during the day to be logged directly onto the screen.

- Screen-based scripts providing prompts for the staff member when dealing with the customer. Different scripts should be capable of being summoned up according to the different types of enquiry.

- A facility to speed the process of taking the customer's address. This requires the package to incorporate a comprehensive database of addresses corresponding to postcodes. This means that the member of staff only needs to ask the customer for his or her postcode and house number rather than the whole address.

- The opportunity to build up a comprehensive database of the organization's customers.

- The potential to scan into the system any documents relating to a particular customer's requirements. This is a particularly important resource for bankers whose customers' complaints and queries usually need to be investigated. This scanning facility naturally saves the banker storage space and makes retrieval of images much easier.

- The provision of a screen-based daily diary which enables the staff member to diary in actions for the future and which will also provide a reminder of what needs to be done. This is an especially important resource for cementing the customer relationship, as customers will understandably be seriously annoyed by failure on the part of someone in the customer service department to do what was promised.

- A tool for prioritizing specific tasks which the department needs to undertake in terms of their urgency. These tasks would normally be highlighted on the screen-based daily diary.

- The provision of a variety of tools which will enable the banker's management to analyse data generated within the customer service department. The different bases for the analysis would vary depending on management requirements. For example, an analysis could be made of product groups to which enquiries or complaints related, and of specific brand categories within these groups. Ideally, the customer service package should provide considerable flexibility here.

In summary, what a financial bank ideally needs is a customer service system which efficiently, rapidly and professionally manages widely disparate complaint and contact types in the front and back office, and facilitates learning from them.

These standard features which a bank can reasonably expect to obtain from its customer service system are not, however, the full story, for there is a new type of customer service system resource which integrates the computer and telephone even more efficiently than when the staff member has access to the standard features above. This additional resource is – reasonably enough – known as 'Computer Telephone Integration' (CTI). Its aim is to enable the organization operating the customer service facility to make its customer service even more efficient and customer-friendly.

Customer service systems featuring CTI can reasonably be described as representing 'advanced' technology by today's standards. The advanced functions facilitated by CTI would typically include the following:

■ A facility to enable the location of customer records automatically from the incoming phone call (which it will match to the customer's telephone number), thereby enabling the staff member to have the customer's details on the screen immediately when he starts to take the call.

■ A facility to transfer calls and the associated customer information to the customer service system from other departments.

■ Where customers are likely to be phoning in with relation to different promotions or products, and where different response numbers relate to different promotions or product lines, it is now possible for CTI systems to detect from the number the customer is phoning what the subject of a customer's particular enquiry is likely to be. The system can then automatically provide the staff member with a screen-based script relating to that particular enquiry. Again, this saves time and creates customer goodwill.

Finally, what about likely future developments in customer service technology for bankers?

There seems little doubt that e-mail and the Internet potentially represent the dominant new technologies in implementing customer service strategies. Even as we write, both these technologies are well on the way to achieving serious levels of penetration in private homes as well as in offices, although this process clearly has some considerable way to go yet. Still, we can be fairly certain that the relatively short time between now and the end of the century will see private access to e-mail and the Internet become about as unremarkable as having one's own private mobile telephone.

The question of the extent to which the Internet will play a major role in the future as a delivery mechanism for retail financial services is far from being easy to answer. Despite the great media interest in the Internet and related technologies such as e-mail, the fact remains that interest in the Internet is disproportionately greater among high net worth individuals compared with people who are not in this category.

Certainly, the hardware required to obtain access at home to the Internet is not cheap – it is unlikely to cost less than £1,000, and may cost considerably more, plus a regular monthly fee. At present prices, it is difficult to see how the Internet could attain anything like the level of penetration among all sectors of bank which all electronic delivery systems *must* attain if they are to be a major mechanism for delivering retail financial services.

On the other hand, it is surely inevitable that the cost of hardware for gaining access to the Internet will come down in due course as the Internet becomes more popular: the one development reinforcing the other. The problem of the security and confidentiality of Internet transactions and balance enquiries must also be solved if the Internet is to be a successful delivery mechanism, but there is every reason to believe that this problem will be solved before long. Generally, the prognosis for the Internet as a new delivery channel for electronic financial transactions must be a good one. Similarly, nascent technologies such as interactive television are also likely to have a future as mass-market delivery mechanisms for financial services. Ultimately, customers will always want convenient means of obtaining access to financial services, and if these services can be provided to the customer at the most convenient location of all – the customer's home – and if the technologies work reliably and are cheap and easy to use, there is every likelihood that they will gain wide acceptance among customers: indeed, become seen by customers as essential.

Whatever the nature of the new channel, they can give banks important new opportunities for handling customer contact and for delivering customer service. In the meantime, banks ought to give serious consideration to making sure that their telephone banking facilities incorporate all the 'standard' features outlined above, and that – ideally – progression to 'advanced' features incorporating CTI happens before long.

Current issues in the planning and implementation of call centres

First thoughts

For many banks seeking to maximize the competitive impact of their use of virtual financial services, the use of a call centre will – as I have suggested – be central to their plans. Here, we look at the strategic aims behind setting up and operating a call centre, and examines the principal practical issues involved in giving the bank the best chance of putting its plans into action.

The first point to make is that banks should not primarily see themselves as having the aim of setting up a call centre, but rather they should have the aim of finding a method for achieving what they want to achieve in delivering virtual financial services to their customers.

The objectives which banks will have in this respect have been analysed in detail earlier in this book. They can, however, usefully be summarized here as:

■ giving customers access to their funds (principally for cash withdrawal);

■ giving customers access to information about the state of their accounts;

■ giving customers access to payment facilities;

■ giving customers information about products and services the bank may want to supply to them.

The difference between the fourth objective and the first three is that supply of such information will usually be initiated by the bank, whereas the others will be demanded more pro-actively by the customer.

What exactly is the fundamental nature of the functions carried out by a call centre? In essence, it is to provide the customer with an interactive service which enables the bank to get into meaningful conversations with customers on all matters relating to their account. These matters need not be confined to the handling and enactment of routine transactions; indeed, one of the main reasons for establishing the interactive connection with the customer is so that the bank has an opportunity to tell the customer about other services it is offering.

For example, First Direct's staff will ask new customers when their various insurance policies come up for renewal. The purpose of asking this question is not so much to try to make an immediate sale, but rather to ensure that First Direct has the opportunity to quote for customers' insurance business when the renewal comes up. Customers are, of course, not obliged to reveal the date of the renewals, but in practice they are likely to want to, for First Direct's approach to this matter is not based around a 'hard sell', and if customers have sufficient faith in the quality of First Direct's service to want to open up accounts there, it is likely they would also have faith in the (in fact highly competitive) prices of First Direct's insurance policies and in the accompanying service level they could expect. This kind of pro-active identification of a customer's more complex needs alongside the provision of a routine service lies at the heart of the interactive relationship with the customer that represents the best that virtual financial services can offer both the customer and the bank.

The establishment of a call centre is an important – indeed often essential – element in the virtual financial services resources of bank, but it is rarely, if ever, a complete solution to the need to deliver these services. There are areas of customer need which call centres cannot address, in particular:

■ the need for cash withdrawal;

■ the customer's need to pay in credit items;

■ the customer's need for face-to-face contact to discuss complex and personal financial transactions. Whether or not this contact will be necessary will vary to some extent from customer to customer – for example, some customers will be happy to discuss a mortgage application over the phone, while others will feel that this is too momentous and personal a matter for telephone discussion and will prefer to talk about it face-to-face – but probably all customers have some area of their financial life they would not want to discuss over the telephone.

None the less, even though it is not a complete solution to the provision of virtual financial services, the call centre remains an extremely important element. Most banks with an ambitious approach towards implementing virtual financial services will wish to set up a call centre, and often this need will arise sooner rather than later.

Formulating the specifications of the call centre

The first step in deciding what nature the call centre will have is to ask the fundamental question, what are we trying to achieve from our virtual financial services?

If, as is often likely, one of the answers to this question is, we want to use interactive conversations with remotely located customers to deliver services to them and to ascertain their needs more precisely so that we can sell them the products and services they want, it is likely that a call centre will be an asset to the bank.

Furthermore, as has been seen on several occasions in this report, new types of virtual resources such as remote banking networks or, as here, the call centre may be capable of delivering services which supersede a large part of the functionality of a bank's legacy of bricks-and-mortar branches. It therefore follows that there is little point in a bank looking at the possibilities for setting up a call centre if it is not at the same time ready to re-evaluate the usefulness of its branch network, and to consider where functions currently carried out by branches can be wholly or partially replaced by the call centre.

Once the bank has decided what it is aiming to achieve from its use of virtual financial services and how the use of a call centre fits in with this fundamental commercial objective (if it does), the bank can go on to specify the precise tasks the call centre will need to carry out. These will typically include the following:

- using authorization techniques to do the utmost to ensure that the customer who is making or receiving the call is the bona fide account holder;

- receiving telephone calls from customers and acting on instructions received;

- making telephone calls to customers in order to action whatever banking function is involved (it is worth noting, however, that most call centres tend to be geared to receiving far more calls than they make);

- having access to customers' account details so that information can be given on the telephone to bona fide customers (note: this information will almost always be provided for the call centre member of staff on a computer screen);

■ having access to funds transfer facilities so that customers' instructions regarding the making of payments to third parties can be acted on.

These tasks – and any other the bank specifies – must be kept firmly in mind as objectives at all times during the setting-up of the call centre.

The location of the call centre

The decision about the location of the call centre is, as might be expected, extremely important. One of the important advantages to a bank of being able to deliver service to its customers via a call centre rather than via bricks-and-mortar branches is that call centres give the bank the option of 'killing geography' and removing all the problems contingent upon the need to locate in a specified area.

Certainly, there is no sense whatsoever in siting the call centre in some location where the cost of freehold or leasehold premises is likely to be high, and where the cost of labour is also likely to considerable. It may be possible for the bank to gain considerable tax allowances and even grants from siting the centre in an area of the country where the government is doing its utmost to encourage the location of precisely the kind of labour-intensive organizations that the call centre would represent.

This does not, however, mean that every call centre operated by a financial bank ought to be located in some remote part of Britain.

The availability of an articulate, educated, pool of labour will also be a factor, as will the reliability of local telephone exchanges (which for maximizing the efficiency of the call centre will need to be digital rather than manual). Many banks also prefer to site their call centres near principal points of geographical communication, such as (for example) within reasonable access of a major motorway, or reasonably near to the bank's head office.

After all, the call centre is not going to operate in a vacuum, but will be visited by senior managers of the bank, consultants providing advice, interviewees seeking employment, training advisers and so on. The call centre should, therefore, be located somewhere where it can be an integral part of the bank's entire operation.

That said, siting a call centre in prime office space would be foolish unless there were extremely strong reasons for doing so.

Another key initial consideration is the space required for the call centre. First Direct, for example, as we have seen, employs about 800 staff for interacting with customers via the telephone. It is not likely this or similar numbers of staff will work happily in cramped, stuffy offices where they all feel that they are working too close to one another and cannot concentrate on their own conversations and related work.

The structure of the call centre

All call centres have the same fundamental structure. This consists of the people who staff it (primarily meaning those who talk to the customers), the processes the call centre carries out (i.e. the tasks it performs for customers) and the technological systems it uses to carry out those processes and thereby meet customer needs.

In effect, these three elements of the structure constitute the embodiment of the bank's customer service strategy. They all add up to the 'culture' of the organization. It is this personality with which the customer comes into contact when he makes his telephone call.

Figure 8.5 shows this relationship in diagrammatic form.

The three elements of the call centre are now discussed in turn.

People

As we have seen, banks nowadays tend to agree that even where they use automated voice response systems to deal with routine telephone banking transactions, human operators are needed to handle more complex transactions, or anything related to sales. Furthermore, some banks use human operators for all transactions.

FIGURE 8.5 *Customer perception of the elements of the call centre*

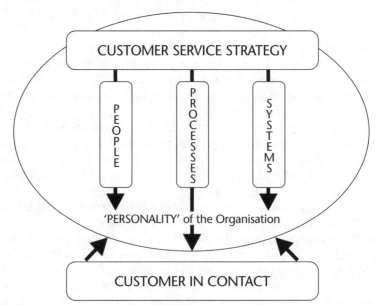

(Source: Syntega)

Whatever option the bank chooses, the importance of people at the call centre is unarguable.

Where real people are being used to deal with telephone transactions, it is essential that the people are:

■ courteous and helpful to customers at all times – not only when the operators are relaxed at the start of a shift or in a good mood;

■ professional and efficient – the service being provided relates to the customer's personal finances. Staff should not be monotonic in their tone or manner, but neither will the customer expect to encounter frivolity or flippant levity;

■ accurate and reliable in terms of the information they provide;

■ able to develop a friendly and harmonious interactive conversation with the customer, and thereby have the opportunity to spot possible selling opportunities for the bank.

Staff of a high calibre are therefore required. Generally, the kind of people who are best at this job tend to be young – up to, say, about 30 years old – intelligent and confident. A careful and thoughtful approach to recruiting staff is required. Sometimes temporary staff – such as students and 'resting' actors – can be very good at this work, although they do of course carry with them the drawback that time spent training them may be less well-spent, if they are not going to work for the bank for long.

Intensive staff training will be required. This is frequently best provided by external organizations which specialize in training call centre staff.

No matter how well trained and highly motivated the staff members may be, they will on occasion suffer troughs in their morale. Since the success of the call centre operation depends substantially on the quality of service being maintained at all times (and in particular not just during the early honeymoon months), it is important that refresher training is provided to staff on a regular basis.

Incentive schemes can also be introduced, with the proviso that these should somehow be made to focus on the quality of the service provided (i.e. by assessing staff on the number of new accounts they had set up within a certain period or on products sold) rather than on banal numerical targets such as number of calls answered. Indeed, it is a mistake to give staff high numerical targets for taking calls, since, again, what is required is the quality of the staff–customer interaction rather than the number of such interactions.

A pleasant and congenial working environment is also extremely important for keeping staff motivated. Air-conditioning, bans on smoking, plants in the vicinity, subdued lighting, sufficient space available for each staff member, and generally an agreeable internal decor for the call centre are all important facets in helping staff to be happy to do what they do. This happiness should translate into a pleasant telephone manner and into the maximum proportion of satisfied customers.

Finally, what about scripts? Do they have a role to play in the staff–customer interaction?

Generally, the advice here is that the use of scripts should be avoided. They can be important in staff training, but in real-life staff–customer interactions they are too restrictive. Not only is there a serious danger that they will prevent the conversation from running into areas that can allow the staff member to spot an important opportunity to sell a product or service, but the use of a script is usually readily detected by customers on the other end of the line, and they will usually feel demeaned or even insulted that they are being spoken to in this way. Neither feeling is likely to make for a happy customer, receptive to what the staff member has to say or has on offer.

Of course, just because it is inadvisable to use scripts, it does not mean that staff members should not be given lists of objectives to try to attain during the call. They should be, and it is part of the skill of a call centre staff member to try to fulfil these objectives during the conversation without making it obvious to the customer that this is happening.

Processes

These are the hub of what happens at the call centre. They are the deliverables with which the customer is supplied.

Having courteous and professional staff who deal with customers is only one part of the operation of a call centre. The actual tasks carried out by the bank as a result of the interactive staff–customer conversations must be carried out with complete efficiency and attention to detail. In particular, the bank must always carry out whatever task the member of staff has told the customer will be carried out.

The great danger of processes being carried out inefficiently is that good customer service on the phone will seem superficial, even sugary, if the actions arising from the conversation are not followed up.

Incidentally, no process should be initiated at all unless the bank can be sure the person telephoning the member of staff is the bona fide holder of the account.

This important security requirement is usually discharged by the customer being given a code-word or code number. Ideally, the member of staff should not ask for the entire code-word or number but rather for one or more particular numbers in the code or letter. This way, no one overhearing the conversation would know what the number or word was.

Another key point to make about processes is that the bank should record every incoming or external call. This is to protect itself if customers claim they did not give a particularly sensitive instruction after all, and the bank says that they did.

Systems

These are the technological systems used at the call centre. They consist of:

■ the means by which the customer contacts the call centre by telephone;

■ the in-house systems used.

These are now examined in turn.

The means by which the customer contacts the call centre by telephone
There are three options here. They all relate to the type of telephone number given to the customer to contact the organization.
   The options are:

■ the caller can be given an ordinary telephone number – this would involve the caller paying the usual telephone rate for the call;

■ the caller can be given a special 'local rate' telephone number;

■ the caller can be given a free telephone number.

Occasionally a telephone banking service will make use of a 'premium' line (i.e. one that is more expensive than usual) for certain services (sometimes for a service with 'prestige' attached to it) but the inevitable customer resistance encountered here means that such a premium facility should never be used for more than a short period.

   Of course, the bank should at the outset make a choice of which type of telephone number to give customers and stick to it; customers will hardly be enchanted with a bank which starts out by using, say, a free number and then changes this to an ordinary-rate number or premium-rate number.

   Which option the bank chooses obviously depends on the bank's attitude towards its virtual financial services initiative and its customers. Some banks believe customers ought to pay for the privilege of having a telephone-based service; others believe the bank itself is privileged to have them as customers. My view is that regarding a telephone-based service as something customers should be privileged to use is short-sighted and stems from the fundamentally erroneous notion that the phone-based service is an adjunct to the branch-based service rather than a substitute or replacement for it. This is an incorrect notion, for it reveals a failure to assimilate the idea that virtual financial services aren't just an attractive add-on to a bank's existing services but are changing the entire nature of the service.

In-house systems

These will need to cover the following functions.

Providing assistance to telephone staff
This will include such items as:

■ headsets;

■ means for recording and receiving calls;

■ screen-based systems for use when finding out details of customers' accounts;

■ screen-based systems for use when handling funds transfer transactions for customers.

Providing management information
This will include all systems which allow the call centre's management to monitor the activities of call centre staff.

Providing account-handling information
This will include all systems that allowing customer accounts to be handled, with the status of accounts being modified to accommodate transactions.

Providing interface facilities
The customer information held at a call centre will often need to be interfaced with other networks run by the bank, such as the ATM network and the debit card network.

If the central computer for the call centre is not the same as that for the entire bank, there will, of course, need to be a real-time link established between the two computers.

Conclusion

The successful call centre will feature all of the following characteristics:

■ it will employ courteous, professional and capable staff;

■ it will focus on the needs of the customer;

■ it will operate consistently and reliably;

■ it will be supported by technology but will make this technology strictly subservient to the guiding directive of meeting customer needs. The implementation of technology in a call centre must be a means to an end, and not an end in itself.

Strategic guidelines: making the most of telephone banking

The key strategic guidelines relating to telephone banking should be clear from the material in this chapter, which is a little more didactic than some of the other chapters.

In addition, I think this chapter already demonstrates my belief, which can usefully be stated explicitly here, that telephone banking is an important element of the virtual banking revolution and that any bank which wishes to succeed in the revolution should exploit telephone banking to the full as a way of providing customers with a comprehensive banking service that they can access from that most convenient, and generally private, of communications tools – the telephone. Furthermore, banks should build within themselves and their attitude to telephone banking the confidence that in time to come, numbers of customers who are not only willing to use this service but are positively enthusiastic about it, are certain to increase.

The card that thinks for itself

Introduction

Smart cards fascinate me, and I hope that by the end of this chapter they'll fascinate you, too, if they don't already. The idea of a bank card incorporating a microchip which gives the card the facility to handle numerous applications and store a tremendous amount of data, is bound to be an exciting one in anybody's language. It take us into a dimension of truly exciting applications which may wind up playing a key role not only in terms of how we use plastic cards, but also in terms of how we relate to technology generally.

The possibilities for using smart cards are so exciting that it is – unfortunately, perhaps – important not to get carried away and forget that of all the virtual banking technologies explored in this book, smart cards operate under the heaviest burden of having to prove the customer appeal of the application. That is, the very fact of the underlying technology being so interesting means that there is a serious danger of letting ourselves get carried away by the technology and forgetting that it must prove itself in the real-life banking marketplace.

In both this chapter and the next one, I am careful to avoid an undue amount of speculation but rather to focus on what has happened with smart cards to date and tentatively suggest how things might develop in future. There is no doubt that a strong speculative case could be made that in 20 or 30 years' time, we may all carry smart cards, which quite apart from being an essential and powerful tool of the bank/customer relationship, could be loaded with a whole range of information relating to all aspects of our professional and leisure lives. However, I see that kind of speculation as belonging more to the realms of science fiction – if plausible science fiction – than to the kind of sober applications which I have scrutinized in this book.

One particularly important point to make about smart cards right away is that they differ from all the other elements of the virtual banking revolution examined so far because they are not a complete delivery channel themselves but rather an element of a potential delivery channel. The justification for setting aside an entire chapter for them is that they are an extremely important element of potential delivery channels because they can be used in conjunction with the three principal channels I discuss. That is, they can be used as ATM cards, debit cards and also in conjunction with a telephone banking service.

This last potential application is one of the most exciting of all. I have already mentioned the fact that certain types of telephone banking system enable a smart card to be 'loaded' with electronic cash by means of a specially designed terminal. The type of smart cards which can be loaded in this way are known as stored value cards do (SVC). This particular application is widely recognized as being of the utmost importance for the future of virtual banking. Most of the smart card pilot projects currently going on in the world feature the use of the SVC.

Smart cards are widely regarded within the retail banking arena as one of the most exciting and important current trends – indeed, many bankers would have no hesitation in describing them as the most important trend of all. In this chapter I only have space to look at some of the major issues relating to smart cards and to present an overview of smart card usage and a case study. I do, however, also include a fascinating interview with one of the leading authorities on smart cards today.

Readers wishing to find out more about current trends in smart cards would do best to attend one of the many conferences on them which are frequently being held around the world. Another good source of information about current developments in smart cards is the excellent magazine *European Card Review*, published in the United Kingdom but with a global as well as European remit. I provide contact details for this journal at the end of this chapter.

Defining a smart card

The term 'smart card' is used to describe any bank card which, rather than having a magnetic stripe as the medium on which information is stored and by means of which a terminal can interface with the card, a tiny microprocessor (i.e. semiconductor) is used instead. Some cards are 'hybrid' cards in that they feature both a magnetic stripe and a microprocessor: these cards are also known as smart cards.

The strength of the microprocessor in terms of memory and processing power varies greatly. Some smart cards – especially those used as tokens for assessing such facilities as pay-phone services and not capable of being reloaded – have little more storage and processing capacity than the more advanced types of magnetic stripes. Other cards are extremely powerful, with ample capacity to handle not only the customer's banking facilities but also a range of other services the customer may want.

Such is the speed of development of smart card technology that any parameter I give now indicating the strength of a typical smart card processor is certain to be outdated within a few months of writing, let alone of publication. All I will therefore say is that given the need to keep the cost of the smart card within realistic boundaries, there is a continual impetus for the processors they contain to be increasingly powerful.

Incidentally, it is pertinent to point out that many banks and card organizations prefer to use the term 'chip card' to describe what I refer to as a smart card. While having no particular axe to grind here, I prefer the term smart card myself, for two reasons. First, it seems to me an inherently more interesting way of describing what is certainly a fascinating facility. Second, focusing on the nature of the technology in naming these cards seems to me a basic error and typical of the way elements of the virtual banking revolution are viewed by their creators in the early stages of their development. It's always better to focus on the benefits the facility provides to customers, and I think the word 'smart' does more justice in this respect.

The origins of smart cards

Plastic cards containing electronic chips have been around since the early 1970s, although the first prototypes were inevitably extremely limited in their functionality. There was always considerable enthusiasm in creating such cards, which were in a sense a solution looking for a problem until the 1980s, when a severe escalation in magnetic stripe credit card fraud induced the leading credit card organizations to look very hard at how smart cards might solve this problem. Twenty years of slow evolution via simple pre-paid telephone cards led, in the late 1980s, to many banks around the world selecting smart card technology because of the significantly better security potential it appeared to offer.

Smart cards and security

The potential of smart cards from a security perspective stems from the fact that whereas a magnetic stripe card can easily be copied, it is much more difficult to copy a smart card. Even if this could be done, it is almost impossible to copy the *information* contained on the card. Even if this could be done, the use of encryption techniques will almost always prevent a would-be fraudster from reading the information contained in the chip.

Since the late 1980s, techniques available to fraudsters have inevitably become more sophisticated, but the difficulty of copying and reading the smart card microprocessor remains.

Another security advantage is that because the chip can contain far more information than could ever be placed on a magnetic stripe, more sophisticated authentication methodologies can be used to reduce the problem of unauthorized people making use of the card. In particular, the great processing power of the chip makes 'biometrics' personal identification methods (I discussed these in the chapter on ATMs) readily available.

Another important point to make about the security of smart card transactions is that the power of the processor and its memory capacity are ideal for authorizing transactions on off-line smart card networks, because the customer's personal identification number can be stored within the chip and, as long as it is encrypted, be impervious to being copied by fraudsters or being read.

This particular advantage of smart costs has, as I illustrate below, been especially popular in countries – such as those in the central European region – where the quality of national telecommunications networks does not yet compare with those in the West (although it is getting better all the time) and where as a consequence bank card networks often have to run off-line for part of the day. In many respects the smart card eliminates the serious security problems which off-line magnetic stripe cards invariably incur. I looked at those problems in Chapter 6.

Smart card technology

As things stand at present, the capacity of magnetic stripes is only about one-tenth that of the more powerful smart cards available today. This differential is changing all the time as the chips used on smart cards become increasingly powerful. From a technological perspective, large improvements in the price/performance equation relating to smart cards have been achieved by squeezing the memory and processor circuits onto ever smaller pieces of silicon. This process is not yet exhausted.

Smart card applications in banking

The basic application of a smart card in the banking industry is to use the card as a complete replacement for all types of magnetic stripe cards. That is, cards which are currently being used for any of the following purposes can be readily replaced by smart cards:

- ATM cards;

- debit cards;

- charge cards;

- credit cards.

Furthermore, because the chip on a smart card is so much more powerful than a magnetic stripe, it is perfectly feasible for just one smart card to carry out all the above functions, or any combination of these. An additional point here – not often mentioned by banks and card organizations – is that it is perfectly possible for a single smart card to 'contain' the functionality of several different types of cards issued by different banks and running on different types of network. The implications of this particular potential feature are clearly revolutionary for the plastic card business and have yet to be explored.

The addition of the SVC potential to the above list means that a smart card could be a truly powerful financial token, given its user access to ATMs at a national and international level, access to debit facilities at a national and international level, access to charge and credit facilities and also to electronic purse business.

But this impressive range of functionality is only the beginning, not the end. Even if a smart card offers all these features, it may still have spare memory which can be used for other purposes. These other purposes are many and varied. The most obvious ones would include any functions where it is in the user's interest to have access to some readily portable token in order to obtain certain privileges. For example, the smart card could also contain 'loyalty' features (that is, token-based rewards for regularly using a particular supplier or retailer). The card could also contain details of airline tickets and hotel reservations: not only as a source of information to the card-holder – with this information being read by a portable card-reader such as one that would fit on a key-chain – but also with the card constituting the actual 'voucher' access to the travel facility or hotel room.

Nor is *this* the end. There is no reason why a smart card with all these functions could not also be used to gain access, on a prepaid or pay later basis, to a range of functions such as telephone services, petrol from a garage, and many functions relating to access to remote remotely delivered information such as Internet services. The card could also been used to store detailed information about the card-holder, with the card-holder being able to modify this information at will using some form of card-writing device in conjunction with a card reader. Earlier in this book I mentioned the 'super-smart card', which features some way of writing onto the card such as by using tiny number keys that give the card the appearance of a credit-card-sized electronic calculator. Super-smart cards have not yet been used to any extent, no doubt because there is so much else to do to make smart cards part of our everyday lives, but they certainly have immense potential.

The situation today

The undoubted leader in using smart cards within the banking industry is France, where even by 1985 more than 20 million smart cards were issued to banking customers. By 1995 it was estimated that numerous applications of smart cards around the world – it must be said that many of these applications were pilot projects rather than national initiatives – were consuming more than 500 million chip cards. Incidentally, another major use of smart cards, although not related to banking as such, is in satellite digital phones. There is obviously potential for linking these two applications, and it is already perfectly feasible for a customer to load an SVC via a mobile telephone unit which has been specially designed to do this. Clearly, such an application is extremely exciting as it means that an SVC could be loaded wherever the customer is located, without the customer having to find a special terminal to do this.

Since 1995 there has been a great surge in the general recognition of the exciting potential for using smart cards in financial applications. In particular, as we have seen, 'pay before' applications have been added to 'pay now' (debit) and 'pay later' (credit) types of consumer transactions.

There has also been a comprehensive recognition of the potential which smart cards offer to utilize spare capacity on the chip for non-financial tasks. Many non-financial organizations are establishing schemes with the necessary infrastructure for processing financial transactions. Smart cards undoubtedly offer newcomers opportunities to gain a considerable amount of market share at the expense of traditional banks because the newcomers are not handicapped by an existing (and increasingly obsolete) magnetic stripe infrastructure. As the reader might imagine, the existence of this infra-structure is one of the major inhibiting forces to the progress of smart cards, although such are the attractions of smart cards that even this factor is rapidly being seen as an entirely surmountable obstacle.

Overview of current developments around the world

In this section I take a look at current progress with smart cards in some of the world's leading economies.

United Kingdom

As with all aspects of the virtual banking revolution, the United Kingdom is one of the forerunners in the progression towards making smart cards the central standard for plastic bank cards.

The most noteworthy scheme currently running in Britain is Mondex, of which I will say no more at this stage other than it is an ambitious and generally successful SVC scheme. I devote an entire case study to Mondex later in this chapter.

Another major smart card initiative in Britain started on October 1 1997, when 15 members of the UK banking industry joined forces in a project to introduce chips on plastic bank cards, with trials starting in Dunfermline in Scotland and Northampton in England under the auspices of APACS (the Association for Payment Clearing Services). The trials are involving a range of debits, credit and ATM cards.

During the course of the trials more than 100,000 cards are being issued and more than 600 retailers will operate terminals capable of taking the new cards. Card-holders issued with the new cards will be able to use them in cash machines and at all shops and businesses currently accepting card payments, not just those taking part in the trial. The existing methods for identifying cardholders – signature at point of sale and PIN at cash machines – will be retained.

APACS says that a major advantage of the new cards is that they provide security against counterfeit card fraud, a growing problem in many countries. As APACS rather didactically puts it: 'Chip cards are part of the long-term technical answer to this threat and incorporate highly sophisticated processing to identify genuine plastic cards and make counterfeiting difficult and expensive.'

The cards being used in the trial are hybrid ones which retain magnetic stripe technology so that they can be used in all locations where bank cards are accepted.

The significance of this pilot project stems from the fact that it shows that APACS has made a real commitment to work with terminal and software manufacturers, retailers and retail organizations to establish the most suitable mix of equipment, cards and retail outlets to ensure the smooth introduction of the new technology. As APACS adds: 'The infrastructure to support chip cards has been designed with the flexibility to cater for future developments in card technology.' And my source at Apex added: 'This initiative is an important step forward for all those involved in the card payments industry. The new cards, developed in collaboration between APACS members and international card schemes, will enhance the security of transactions and, over time, the range of services available to cardholders from payment and cash cards.'

Late in the spring of 1998 the results achieved by the trials in Dunfermline and Northampton will be reviewed. This review process will incorporate feedback from all parties involved, including retailers and cardholders. Assuming that no particular problems emerge, it is likely that an industry decision will be made in Britain to begin a rolling programme of producing chip cards over the next two or three years. This will involve re-issuing existing credit, debit and cash machine cards together with the installation of smart-card-enable terminals. The precise timing of these actions will be a decision for individual card issuers and acquirers.

Another important UK initiative involving smart cards is the Visa Cash pilot programme which started in Leeds, West Yorkshire in October 1997 and is scheduled to last about 12 months. It is involving up to 70,000 Visa Cash cardholders who have access to around 2000 merchant terminals in Leeds and the surrounding areas, with acceptance at a wide variety of locations including car parks, newsagents and fast-food outlets. There are about 60 locations where people will be able to load value onto their Visa Cash cards.

Visa Cash is an SVC system. It is the UK's contribution towards Visa's extensive world-wide pilot programme of smart cards.

Why was Leeds chosen? The answer reveals useful insights into what criteria smart card operators think are necessary for a town to be a success as a location for a pioneering electronic payments initiative.

According to Visa, Leeds was chosen 'after extensive research' which showed that Leeds had the right attributes. These attributes are listed by Visa as:

■ A good mix of suitable retailers, with more than 1000 shops, plus excellent public transport and, parking facilities. Visa noted that its retail consultants, Management Horizons Europe, recently ranked Leeds just behind London's Oxford Street in terms of quality and choice of shops.

■ All the participating banks have a significant presence in the city.

■ Leeds is a progressive city embracing new concepts in shopping, entertainment, recreation, business and industry.

■ Located midway between London and Edinburgh, Leeds has excellent transport links with the rest of the country and with the immediate surrounding area.

■ Leeds is considered to be the North of England's leading business centre. Leeds is also the second largest metropolitan district in the UK.

Visa Cash began a world-wide programme in April 1995. Today there are more than 6.47 million Visa Cash cards in circulation. The largest Visa Cash implementation to date is taking place in Spain. Following a successful series of in-house and university pilot schemes, Visa Espana decided to launch Visa Cash nationwide in December 1995. Today, Visa Cash is issued by more than 40 banks in 26 provinces across the country and used in Spain's major banking cities Barcelona, Madrid and Seville.

Visa Cash is currently being used in 12 countries – Argentina, Australia, Brazil, Canada, Colombia, Germany, Hong Kong, Italy, Japan, Spain, the UK and the United States. Further programmes are being planned for Mexico and Taiwan.

France

France, the world's leader at present in terms of implementations of smart cards in the banking sector, currently has more than 27 million smart cards in circulation, with these cards competing for a volume of nearly one trillion francs annually in terms of transactions.

A major consequence – and causation factor – of the boom in smart card use has been a continual dramatic expansion in the number of acceptance points throughout the country. There are currently more than 900,000 of these, and reliable industry sources in France estimate that this figure will reach eight million by the year 2000.

The principal contribution to this increase is expected to come from new applications from retailers rather than simply proliferation of terminals at existing retailers who accept the French smart card. By the year 2000 there are also expected to be two million telephones and terminals with smart card readers and three million pay television systems using smart cards.

As a result of the widespread use of smart cards throughout France, card fraud has been enormously reduced. Furthermore, the French banking industry reports major cost reductions in the area of authorization as well as reductions in card manufacturing costs due to the high volume in which banks issuing smart cards can afford to order them. A source in the French banking industry told me that card manufacturing costs there are only about one dollar per year per customer in excess of those for magnetic stripe cards. This gap is apparently narrowing year by year.

There is no doubt that France is the world's leading pioneer in smart card implementation, and will continue to be for the foreseeable future. As has often been the case with their attitude towards new technology, the French have shown considerable resourcefulness in adopting new and exciting technology to practical uses, and have backed up this resourcefulness with a central direction that generates a consensus of purpose, the necessary infrastructural changes, and the requisite funding to make the changes happen.

Belgium

Belgium, despite being a small market numerically, has made remarkable progress with an electronic purse scheme known as Proton. Launched in 1995, more than one million cards have now been issued. The scheme, which was started in a pilot project involving three cities, was extended in May 1996 to a national roll-out. Today, there are 939,000 proto cards in use in Belgium, with 10,800 point of sale terminals and 1563 loading terminals available to the public.

The Proton card has been designed to allow for a multitude of applications in addition to the electronic purse function. These applications include telephone calls, telephone-based loading of the card, and use in vending machines, ticketing, transportation and other applications.

A competitor to Proton on the Belgian market is the Postcheque card. This multi-service client card has been developed by Postcheque, the financial division of the Belgian post. This new smart card will be used as a replacement relationship card for the customer base of the Belgian post (currently more than 400,000 magnetic cards have been issued) and is also available for any commercial organization interested in issuing its own private card with payment facilities and its own logo.

Germany

There are currently three German SVC schemes. Known as Geld-Karte, Pay-Card and P-Card, the three schemes are competing with one another. The Geld-Karte system is the forerunner at present, with about 35 million cards issued by the end of 1997.

Note that Visa Cash has also run a pilot smart card scheme with the Bankgesellschaft Berlin Bank.

Industry sources indicate that by the end of 1998 Germany will be well on the way to achieving smart card penetration among a majority of the country's bank customers.

The Netherlands

The major implementation of smart cards here is in the field of stored value cards. Two different programmes, namely Chipper and Chipknip (smart card schemes severely task the imaginative powers of brand name experts) are currently operational.

Chipknip, a licensee of the Belgian SVC system Proton International, was introduced in January 1996 by Interpay, the Dutch bank group. Today, Chipknip is being rolled out nationally, with more than three million cards in circulation in the country, usable at nearly 60,000 point of sale terminals and reloadable at 5000 loading points.

The second Dutch SVP scheme is Chipper, which is being run by two local operators, the PTT and Postbank. Chipper is currently being rolled out, with several million cards expected to be in use by the end of 1998 and 150,000 terminals.

Central Europe

There are currently several different smart projects in central European countries, although the pace of growth of these projects is relatively low. Even so, there is a general recognition in the region that off-line smart cards are of great interest in areas where telecommunications networks are poor. I have had reports that there are successful projects in the Czech Republic, Hungary and even the Commonwealth of Independent States. The major players in the market are, as might be expected, Western organizations, including the Austrian smart card integrated BGS and the French organization IDS. These companies have been installing closed smart card systems in large banks in the CIS and in other Central European countries.

United States

Smart card implementations, whether full-scale or pilots, are not as common in the United States as might be expected. As is often the case with the virtual banking revolution, progress with smart cards is hampered in the US by the difficulty of generating a centralized impetus to infrastructure change and by the essentially regional nature of banks. No doubt in due course the United States will be an important area for smart card implementation, but we are still a few years away from that situation.

Currently, the most numerous types of smart card implementation in the US are SVC projects for use in closed environments such as high schools, stadiums, mass transit systems and so on. These are not always strictly banking systems, but as they feature SVC smart cards they are certainly a useful indication of what seems to be clear: that stored value cards are going to be the first type of bank card smart cards used in America, with most such projects probably featuring some kind of joint venture between a bank and a group of major retailers or other consortium.

Canada

Here, as in the United States, the major current application of smart cards is stored value cards. During the summer of 1997, a war for leadership took place between the main players in the market: namely Banksys with its Proton technology (known as the 'Exact' card on Canadian territory), Mastercard with the Mondex scheme and Visa's Visa Cash system. A version of Mondex is also being implemented in an ambitious pilot in Britain – see below for details of this.

All these three schemes are currently planning nationwide roll-outs. Sources suggest that it looks as if Mondex – which was first piloted in the city of Guelph in an initiative that started in September 1996 – will achieve major national roll-out status in 1999 and may become the dominant smart card for SVC transactions, with the Exact card close behind, while Visa Cash looks set to dominate the 'smart card as credit card' market.

The future of smart cards

During the next decade, it is likely that improvements in manufacturing the chips used on smart cards will lead to chips that are at least twice as powerful as the most powerful available at present and very likely several times more powerful. In particular, technologists are optimistic that a new type of chip – known as the 'quantum effect' chip – will amount to a real breakthrough in memory and processing power.

In parallel with this particular development, research is going on into looking at alternatives to silicon for data processing to meet the demand for electronic devices that are physically more flexible than a silicon chip (a singularly physically *inflexible* device) as well as chips that are smaller, cheaper, faster, more reliable and require even less power than a silicon chip needs. The question of power is always going to be important because even a tiny chip on a smart card requires a power source. Microprocessors based on DNA, a protein or optical circuits using polymers are being investigated, especially in view of their potential for creating flexible microchips.

Other technologies are being planned to provide computers that are as little as one-fiftieth the size of today's machines and more than one hundred times faster. For example, in Britain BT recently announced a base station for mobile telephony which is powered by the light transmitted to it by an optical fibre cable. These technologies could apply to the smart card of the future as they move from the realm of science fiction to commercial applications.

Another important likely future development is the introduction of what are known as 'contactless' smart cards. As the name indicates, these do not need to go into a slot to communicate with a host terminal. Instead, all signals and operating power is transmitted between a coil on the clock and a similar coil on the terminal.

The main advantage of this type of card is that the chip is encapsulated within a protective barrier (typically a thin layer of clear plastic) and completely isolated from human handling. With current smart cards, the electrodes of the chip obviously need to be exposed to interface with the terminal, but with contactless cards this will not be necessary. A major limiting factor on the life-span of a smart card is, inevitably, corrosion of the electrode caused by dirt and by sweat from the user's hands. Contactless cards will eliminate this problem and so greatly extend the lifetime of a smart card. It is estimated that most of these cards will operate at a distance of about ten centimetres, any way up and any way round.

Contactless cards are more expensive than ordinary smart cards at present and require a special terminal, but the advantages they offer suggest that their introduction is inevitable at some point in the future. Probably this introduction will be initiated by creating a hybrid form of smart card containing both contactless and standard chip functionality, but I suppose this kind of development must be at least five years away since we are still very much in the position where migrating from magnetic stripe cards to smart cards is the order of the day.

My overall belief is that ultimately what is powering the relentless move to widespread smart card implementation is not so much their ability to provide much greater levels of security than ordinary magnetic stripe cards provide – even though this is certainly a factor – but rather the potential they have to be loaded with vast amounts of customer information and to act as multi-function cards. Their role as loyalty cards is also only now being explored to any serious extent.

Beyond this, I have a great deal of faith in the ability of stored value cards to change the way we pay for products and services costing less than $10. The point is that cash is a most unsatisfactory way of paying for anything, and once stored value becomes the name of the game, the days when cash was king of the payment methods for small transactions may be numbered, at least in major developed economies. It is clear from the success of pilot projects world-wide that, as with many elements of the virtual banking revolution, people simply *like* using stored value cards.

Certainly, there is plenty of room for progress in this respect. Despite there being about one billion credit/debit cards in the world, 98 per cent of sales transactions world-wide are cash-based, and 90 per cent of these transactions are for less than $10. Smart card technology is likely to be as much part of our future as technology itself.

Case study: Mondex

Introduction

On July 3 1995 in Swindon, Wiltshire, a 72-year-old newspaper vendor called Don Stanley became a minor historical figure in the UK's virtual banking revolution when he exchanged a copy of the Swindon newspaper, the *Evening Advertiser*, for 'cash' stored in the microchip of his customer's 'Mondex' stored value card (SVC).

Mondex is the UK's first major smart card pilot. It was launched on July 3, 1995, in Swindon, a busy and growing town in the county of Wiltshire, UK.

The choice of Swindon was made after careful consideration of the town's features. According to Mondex, the reasons why it was chosen were:

- The total population (190,000) made Swindon the right sort of size: not too small and not too large.

- The Mondex was developed by Midland Bank and NatWest Bank. Both banks have a firm footing in this town: there is a total of 40,000 NatWest and Midland account holders in Swindon. (Note the similarity with the reasons for choosing Leeds for the Visa Cash scheme, above). Swindon was therefore adjudged to provide a good potential customer base for the pilot, which Midland and NatWest have run in conjunction with British Telecom.

- The town was regarded as containing a representative cross-section of the British population by income group and social class.

- The town also contains a selection of high street shops and other outlets that is highly representative of the British population as a whole.

- The town was seen as offering convenient access (less than one hour's drive) from London and Heathrow Airport: a useful attribute bearing in mind that the organizers expected numerous domestic and overseas visitors to come to see the scheme in action.

- An initial survey of customers and retailers in the town showed that there was considerable enthusiasm for the Mondex scheme.

While a smart card scheme, Mondex is above all a stored value card (SVC) scheme: that is, it features a smart card which is 'loaded' with cash electronically, with the cash being available to the customer when using a special payment terminal.

Mondex was not the first stored value card scheme in the UK, but it was by far the most significant to date. In the 1980s, Barclaycard had tested a stored value card at the Dallington Country Club in Northamptonshire (the county where Barclaycard is based). The scheme allowed members of the club to pay for sessions, and for food and drink and sports equipment, by the use of an SVC. The Dallington scheme was seen as successful, and its success was unquestionably a factor in the inauguration of Mondex. The Dallington scheme was, however, severely limited as it was only open to members of the club, whereas Mondex is open to the public.

As of March 1998, there are 13,000 cardholders in Swindon, representing over 30 per cent of 40,000 targeted Midland and NatWest account holders. It is obviously unrealistic that every Midland and National Westminster cardholder would want to become a Mondex user; Mondex are calling the 13,000 take-up rate a big success.

What reinforces this argument is the fact that Mondex cards are not distributed freely to customers. This is partly because to do so would not reveal any useful information about the acceptability of the scheme to customers, but more importantly, because Mondex needs to be loaded with cash by the customer and therefore requires a considerable degree of understanding of the scheme by the customer and a responsibility for using the card properly. Customers not only of Midland and NatWest, but of all other banks and building societies can apply for a Mondex card. Cards can also be obtained from the Mondex Centre in Swindon.

Status checking of customers prior to acceptance on the scheme does not need to be rigorous, as one of the many advantages of Mondex to the banks is that there is no risk (apart, at least, from the risk of the cost of setting the scheme up in the first place). There is certainly no credit risk, as no credit lines or even three-day debit clearing floats are offered to customers, who must transfer cleared funds onto the cards before the cards can be used.

Mondex equipment

Naturally, any stored value card scheme must provide for a way for cards to be loaded and unloaded. Mondex facilitates this by means of two types of terminals.

Retailer terminals. These are located in retailers' premises (or, in the case of street vendors, in some convenient part of the stall). Their function is to 'unload' from the card the cost of whatever is being spent (i.e. facilitate the payment process). The transaction takes place by the simple procedure of the retailer keying in the relevant amount and swiping the card through. The cardholder receives a receipt and can therefore check that the amount taken off the card is correct. The process is therefore similar to the electronic use of a debit or credit card at a terminal, with the exception that the user does not have to use a signature when making a Mondex purchase. Again, this is because Mondex is conceived of as a cash scheme: the card is used like cash. Note that Mondex uses no paper vouchers; it is an entirely electronic scheme.

Payphone terminals. One especially interesting feature of the Mondex scheme is that the cards are not, as might be expected, loaded in bank branches. The reason for this is that the organizers feel – not unreasonably – that there is very little point in customers having the cards if they need to go into branches in order to use them. After all, customers can obtain cash from branches anyway.

Instead, Mondex is essentially conceived of as offering customers the opportunity to gain additional access to their funds. The access points are, therefore, additional to the familiar access points to funds which branches represent.

Mondex is loaded through BT Payphones and ATMs modified for use with Mondex, and through specially adapted Screenphones.

Nine NatWest ATMs and 11 Midland machines in Swindon (including one site at the local branch of Sainsbury's and at Swindon railway station) have been adapted to act as Mondex terminals. However, the main access points – and here the involvement of BT starts to become clear – at which Mondex cards can be loaded and other functions can be carried out at specially modified payphones located around Swindon. Mondex UK has stated that is very encouraged by consumers' adoption of the telephone as a cash machine.

These payphones (which, incidentally, can also be used as telephones if required, with calls being paid for by Mondex) enable cardholders to carry out any of the following functions:

- loading the card with cash from cleared funds from their bank account (up to a maximum of £500 per card);

- remote Mondex Cash transfers to another cardholder;

- depositing of cash into cardholder's own bank account;

- locking or unlocking the card;

- changing the PIN (this convenient function means that cardholder's can choose a PIN they are unlikely to forget);

- checking their bank balance;

- checking last 10 transactions.

Note that when a cardholder is using a payphone, he does need to use his PIN, as the payphones give him direct access to his bank account.

The 'lock or unlock' function refers to the principle that Mondex cards can be 'locked' electronically by customers in order to prevent an unauthorized person using the card (which can of course include spending money from the card), but if the cards are lost, the cash that has been loaded onto them is lost and will not be refunded. This is even so in cases when the card has been locked by the customer and could therefore not be used by an unauthorized person who found it. Locked cards have been handed into the Swindon Mondex Centre during the pilot as they are of no value to the finder.

There is now an insurance policy which enables cardholders who have lost a card loaded with cash to claim back up to £100 in Mondex Cash. The value of the refund is based on the last Mondex withdrawal from the cardholder's bank account.

The principle that 'a lost card means lost cash' prevails because the banks operating the Mondex scheme regard the funds as having left their custody at the moment when the card is loaded: in this sense the card is exactly like cash that has been dispensed to a customer through an ATM or over the counter in a branch.

While it would theoretically be feasible for the banks to implement some kind of tracking of spending procedure which would enable them to refund money that has been loaded onto a Mondex card but not yet spent, in practice this is unfeasible, as not only would such a procedure dramatically escalate costs, but it might also involve cardholders in breaches of privacy. Customers do not receive a statement of what they spent, and where and when they spent it: another way in which the card is used like cash.

Other 'Mondex equipment' includes Mondex 'wallets'. These are devices which in effect act as portable retailer terminals, although they are principally designed for use by cardholders. They resemble pocket calculators and are approximately the same size, with the difference that they contain an access slot for a Mondex card.

The Mondex wallet allows a third party to make a payment to the holder of the wallet. So, for example, if Mr Smith owes Mr Jones £10, Mr Smith could pay him by inserting his card into Mr Jones' wallet. Mr Jones keys the amount into the keypad on the wallet, and the transaction is made.

The wallet will if necessary display details of the past 10 transactions that went through it, so that queries can be checked. The money accumulated in the wallet can be loaded into Mr Jones' bank account when he next checks his balance.

The beauty of the wallet notion is that it can, obviously, be used by retailers for whom a power source is not available, such as market traders, taxi drivers, milkmen and pizza delivery men. The usual upper limit for the Wallet, as with the Card is £500. However, retailers are issued with special retailer cards with an appropriate upper limit. This enables them to accumulate Mondex Cash and transfer it directly to their account whenever convenient, either by phone or through an ATM. The first Mondex transaction at the news-stand run by Mr Stanley was made via a retailer's terminal, but in many respects would have been more conveniently made via a wallet.

Figure 9.1 gives a diagrammatic summary of all the Mondex equipment and illustrates how this interrelates to form a complete payment scheme.

FIGURE 9.1 *Elements of the Mondex scheme*

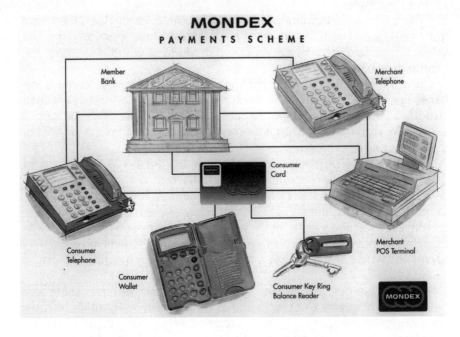

In Figure 9.1 you will see a keyring balance reader and home screen phone and payphone, which need further explanation. The *key ring balance reader* is a small device which cardholders use to enable them to read the balance off their card at any time. Balance readers are given to all cardholders as part of the package.

The *home screen phone and payphone* is a device which allows a cardholder to make all the Mondex transactions at home i.e. he can load his card with cash from his bank account, unload cash from his card (or wallet) directly to his bank account, lock or unlock the card, change the PIN and check his balance. Mondex users can have screenphones installed in their houses. They carry out the same services as the payphones on the streets of Swindon and can also be used for domestic calls.

What is exciting about the home screenphones is that they amount to an 'ATM at home'. Indeed, a cardholder could use the home screenphones, street payphones and retailer terminals, and never need to visit an ATM at all, let alone a branch.

Mondex has installed 1000 home screenphones as part of the trial. Their distribution is being arranged by BT, which mails a cross-section of Mondex customers and invites them to install a home screenphone.

Note that, in order for the trial to proceed smoothly and for the equipment to be distributed without delay, there is no charge made to any cardholder or retailer for participating in Mondex or for using any of the equipment.

On the face of it this may seem the one area of the pilot scheme that is not realistic. However, it is important to bear in mind that institutions running a stored value card scheme such as Mondex will not necessarily need to charge for the equipment even when a scheme becomes a major national initiative.

The institutions could use the scheme as a way of winning new customers and relieving the pressure on branches. If they perceived it in this way, they would not necessarily need to charge customers for the service at all. Alternatively, they might charge customers a nominal sum for renting the equipment and having the card, and charge phone calls out at a special local rate, or sell some equipment to customers.

Clearly, there is a wide variety of different charging options. Participating institutions (plus telecommunications providers) would need to strike a balance between the need to avoid raising charges to a level that they put off customers who may be nervous and hesitant about using a new stored value card scheme anyway, and the almost equally pressing requirement to avoid subsidizing the scheme to such an extent that the financial and commercial benefits of launching the scheme are largely or partially eroded.

Promotion of the Mondex scheme

During the summer of 1995 four trailers, equipped with BT staff and Mondex phones, were stationed in Swindon to give the public the chance to become familiar with the new technology. The Mondex Centre, in the centre of Swindon was a key focus of Mondex's presence in Swindon. The centre gave potential cardholders a source of information about the scheme, as well as an opportunity to view and try the technology and apply for the cards.

For stored value cards, as with other types of new virtual financial service, the need to familiarize users with the service is far from being a trivial concern. The vast majority of members of the public would have no experience whatsoever of stored value cards; the education requirement faced by Mondex was a considerable one.

Note, incidentally, that the following methods are the principal ones whereby users get to know how to use a virtual financial service:

■ *By word of mouth*. People's friends and/or relatives tell them about the new service and how it works.

■ *From advertising*. The organization implementing the news service will often advertise locally (or, where appropriate, nationally) in order to explain how the service should be used.

■ *From in-branch demonstrations*. Users are often amenable to taking the trouble to find out about the new service when they are in their branches.

■ *From other types of demonstrations.* Branch demonstrations are all very well, but they confine the time during which the demonstration is available to the branch opening hours; a flaw which is in many respects at odds with the whole idea of 24-hour virtual banking. It therefore makes sense to locate other types of demonstration facilities elsewhere; typically in places (such as car parks and shopping malls) where large numbers of members of the public congregate.

Benefits of Mondex to customers

According to Mondex – unfortunately the only source of information on this subject – these are as follows. (Additional comments in brackets are by the author).

Convenience

■ The customer will in effect always have the correct change and will not need to sign or wait for authorization. (Mondex does not make use of PINs for authorization but in order to confirm that the person using the card is the bona fide customer).

■ The customer will be able to load or unload cash both from ATMs and telephones. In effect, any Mondex telephone is also a cash machine.

■ Mondex is cleaner and less bulky than notes and coins.

Flexibility

■ Mondex is suitable for high and low cash payments.

■ It gives users the ability to make payments via the card to a third person.

■ Mondex is accepted widely at retailers' premises – more than 700 have agreed to participate.

Safety

■ Cardholders can choose or change their personal code at any time; the store of cash can be locked to prevent money being removed. Cards are unlocked by keying in the PIN. Retailers provide a machine, located away from the counter where customers can put their card in to unlock it before going up to the counter to pay. This saves the congestion which would occur if customers kept going up to pay for things with locked cards.

(Note, however, that – as we have seen – the fundamental nature of Mondex as a cash replacement means that:

(a)   cash on an unlocked Mondex card which falls into the hands of an unscrupulous third party can be spent by that third party, as there is no requirement for the cardholder to key in his PIN at the point of purchase;

(b)   cash on a locked or unlocked Mondex card which is lost by the cardholder is irretrievable, even if the card is never found by an unscrupulous third party and used.

It is important again to point out here that there is now an insurance policy which covers the loss of a Mondex Card and which will give the policy holder up to £100 Mondex cash if their card is lost.)

Control and independence

- Cardholders can manage expenditure by limiting the value on the card; like cash, you can only spend the amount you are carrying with you.

- The Mondex wallet can be used as a secure, portable bank of money.

- It's easy to keep track of spending because the last 10 transactions can be checked with a wallet, a home screenphone or a street payphone.

- Assuming the pilot scheme turns into a national scheme, it may at some point be possible to send and receive money on a stored value card across national borders.

- One important application of stored value cards is that they can be used to control the spending of people whose spending needs to be monitored. For example, parents might wish to control their children's spending.

With the foresight and ingenuity with which, it is fair to say, Mondex operators have approached this pilot scheme, they have provided for this, too. Cardholders need to be a minimum of 16 years old to apply for a Mondex card, as the card must be linked to a bank account. However, it is possible for cardholders to apply for additional 'associated cards', which are Mondex cards that are not linked to a bank account.

They can therefore be spent by whoever has the card but can only be loaded under the supervision of the primary cardholder. Associated cards are ideal for children, who could be given their pocket money on a card and have some control therefore imposed on their spending (the lout selling violent action comics or even drugs outside the school isn't likely to have a retailer terminal or wallet). Children can also get introduced to the payment system of the future, too.

Benefits of Mondex to retailers

These are listed by Mondex as being the following.

Increased efficiency

■ No need for customer identification, authorization or signatures.

■ No clearing period – unlike cheques and credit cards – and the value of the transaction is guaranteed (i.e. there is no danger of a cheque or credit card transaction being subsequently found to be fraudulent).

■ Less time is wasted than is often the case when handling change.

■ fewer mistakes are likely to be made – either those which irritate the customer or which result in the retailer incurring loss – than when handling cash.

■ No counting is needed to check how much is on a retailer terminal.

■ Mondex payments are faster and more accurate than others.

(There is no doubt that the cash transaction nature of Mondex is an immense boon to retailers all too familiar with taking debit and credit card transactions and paying commission on these. Becoming a Mondex user in the pilot scheme does not cost retailers anything at all, and while this may change as the scheme widens beyond Swindon and becomes part of a national or regional initiative, it seems likely that it will always be less expensive for a retailer to take a stored value card than to take a debit or credit card. This must be so, since if it were not, there would be little incentive for the retailer to take the card.)

Lower cost

■ Less of a need to handle, store and transport cash.

■ Improved security and potentially lower insurance premiums.

■ Reduced pilferage from cash tills if the retailer's card is locked, and less risk of fraud.

Better financial management

■ Totalling, analysing and reconciling takings is quick and easy.

■ Money can be banked in a designated account at any time.

Lower risks

■ Reduced likelihood of raids and attacks on staff.

■ No need to store large amounts of cash on site overnight.

■ Mondex is more impervious than cash to fraud, forgery and theft.

■ Retailer terminals have both physical and electronic locks.

Assessment

The Mondex pilot scheme is an ongoing one. The three organizations that are operating it will be announcing in 1998 a programme of national roll-out.

At this stage it is possible to draw some conclusions on the success of the pilot. Since its launch in July 1995, Mondex has become recognized as a global payment system, with MasterCard International acquiring a 50 per cent shareholding in Mondex International and with the following organizations taking a shareholding in Mondex International, with a view to introducing the system in their respective territories. These include: National Westminster Bank, Midland Bank, Royal Bank of Canada, Canadian Imperial Bank of Commerce, The Hongkong and Shanghai Banking Corporation, Wells Fargo, AT&T, Chase Manhattan, First Chicago NBD and 10 major banks in Australasia.

Furthermore, it is greatly to the credit of the organizers of the scheme that every aspect of the pilot has evidently been thought through with great care in advance. Far from being a mere 'smart card-as-cash' scheme, Mondex amounts to a complete and comprehensive payment system that uses a wide variety of devices and equipment to achieve its objectives.

Mondex is in effect about as virtual a banking system as it is possible to have with current readily available technology. It is easy to forget – as Mondex is, despite everything, still a pilot scheme – that it provides proof of the dramatic suggestion that a banking system could be created, with the stored value card at its core, which does not really require banks at all. Why should banks be necessary, if employers can pay their employees' salaries into the system and employees could draw on those salaries and spend them in whatever way they wished?

Admittedly, in this scenario – which is by no means a far-fetched one – there would still be many reasons why banks could remain necessary, but the point is that the system could function without them. This would truly be the ultimate in virtual banking, as no banking scenario is more virtual than one which doesn't even involve banks.

Without doubt, it is very much in the interest of the banks to become involved with stored value card schemes at an early stage, and for them to establish a track record of running these schemes. If they don't, large retailers and large employers (including major public organizations) might start to reflect that they might be able to start stored value card schemes which don't involve banks at all.

At the very least, there might be incentives for the largest employers in a town to band together and create stored value card schemes which involve the town's retailers (particularly the big supermarkets and department stores) and where some portion of the employee's salary could be paid into the scheme. (Incidentally, in any 'employer/retailer stored value card scheme' it would make more sense for the employer to 'drip-feed' the employer's monthly salary into his account on a weekly or even daily basis than for it all to arrive as a lump sum on a particular day. This is because most employees would probably feel happier and more secure about using a card that was regularly being reloaded with a certain amount of cash than one which was loaded with a large amount of cash on one particular day of the month.)

Clearly, as a pioneer pilot scheme, Mondex plays an essential role in investigating how the entire concept of the SVC and the smart card could be developed in future.

Mondex told me that in their view the following pointers to this have been learned from the pilot implementation to date:

- Giving customers access to electronic cash is clearly a successful and important application of smart cards. But there still appears to be abundant scope for combining the functions of the SVC with a wide range of other useful features. These can include: Access control, monitoring of who accessed premises at a certain time, personal credit records held on card, personal health records held on card, computer service control, details of marketing services which card-issuer wishes to promote, and other features which could be stored in the chip held on the card.

- The pilot project has also found that an important application of the technology concerns its use in unattended point of sale. The technology is secure enough for this to function with both parties being protected against fraud. The car-parks and photo-booths in the Swindon pilot have demonstrated the advantages of this both to the consumer and the provider.

The pilot also demonstrated that a fundamental problem with introducing a completely new payment method of this kind is the need to win retailer support and to create a standard for terminals. Mondex has spent considerable time and effort to win retailers over to the new system and to create alliances with manufacturers based around the creation of a single standard terminal. Mondex has also made strategic alliances with organizations to secure the supply of the chip card through to the peripheral hardware such as wallets and key fobs. Such standardization and alliances will be necessary in all major SVC implementations. Ideally, a national standard is required.

The Mondex pilot has raised the important question of whether SVC technology could be used in Internet commerce. Very likely it will turn out that this payment method is ideally suited for commercially viable low-value Internet transactions. Clearly, the SVC has the advantage that even if the message is intercepted, only the person with the SVC can make the transaction. There is obviously scope for further investigation of possibilities here.

I conclude this chapter with a telephone interview with Glenn Weiner, vice president of industry relations in the Electronic Commerce Centre of Excellence at American Express (Amex).

Amex is one of the world's most ambitious pioneers in the implementation of smart cards, especially in the area of multi-function cards. In October 1997 Amex announced a pilot programme using smart corporate cards for faster airport check-in with Continental Airlines Electronic Ticket Machines. The multi-function cards also offer an application for storing electronic passes on the computer chip embedded in the card. These passes will grant American Express, cardholders access to Continental Airlines 'President's Club' lounges at six United States airlines. Several thousand American Express Corporate Card customers who are frequent business travellers have been hand-picked by their companies to test the new applications in the pilot, which began on November 1 1997. In addition, test participants will be able to join an ongoing pilot, which began on June 1 1997, in which they can use their smart card to quickly and easily check in and out of eight participating United States Hilton hotels using self-service kiosks in the hotel lobbies.

I regard these initiatives as momentous for the future of smart cards and I thought it would be interesting to talk to an executive at American Express to find out about the approach to smart cards which is being taken there. I am grateful to Allen Gilstrap, a smart card specialist at Amex and an energetic and thoughtful advocate of the potential of these cards (his superb talk about Amex and smart cards at the Unisys conference on smart cards at St Paul de Vence in France in October 1997 was one of the highlights of my research for this book) for putting me in touch with Glenn Weiner.

Interview with Glenn Weiner

JE: How do smart cards fit in with the Electronic Commerce Centre of Excellence?

GW: The idea behind Amex's Centres of Excellence is to integrate all different relevant disciplines under one roof and to apply to them our best resources in terms of know-how, marketing expertise and developmental ingenuity to maximize the success of the projects each Centre handles. Smart cards are a big part of what the Electronic Commerce Centre of Excellence does.

JE: Generally, do you regard the United States as a smart card pioneer?

GW: No, I don't think we can see the US in that light. You in Europe, in general, and in Britain are much more of a pioneer. The smart card initiative which APACS has taken comes to mind. It is a project which clearly is intended to become a national roll-out. The regional nature of the United States market, and the sheer number of banks we have – more than 9000 – makes it difficult for a centralized smart card infrastructure to be developed and makes it likely that other countries will lead the way in smart card implementation. That said, American Express obviously has the market here to make smart cards a really big thing once the US is ready for them in a national sense.

Of course, as an international organization Amex has to take a view on smart cards which goes beyond what is happening in the United States, even though – as you might expect – many of our smart projects will be trialled here.

JE: What potential do you think smart cards have?

GW: They have so much potential that I can't answer that question straightforwardly, I need to go through the different areas where smart cards offer the prospect of truly exciting applications.

JE: Be my guest . . .

GW: Well, first, I think the potential the smart card offers for many applications running on the same card is extremely exciting. In particular, smart cards can be used to marry payment functionality with other functionality an individual requires as part of his or her professional and leisure life. For example, you can put an airline ticket or hotel reservation onto a smart card together with banking functionality. Many Amex smart card pilot schemes have been multi-application schemes. In a very literal sense, the smart card allows you to cut across a wide range of industries and tailor-make a package of functionality which should have a very high level of appeal to the individual.

Second, they offer the opportunity for issuers to create an open infrastructure on which all compatible cards will operate. Clearly, by definition, the more open a smart card infrastructure is the more useful it is both to issuers and customers. I believe that this issue of openness is crucial to the future of the smart card industry.

Third, they will offer the exciting feature that allows changes to the applications themselves on the card, through connection to a remote host, without the need for the card itself to be recalled. You could even extend the functionality of a smart card remotely, without needing to issue a new card and recall the old one.

Fourth, there is the sheer memory and processing power of the card. After all, a smart card amounts to a portable computer in one's wallet. There are many big implications of this, such as greatly improved security due to the difficulty of accessing the chip, and the opportunity to base authorization upon more criteria. But even more important than these benefits are, in my view, that smart cards give you the facility to broadcast a sales message or deliver some other benefit to customers on an individual basis. The process is precisely the opposite of electronic delivery channels which broadcast to many people: with smart cards you can 'point-cast' to just one person at a time, and tailor everything around that person's needs.

JE: What particular contribution do you think Amex is in a position to make towards the development of smart cards?

GW: We have been a leader from the outset promoting an open infrastructure in smart card deployment. We are currently licensing our multi-application smart card file structure so that other players can 'safely' tie into an open, global infrastructure for multi-application smart cards. Beyond this, we are committed to being a pioneer in development of smart cards, especially in the area of combining financial and travel functions on one card. Our basic attitude to smart cards is that they are certainly coming, and therefore we need to be leaders in implementing them. Besides, we constantly aim to improve our products and services as a matter of course, and smart cards undoubtedly offer the scope to effect major improvements in how banking, travel and payment services are provided.

JE: What functions do you expect smart cards to contain in five years' time?

GW: I imagine that in the first wave of multi-functionality you will find payment, travel, accommodation, telecommunications and information technology functions (such as for accessing the Internet).

JE: How should a financial institution get the most out of smart cards?

GW: An institution should take stock of its own competitive position, look hard at its commercial objectives, and decide exactly how smart cards fit in with these two essential aspects of its operation.

JE: Do you expect use of smart cards in the United States to replace magnetic stripe cards?

GW: I imagine that this will happen eventually, but I think the process will take a long time to complete. The most likely situation is that for many years hybrid cards containing both a chip and a magnetic stripe will co-exist. But yes, I do believe there will come a time when the magnetic stripe card will become a thing of the past.

Strategic guidelines: smart cards

Much of the material in this chapter focuses on strategic issues relating to an institution winning an edge from smart cards. Without repeating matters that have already been discussed, it is useful to summarize these strategic issues here:

1   Smart cards are already a major part of the virtual banking revolution and sure to play an even more important role in the future. You should look carefully at the possibilities they offer for your own bank and seek to capitalize on those possibilities.

2   Stored value cards are clearly particularly attractive to customers. It may therefore be in your interests to launch a pilot for this type of card or participate in a shared pilot.

3   There is much to be gained from using smart cards to reduce card fraud.

4   Even given your natural desire to win the most benefit from smart cards, there is no avoiding the fact that infrastructure changes are so gigantic an undertaking that it is questionable whether one individual bank should be paying for them. The cost of these changes should be spread around the entire banking industry of the country in question. Consequently, you need to balance your understandable desire to win the largest competitive advantage from smart cards with the need to band together with other banks to create the necessary infrastructure.

5   Multi-function cards are likely to be particularly popular with customers and to give you ample scope for enhancing your marketing activities by creating joint ventures with other suppliers, such as airlines, hotel chains, telecommunications companies and information technology providers. You should therefore look hard at the possibilities for launching an initiative here, possibly featuring a pilot scheme which does not require an enormous expenditure in infrastructure cost.

Note

Contact Details for *European Card Review*:
European Card Review
Middle Barn
Morston
Norfolk
NR25 7AA
United Kingdom

Tel: +44 (0) 1263 741126

10 The future

Introduction

Many business books use the inevitable final chapter about the future as a vehicle for indulging in a variety of often fairly wild speculation. Quite apart from my own belief that wild speculations have no room in a book such as this, I have already indicated in the foregoing chapters what are likely to be the biggest developments in the future of the virtual banking revolution.

Rather than repeating those points here, I will use this chapter to introduce some ideas which I have not yet explored.

Internet Banking

First, what should be said about the prospects of Internet banking? There is no doubt that Internet banking is already high on the virtual banking agenda. For example, on June 2 1997, the Nationwide Building Society launched its first Internet banking service in the UK, which was also the UK's first such service. The idea is to give customers access to their bank account via a web site and to enable them to enact certain transactions on their account, given compliance with stringent security checks.

It is possible that Internet banking may become an important aspect of the virtual banking revolution in the future, but my personal belief is that this may not happen as automatically as some bankers and commentators believe. I realize I have been 'stung' before when being over-tentative about predicting how a new type of virtual banking service will develop (I'm referring to my already documented and erroneous erstwhile belief that EFTPoS offered customers no particular advantage), but I can't help thinking that my reservations with Internet banking have a better foundation.

The basic problem with using the Internet as a banking resource is that in many respects it goes against what the basic purpose of the Internet is. An incredibly powerful research tool, which I readily confess to using almost every day, the Internet is by its very nature designed to be used by the widest number of people. Information displayed on it is designed to be capable of being read by anybody who is interested.

Clearly, banking information across the Internet is information which by its very nature is designed to be accessed by only one or two people. Even if security checks become so reliable that they are completely safe – and at present this is not the case even with the most stringent tests – it is still debatable whether giving customers access to banking services across the Internet is the type of application for which the Internet was designed.

I'm not talking here about banks displaying information about their services on the web: of course this is a superb medium for doing so. I am talking about banks providing *interactive* services.

Another obvious problem with the Internet as a banking service delivery medium is that accessing it requires the user not only to have a PC but also to purchase Internet time, both of which involve expenses that the ordinary domestic user of a bank's services may not wish to incur. The log-on process is also often slow, especially at peak times, and the whole process involves a conscious effort: you can't just pick up the phone and dial a number.

Of course more and more people can access Internet at work, but should a bank really be providing a service which almost encourages customers to steal access time from their employers, and to devote paid time to private business? I don't think so.

Besides, the initial public reception of Internet banking hasn't been conspicuously successful. The one major Internet-only bank launched to date – Security First Network Bank of the United States – has not been a spectacular success, although of course that position may change in the future.

In any event, I don't think that a book like this, which looks at proven successes in virtual banking, should end with an upbeat assessment of the likely success of Internet banking. Instead, I prefer to err on the side of caution and advise readers to seek a watching brief on Internet banking rather than launch a major, and inevitably expensive, Internet banking initiative themselves. By all means have a web site, but this doesn't mean you should necessarily offer an interactive service at this stage.

I would, however, be remiss if I didn't point out that some consultants firmly believe that Internet banking will be an important delivery channel in the future. Furthermore, I might be wrong.

A useful summary of the future of the virtual bank

During my research for this book I got to know the organization Fiserv (Europe), a major supplier of comprehensive virtual banking solutions. I like their summary, from a promotional brochure, of the future of banking and include this here as a Exhibit 10.1.

Exhibit 10.1 Providing solutions for a changing market

The challenge of the virtual bank

The global retail financial services market is moving fast and competition has never been more intense. Deregulation has led to fragmentation of traditional, branch servicing systems.

Many new niche competitors are offering a narrow product range, using third-party or electronic distribution channels to keep costs down and offering excellent customer service over few products.

Non-financial organizations, such as retail chains, are attacking traditional banks by offering products such as mortgages and investments.

Financial organizations are having to open longer hours and provide more products through more diverse delivery channels. Increasingly, products have to be sourced from third parties (e.g. credit cards, insurance products) and delivered through third-party distribution channels, such as call centres.

Consumers have simultaneously fragmented their banking relationships: today, customers want to receive whatever service they deem appropriate, wherever and whenever they find it convenient.

The challenge for a financial services organization is to provide a branded package of services and products through any distribution channel the customer requires and *whenever* they require it, with consistency and ease.

(Source: Fiserv (Europe))

Postal banking

One virtual delivery channel I have not mentioned so far is postal banking. It clearly isn't an electronic channel, but I tend to think it deserves a mention here as a channel likely to find increasing favour with customers in the future.

It is of no real use for the day-to-day delivery of a current account service, but it is ideal for savings accounts where the customer is aiming to to build up a solid reserve of money through periodic contributions by cheque and occasional withdrawals. Both deposits and withdrawals can easily be handled by post – given that the postal system of the country concerned is reliable – and that the customer is confident about posting cheques to a bank in this way. Obviously there are special postal services available if the customer wants to ensure speedy delivery and extra security.

I think every bank ought to remember that while a postal facility is never going to be anything like as important as the principal virtual services discussed in this book, this is a facility which is none the less important and one that should be offered to customers.

The increasing importance of the data warehouse

I have not yet mentioned the data warehouse: a term rapidly gaining increasing importance in retail and wholesale banking as indicating the new focus on the way banks handle their reservoir of customer information. There is a rapidly growing school of thought within the banking technology industry that the data warehouse has the potential to play an immensely important role in how banks win a competitive edge in the future, especially in relation to how they use their customer information and how they integrate customer information with their virtual delivery channels.

As data warehousing is not one of my specialities, I have approached a data warehousing expert to provide a statement of its importance. This expert, Mike Meltzer, is a director of NCR's financial services industry consulting group for the financial services industry in Europe, the Middle East and Africa. Mike also has an impressive track record in retail and wholesale banking, especially in relation to the strategic management of the customer relationship.

I am grateful to Mike for the following succinct account of what data warehouses are, and how they fit in with the types of challenges explored in this book.

Data warehouses

For most banks today, customer information is a severely under-utilized asset. In many respects it is one of the most precious assets a bank has, but few – if any – are making the most of it. The vast majority underestimate how important customer information is to them, and as a result come nowhere near extracting the maximum benefit from it.

Data warehousing is best understood in terms of a bank's essential need to capitalize on the true value of the customer information it holds.

By looking at customer information in this way, we can categorize data warehousing as a means of exploiting the value of what is essentially a hidden asset of the bank.

For banks operating in today's world – and this applies in whatever country a bank is doing business and whatever type of business the bank is handling – the challenge to retain the most profitable customers, sell them more products and services and to find more of them is becoming increasingly difficult to meet. This is partly a result of the increasing sophistication of the customer, partly the result of a broadening in the traditional market-place (e.g. UK building societies now offer a comprehensive range of banking services) and partly a result of the fact that retailers, supermarkets and entrepreneurs of all kinds are offering ever more appealing packages of services to customers. The traditional providers of banking services know that they must rise to the challenge or risk being eliminated.

In order for any bank or other type of financial services organization to compete successfully in a highly competitive industry – and for newcomers to the industry to make the most of their competitive challenge – it is essential that organizations offering banking services are able to identify who their most profitable customers are.

The types of questions which banking organizations must get into the habit of asking and be able to answer are:

■ Who are my customers?

■ What products and services do they want?

■ What is the lifetime value of specific customer types?

■ How can I improve the lifetime value of individual customers?

■ What products/services are most profitable and how should we be assessing this profitability?

■ What services can we expect the customer to want to buy?

■ Where can we find new customers and how can we identify them?

■ How can our marketing campaigns by more effectively targeted?

■ How can an assessment of a product's value be made, both in terms of the product's value to the customer and to the bank?

■ What delivery channels shall we use?

■ How do we manage these delivery channels to our greatest competitive effect?

■ How do we make our marketing more effective?

■ How do we develop our entire commercial activities and culture to maximize the value of the customer information we currently hold?

Today, banking is all about focusing on the customer and managing the customer relationship with energy, creativity and real dynamism. Data warehousing plays an essential role in this challenge. To understand the precise nature of the role we need to think about the data which banks have on file, which principally means data they hold in some form of electronic storage and retrieval system.

It's no exaggeration to say that the information mine which banks own is a real diamond mine, with this mine constituting the data they have about their customers. Most banks hold vast amounts of data about customers and the products they buy. Every processing system, from payments to cheque processing, creates volumes of detailed data: data on the customer, the transaction, the process, the place and the time. This data is a valuable asset that needs to be hoarded, mined, manipulated and interpreted so that the bank can use it for differentiating itself from its rivals and thereby winning a competitive advantage.

Indeed, we believe there is a strong argument for a bank looking at *data* in a completely different light to *information*. *Data* is the raw and unanalysed stuff generated and printed by the bank's technology; *information* is what data is magically transformed to when human beings attempt to interpret it. *Information* is what banks really need if they are to maximize their competitive edge.

There is significant empirical proof within the banking industry that when this data is turned into refined information to support management decisions there can be an enormous potential positive impact on a bank's bottom line. Data when transformed into valuable information moves from a strategic dimension into tactical implementations in one-to-one marketing contexts, above and below the line campaigns and potentially improved customer service.

As banks have become aware of the opportunities locked up in their data, the computing industry and consulting gurus have come up with a popular if hotly debated term to describe this whole process of seeing data as a dynamic and potentially extremely valuable tool: data warehousing.

Initially, banks which were pioneering data warehousing techniques tended to focus on the utility of the data in a particular area of marketing activity. The success they won from this approach led them to add more and more data into their analysis until they were starting to create an enterprise-wide view of their banking operations. Enterprise-wide data warehousing therefore began.

Naturally, this required a targeted and technologically advanced approach to finding the right type of data from the very large data warehouses that were being investigated. Consequently a new term, 'data mining' has come into use to describe the process of searching for hidden patterns in large databases.

The beauty of data mining is that it can be undertaken at several different levels, depending on the evolutionary state of the bank from an operational and technological perspective. Even poorly-resourced banks in emerging markets can undertake a form of data mining, while more advanced banks can apply extremely sophisticated tools to it. There are ample opportunities for marketing to be based on various data mining methodologies, with the bank having considerable choice on which methodology it adopts.

Recent years have seen a particular surge in the power and sophistication of data mining tools used to access large data warehouses. These tools range from executive information systems, decision support systems, neural networks and artificial intelligence.

A data warehouse typically contains data that can only be accessed but not changed by the user. It is linked but not integrated into departmental or central operational processing systems. It often comprises data collected from distant systems that are spread all over the bank. The data is held separately and is often based on powerful parallel processing computers. Users expect a fast turnaround when they want to investigate their data warehouse. Experience has shown that it is necessary for the data to be investigated at a level of detail which enables patterns and connections to be found. Summarized data is an unreliable source when looking for those elusive diamonds.

Data warehousing has become big business and every computer manufacturer and consulting firm has created their own solutions and methodologies to enable customers to create a data warehouse which is susceptible to rapid, detailed data mining and which can produce precisely the type of information which is so useful in all aspects of the bank's activities. The data warehouse itself, coupled with the highly skilled managers who know how to use state-of-the-art data mining tools, is now an essential part of a bank's competitive armoury.

It is no exaggeration to say that there is no part of a bank's activities which is not to some extent affected by the latest data warehousing techniques. Naturally, the marketing department is a particularly fertile field for the implementation of data warehousing techniques, but in essence these techniques are relevant throughout the bank because they relate to the entire issue of the bank's relationship with its customers. This relationship is the hub of all banking activity today, whether we are talking about traditional banks or newcomers who have only joined the industry in recent years.

Systems which are designed to integrate information

In my research for this book, I have become increasingly convinced that an extremely important type of computer system for the future of the virtual banking revolution is one which allows the bank to integrate all its customer *information* (as opposed to the less useful *data*, according to the definition above) and make that information available across all the different delivery channels which the bank uses.

I have looked around the industry for a product which does this, because while I have comprehensively avoided mentioning vendors' products here except in case studies, I do think that this information integration resource is so important that it should be featured here.

After careful consideration, the only product I have been able to identify which carries out this particular objective along the lines which I think would be most useful for banks is the Composite Banking Desktop (CBD), developed by Henley-on-Thames software house AIT. Supported by AIT's core product, the Teledirect Service System (TSS), CBD is a single desktop application designed to support multiple distribution channels.

Distribution channels which have traditionally been very much operated as individual entities – such as the branch or call centres – have dealt with processing of data independently and in different ways. As a result, data can frequently be duplicated or hard to access. The CBD provides a more integrated approach, and enables the data to be transformed into information in the best sense.

In essence, the data which the application holds will be the same whether it is being viewed by a call centre operator, a customer in the home, a teller in a branch or a customer using a self-service kiosk. Only the presentation layer changes in accordance with the user's needs.

For example, information entered into the main computer system by a customer using a branch system can be accessed and dealt with via another channel such as a call centre. By integrating information across all channels, duplication of data and transaction processes is avoided, thus improving efficiency and customer service.

The CBD provides a number of standard components, which can be configured to each work station as required. These modules include telephony, customer folder, fax, quotations, product information, scripting and marketing campaign management among others. AIT has a reputation within the banking services business for placing an emphasis on user-centred design and thereby facilitating the development of a system which not only holds all essential functionality, but which is also highly graphical and easy to navigate. The application has been developed in C++ and based around object orientation.

From what I have been able to ascertain, customer service is greatly improved by the level of information offered by the CBD. Staff dealing with customer queries are presented with a complete picture of the customer and the accounts or products which he may already have or may want in the future. With the right amount of relevant information, staff are empowered to perform all the functions necessary to fulfil the customer's request, making the process faster and appearing more efficient to the customer. As AIT put it: 'Improvements in efficiency and customer contact promote competitive advantages and help to improve conversion and retention rates. In a market where customers may be high-value and long-term, retention is crucial to the future stability of the financial organization.'

Interviews with key people

All the following four people are experts in virtual banking, and have, in their own way, played a key role in the virtual banking revolution. I can think of no better way to end this book than with their comments.

I asked them all the same questions, which are as follows. Their answers, presented with their biographical details, follow.

1   How do you define the word 'virtual' in terms of its application to financial services?

2   Do you regard the move towards virtual financial services as being led by public demand, institutions' commercial motivations or technological progress?

3   What do you think consumers really think of electronic banking facilities?

4   How virtual can a bank get?

5   How can banks outperform new non-banking entrants in the virtual world?

6   How can banks outperform other banks in the virtual world?

7   What major structural and organizational changes do you expect to see within the retail banking sector during the next few years?

8   What role, if any, will bricks-and-mortar branches be playing in the year 2008 (i.e. 10 years from now)?

9   How do the senior management skills required within virtual banks differ from those required within traditional banks?

10   What are your predictions for the next 10 years of the development of:
     (a) ATMs?
     (b) EFTPoS?
     (c) Remote banking?
     (d) Smart cards?

The four people interviewed are:

Roger Alexander (48), who joined Barclays Bank as a graduate in 1968 on the information technology side of its operations and has been with the bank for the whole of his career. He has won a wide reputation within the UK electronic banking industry for the acuity of his strategic insights, and is a popular speaker at UK and overseas conferences and seminars on virtual financial services.

Roger Alexander was a key player in the development of 'Barclaysquare', Barclays Bank's virtual shopping program which is available on the Internet and gives the user the opportunity to 'view' the range of goods and services offered by the retailers and then to order items by using a secure authorization process that involves the user keying in details of his credit card. Several additional security procedures are used in order to validate the transaction.

Rob Baldock (41), is a partner with Andersen Consulting and widely regarded within the UK retail banking sector as a key figure in the development of virtual financial services. He has acted as consultant to numerous leading financial institutions over their implementation of electronic delivery and payment systems. His experience is particularly relevant for this report, as much of his time has been spent helping financial institutions leapfrog their competition by employing new business practices and/or technology.

Rob Baldock was a principal figure behind the development of the Nationwide Building Society's pioneering 'Interact' touch-screen banking service, which I profiled earlier in this book. Interact is a full-colour service which uses digitized images and a video image of a member of the branch staff to create a virtual branch on a computer screen. Users touch parts of the screen to progress forwards through the branch, with the option of returning to the general lobby (where the digitized member of staff is there to help them) whenever they wish.

Interact is currently a pilot scheme. It is deployed in seven Nationwide Building Society branches in Southampton and at the Society's head office in Swindon (coincidentally the same town as the Mondex trial is taking place). There is also an Interact screen at Victoria station in London, and in the lobby of the Chesterfield Royal Hospital, Chesterfield, Derbyshire. The Interact pilot scheme does not have a time limit for its completion and for consideration of the response: it will simply be extended to other of the Nationwide's total of 694 branches if and when the Society thinks fit.

Rob Farbrother (49), is something of a virtual financial services guru. Details of his career to date were included earlier in this book. They can be summarized as having worked in information technology operations with the Abbey National Building Society and Citibank before moving to head the ATM consortium Funds Transfer Sharing (FTS) in 1986. As we have seen, FTS has now metamorphosed into Sligos Payment Services Limited, the UK arm of international payment systems organization Groupe Sligos, and then into Atos UK.

In April 1996 Rob Farbrother became managing director of PayPoint, a cash payment facility service aimed at providing a virtual payment facility for unbanked people (i.e. people with no bank accounts) to pay the bills of large utilities such as British Gas, BT and electricity boards.

John Hardy (50), has been chairman of UK ATM network LINK since 1986, and in this role has overseen its progress during its years of competing with MATRIX, the merger with MATRIX, and its successful development and expansion during the 1990s.

Prior to joining LINK, John Hardy worked with Girobank for more than 15 years as head of electronic banking.

Roger Alexander

1   How do you define the word 'virtual' in terms of its application to financial services?

At Barclays we like to define it as 'the bank you see less of, but do more business with'.

In essence, in a virtual bank the traditional bricks-and-mortar paradigm of a customer's interaction with the bank is replaced by an electronic paradigm.

2   Do you regard the move towards virtual financial services as being led by public demand, institutions' commercial motivations or technological progress?

I agree this is a key question, which basically boils down to whether the onward progress of the virtual financial services business is being governed by a 'customer-pull' or 'bank-push' process.

My feeling is that finding an answer to this question (for which it is quite likely no ready solution can be found) is less important than recognizing that in the electronic banking paradigm, customers inevitably have much more control, and much more choice, than in a bricks-and-mortar paradigm. Recognizing the greater control and choice they enjoy is the first major conceptual step a financial institution must take in deciding how to get the most from virtual financial services.

3   What do you think consumers really think of electronic banking facilities?

The first thing to say is that obtaining an answer to this question from research is difficult because people often haven't got clear views on what they think of a new kind of interaction with technology, and market researchers expect them to have clear views on this.

It is important for bankers to bear in mind that banking is a secondary rather than primary service: we don't visit a bank (whether physically or electronically) because we want money to put up on our walls at home: we visit a bank because we want to buy goods or services with that money. The bank visit is also in some way a 'distress' purchase: like buying petrol, it's something we have to do in order to live rather than because we really want to do it.

For these two reasons it is essential that if an institution wants to maximize the appeal of its services to its existing customer base and to new customers, it makes the delivery aspects of its services as attractive as it can. Generally, virtual financial services contribute towards this being the case. Customers clearly like virtual banking systems, and in particular enjoy the fact of these services being available seven days a week, 24 hours per day and every day of the year.

4   How virtual can a bank get?

It is realistic to expect that between about 80 per cent and 90 per cent of a bank's functionality can be delivered virtually. However, there will always be a need for some branches where customers can enjoy a personal contact with the staff.

5   How can banks outperform new non-banking entrants in the virtual world?

In summary, the answer to this is that banks must leverage their existing skills, which in practice means that they must decide what their strong points are, and then focus on delivering these strong points to customers.

Examples of such strong points would, in the case of most banks, include such factors as:

■ a reputation for being reliable and trustworthy as an intermediary;

■ a reputation for being a safe custodian;

■ 200 years or more as a family name.

6 How can banks outperform other banks in the virtual world?

They have to deliver a better performance in certain crucial areas, which in my view are:

■ the speed to which new products are brought to market;

■ the creativity and energy of their lateral thinking;

■ their ability to rethink the entire nature of what their business is: I strongly believe that among the two most important questions an institution has got to be asking itself right now are: what business are we in? and what business do we want to be in?

■ their ability to speed the decision-making process without being impulsive or irresponsible in arriving at decisions;

■ their ability to maximize the effectiveness of communications between the information technology and operations departments, and ideally for these departments to feature integration.

7 What major structural and organizational changes do you expect to see within the retail banking sector during the next few years?

The sector is obviously going to become increasingly virtual, with networks that are at present proprietorial becoming national and open to all institutions. As well as this, I expect to see institutions working more and more with other non-banking organizations in order to deliver new products and services to customers.

8 What role, if any, will bricks-and-mortar branches be playing in the year 2008?

They will still be important. For one thing, don't forget that banks are committed *now* to have branches in place in, say, 10 and 20 years' time, unless they want to sell leases they have already signed, or freeholds they already own. Of course there will be some reduction in the overall number of branches which banks are operating, but I think most banks will have the sense to look at branches not as a legacy problem but as an asset and an opportunity.

What does this mean in practical terms? It means that while banks will of course be using branches more and more for selling complex financial services or for involved transactions, they will eventually start using them as outlets for the new kinds of business they are going to be getting into. As I have already said, banks need to start asking themselves what business they really want to be in, and it may be that the answer to this question could reveal all sorts of new applications for their branches, which are – after all – key, high-profile retail outlets on the high street. Why should the banks let other non-banks muscle in on their business without the banks making a spirited attempt to muscle in on the non-banks' business?

9   How do the senior management skills required within virtual banks differ from those required within traditional banks?

There will be many similarities between skills required today and those needed in the future: particularly in terms of risk management, which is not going to go away as a problem just because assets are delivered by virtual means.

Other, new skills will become important, though: such as an ability to accommodate the idea that banks should consider moving into new areas of related retail activity; the need to be able to understand and operate an environment which is technology-intensive rather than people-intensive; and the ability to identify mutually profitable joint ventures with other banks or with other non-banks.

10   What are your predictions for the next 10 years of the development of
   (a)   ATMs?
   (b)   EFTPoS?
   (c)   Remote banking?
   (d)   Smart cards?

I would like to give a general answer to this question. I believe that by the year 2008 all the above virtual systems will have reached maturity (ATMs are close to that point already, of course). I would certainly expect there to be just one network for all these delivery systems, and I see cashless cards as being part of everyday life by then.

Incidentally, I believe the cashless card function should be an extension of the credit or debit card function: that is, an extra feature on those types of cards rather than – as Mondex is – a completely separate type of card.

Rob Baldock

1   How do you define the word 'virtual' in terms of its application to financial services?

Virtualization both describes the availability of increased and increasing customer choice through the use of multiple distribution channels, and a movement towards products and services which result from the efforts of many disparate suppliers. This phenomenon is underway across many areas of commerce, but is particularly evident in the financial services industry, where products and services are uniquely suited to the new method of production and distribution.

Customers are able to choose the time, the place and the method by which products and services are accessed, with these being made available directly at the point of need. The financial products and services themselves are produced and distributed by multiple companies which may themselves be widely distributed around the globe, although this may not be apparent to the customer.

2 Do you regard the move towards virtual financial services as being led by public demand, institutions' commercial motivations or technological progress?

I think we can usefully identify two different types of virtualization which impinge on financial institutions. These are virtualization in distribution and virtualization in supply.

Virtualization in distribution is led by financial and non-financial institutions. In a commoditizing market, institutions are using electronic delivery mechanisms to reduce costs (the cost of an ATM transaction can be one-tenth of the cost of the same transaction via a branch teller). The customer obtains easier access to the institution, but the value proposition is a traditional one (product based). Virtualization is therefore primarily for the benefit of the institution – hence 'push' rather than 'pull'.

Some institutions take a longer/broader view and are looking to improve the value proposition (e.g. Nationwide Building Society, Bank of America). Some fall behind and see apparent customer demand for new channels. This demand is often misleading since it is frequently not for new channels at all but for channels which are commonplace. In this current age of rapid change in the retail financial sector, yesterday's innovations are today's 'must-have' features.

Virtualization in supply is likely to be forced upon financial institutions as a result of intensified competition. Extreme specialization will enable suppliers further to reduce costs by focusing on core activities. The alliances between suppliers formed as a necessary part of virtualization will allow suppliers to offer product excellence by incorporating into their offerings the best products available anywhere. Service excellence will also be demanded by customers as global specialists become active and visible in this arena.

3 What do you think consumers really think of electronic banking facilities?

Consumers have high expectations – and on the whole these have been met or exceeded by electronic banking. Customers have come to expect high efficiency, speed, and zero error-rates from electronic channels – service they still would never expect from a human teller. (In service satisfaction surveys, ATMs have been rated by Citibank at around 97 per cent. Branch service never rates above 70 per cent.) Customers expect electronic banking facilities to be cost-effective, and expect banks to introduce new technologies as a matter of course.

A recent National Opinion Poll (NOP) survey showed that customers are more satisfied now with the service their bank is providing than they were 10 years ago. They largely attribute the improved satisfaction to the deployment of technology.

My view is that these survey findings are accurate, but that customers have also come to accept that machines are limited: that, in particular, machines cannot be expected to possess 'intelligence' and will only carry out functions they have been specifically instructed to carry out. I believe that where complex transactions or financial advice are involved, customers will still prefer to do business with a human, although their views on this matter may be changed by contact with new systems, such as Interact.

Two other points I would make here are: first, that the acceptability and popularity of many new systems are helped by many 'early adopters' of a new system being high net worth customers who are often influential in spreading the word about a new system and its reputation; second, that 'technofear' is not such a big problem as it has often been considered to be. In fact, if older people – who are usually regarded as being particularly susceptible to technofear – have the time to become familiar with tools such as Interact, they become enthusiastic users. This rather suggests that technofear is a problem which can always or almost always be solved by familiarization with the technology and education into its use.

4 How virtual can a bank get?

I have answered this question in three diagrams – see Figures 10.1, 10.2 and 10.3.

These diagrams are fundamentally self-explanatory, but can be summarized as follows:

In Figure 10.1 the situation now is set down. There has been considerable progress towards virtualization, but we are still largely in a

FIGURE 10.1 *The situation now – suppliers control delivery*

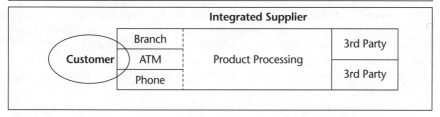

(Source: Andersen Consulting)

FIGURE 10.2 *The situation soon – virtualization of distribution*

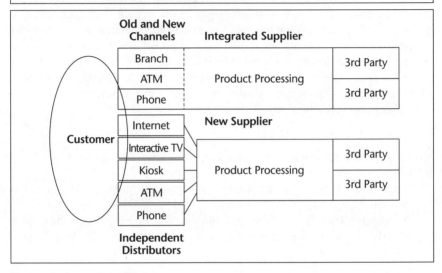

> Traditional and new suppliers increase the number of distribution channels available. Some are owned by suppliers, but more and more are operated independently, *e.g. Microsoft, AT&T*

- Suppliers lose exclusive control of distribution
- Customers gain convenient access to a range of suppliers
- Increasingly sophisticated customers seek more financial services

(Source: Andersen Consulting)

situation where suppliers (i.e. the institutions) control delivery and where they carry out all or the vast majority of the banking functions themselves. However, the idea is well established that an institution can no longer necessarily expect the customer to come to it, but must be prepared to 'go to the customer'.

Figure 10.2 describes the situation where increased virtualization has led to some distribution channels being owned by the suppliers of the services, but by more and more channels being owned independently. The figure makes clear what this means for the customer and for the supplier.

Figure 10.3 describes the future situation where complete virtualization has occurred in supply. The entire notion that the institution has to do any aspect of the transaction processing itself has been questioned: after all, why should the institution not simply act as supplier and outsource most or all of the processing?

I do not want to imply that the situation summarized in Figure 10.3 will inevitably take place for all of the retail financial sector, but rather that it is

FIGURE 10.3 *The end game – virtualization of supply*

Suppliers must be world-class if they are to remain in business. This forces concentration on core competencies. Alliances and outsourcing are used to complete the 'supply chain', *e.g. Virgin PEP.*

- Value-chain specialists complete globally
  - distribution
  - customer relationship
  - product 'manufacture'
- Customers seek satisfaction of needs (financial services are a 'means to an end')

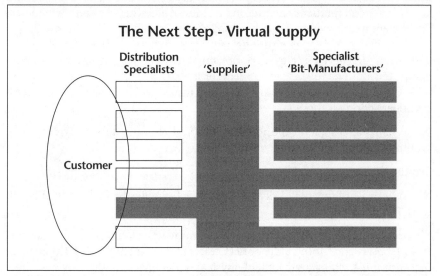

(Source: Andersen Consulting)

likely to occur with some institutions. Of course, it may ultimately become the governing scenario for the entire retail financial sector.

5   How can banks outperform new non-banking entrants in the virtual world?

If the market for financial services becomes highly virtual then banks can only stay in business by intense concentration on what they are really good at. For some this may be customer contact and relationship management (although some utilities are better than others at being a virtual 'shop-front'); for others it may be advice-based services (financial and non-financial) which rely on face-to-face contact (there will surely be a need for branch-based delivery specialists in an electronic world). Other institutions may concentrate on the provision of specialized financial components for other suppliers acting as customer-facing intermediaries.

A few large players may succeed in keeping control of (and even dominating) key financial elements in the commercial supply-chain such as payment processing, but they are likely to face tough competition from outside.

6   How can banks outperform other banks in the virtual world?

Some retail financial institutions will address the problem by becoming low-cost commodity providers. They will deliver the best total cost to their customers by providing low prices, dependability and convenience. However, banks with high cost/income ratios should recognize that this may not be a viable strategy and therefore should not attempt to compete on price, long-term.

Other retail financial institutions will innovate. They will offer customers completely new products through state-of-the-art delivery channels.

Another group of institutions will seek customer intimacy. They will endeavour to develop close relationships with their customers to offer complete solutions to their customers' problems.

The most successful institutions of the future will have won their success by undertaking all three.

7   What major structural and organizational changes do you expect to see within the retail banking sector during the next few years?

See the answer to Question 4.

8   What role, if any, will bricks-and-mortar branches be playing in the year 2008?

My belief is that manned branches will continue to be important, but they will have to be turned into retail outlets. Clearly, any institution with such an objective must retain some kind of physical outlet for providing services where direct human interrelating is required.

Furthermore, it is important to remember that in many countries outside the developed West – such as emerging markets in (say) central Europe and Asia – electronic delivery systems are still several years from having reached a point of evolution at which branch visits are optional for customers.

In countries where they are increasingly an optional extra, we may start seeing institutions charging those customers who visit branches with some frequency. This is already a feature of some US banks' charging procedures.

The future is likely to see more customers being visited by the institutions' staff. Manned branches will need to be positioned in locations where customers are anyway; and in today's society this is as likely to be in the lobby of a supermarket as in a High Street. It is clear that customer propensity to visit the branch cannot be considered to be uniform. Some will never visit the branch but will expect a representative to visit them if face-to-face contact is needed. Others may be prepared to travel to a branch for a specific purpose (e.g. for high-value transactions or for advice). Some may include a visit to the branch as part of a regular activity such as a weekly shopping trip.

9   How do the senior management skills required within virtual banks differ from those required within traditional banks?

Success in an increasingly virtual world (virtual in the sense of supply as well as distribution) will depend on understanding, developing and applying the unique skills of an organization in a rapidly changing market-place. A knowledge of the processes involved in accelerating change will be a major factor; the winners will be those who are able to re-invent their businesses continually based on a sound understanding of how their particular skills can be applied to the needs of their customers – whoever they may be.

A second new requirement will be for senior managers to work in an environment where alliances are necessary for survival, and where these alliances may be short term.

Yet I think perhaps the most important type of skill of all those required will be an ability for managers to start thinking of their product less as a *solution* than as *the means to an end.*

The truth is that productization – that is, placing the full emphasis on the product, whether it be a loan, a mortgage or whatever – can be fatal to banks, since when the entire range of a bank's services has been reduced to a product, it becomes in effect a commodity, and if it's a commodity the lowest price wins.

On the other hand, when a bank perceives that it is providing a means to an end rather than a product per se, all sorts of interesting possibilities for it to develop its business arise. For example, instead of supplying a mortgage, why not concentrate on the need, which is for the customer to obtain a house, and supply the house? Or – since research shows that the overriding use of a bank loan is to buy a car – why should the bank not get into the new cars' business? Barclays Bank already has, and has started a new organization – Cars Direct – which offers customers a discount off the list price of new cars. It is, of course, Barclays which provides the finance.

The point is, managers must understand that the future of financial institutions may not be entirely grounded in the financial industry.

10   What are your predictions for the next 10 years of the development of
   (a) ATMs?
   (b) EFTPoS?
   (c) Remote banking?
   (d) Smart cards?

I would like to offer a general answer to this question. What I expect to see in the future is that virtual delivery channels will continue to improve at an amazing pace. The latest interactive multimedia pages will soon seem as dated as the green flashing ATM screen is already starting to seem to be today. Technological advances will continue to enable an ever-broader range of new delivery channels, which will supersede each other in a never-ending progression of 'S' curves.

Customers will continue to expect their supplier to offer a good cross-section of the available channels at all times. Banks will be forced to maintain a broad range of channels in order to compete. This range will change continuously as technologies develop. Banks will need above all to keep constantly abreast of all this diversity.

Rob Farbrother

1   How do you define the word 'virtual' in terms of its application to financial services?

I'd say that it means a financial service whose most fundamental essence is embodied in its effect rather than in its physical origins. The physical origins matter to the institution, but not to the customer.

2   Do you regard the move towards virtual financial services as being led by public demand, institutions' commercial motivations or technological progress?

My answer to this fundamental and important question is that virtual financial services *is* a technology-led development, but that it is customer demand which pulls it forward. This is not a paradox; what it boils down to is that technological development creates the opportunities for a new virtual financial service, but only customer demand makes implementing that service worthwhile, and profitable.

3   What do you think consumers really think of electronic banking facilities?

I think they use them purely because doing so will make their lives easier. It isn't realistic to generalize about customer attitudes to electronic payment services: the attitudes will vary with how helpful the customer perceives the service to be.

Customer education in the use of virtual financial services is and remains a major challenge, particularly for the more complex types of transactions.

4   How virtual can a bank get?

In my view, the answer to this question is that, as in *Star Trek*, the sky really is the limit, *technologically* speaking. There is no reason why banks should not become entirely virtual, if that's what customers want. But of course it might not be. What matters is that the virtualization process only proceeds in line with customer demand.

5   How can banks outperform new non-banking entrants in the virtual world?

By setting up small business units which are focused on finding ways for banks to capitalize, in a competitive sense, on the competitive advantage they have already won in the market-place by virtue of their trusted relationship with thousands or millions of customers.

These small business units should be set up, organizationally speaking, away from normal core activities, but they should be allowed to feed off, and enrich, those normal core activities.

6   How can banks outperform other banks in the virtual world?

By following the principle of keeping the competitive activities *simple* and *focused,* and by evolving new products and services which aren't based first and foremost on some state-of-the-art technological development but rather on what customers want.

Those banks which will win in the competitive stakes will also be those which are ready to take the time to educate customers in what virtual financial services have to offer them, and how to get the most out of those services.

7   What major structural and organizational changes do you expect to see within the retail banking sector during the next few years?

I think we can expect to see some major shake-outs, due to the following factors:

- Over the past decade or so, it has been extremely difficult for smaller institutions to deal with the problem of bad debts. They have come to realize that they need to be larger to survive this.

- The sheer costs of technology make it easier for large institutions to deploy this effectively without taking unacceptable financial risks.

- The winning of extensive new business for smaller institutions through customers taking on 'secondary' accounts (e.g. a second bank account after their main one) has not been as successful as was anticipated. Institutions realize that it is much better if they can be large enough to win the primary account.

For this reason, by the new century (I don't want to speculate 10 years in advance) I expect to see:

- a reduction in the number of UK clearing banks from about 15 to about half a dozen;

- many more mergers of building societies and more of the larger societies becoming publicly owned banks;

- the creation of a single ATM network in which all ATM cards operate and in which all institutions participate;

- reductions of up to about one-quarter in the number of financial institutions' High Street branches;

- far more financial industry access points at places which customers visit regularly; especially supermarkets, where there will be more ATMs and, increasingly, 'mini-branches' of financial institutions;

- more visits by bank staff to customers in their own homes.

8   What role, if any, will bricks-and-mortar branches be playing in the year 2008?

I would summarize my views on this by saying that I expect fewer branches than there are today to be offering far more functionality to customers than is offered today, with this new functionality very likely including the provision of services and facilities which have little directly to do with the services banks offer today.

9   How do the senior management skills required within virtual banks differ from those required within traditional banks?

Managers of virtual institutions must completely rethink their understanding of what a bank really is. As for new recruits to the ranks of financial institution management, they will very likely end their careers – even if they stay at the same bank – doing tasks that they would hardly have dreamt of undertaking when they first joined the retail banking sector.

On a more technical level, senior managers – and junior and middle management, for that matter – are unlikely to be of much use to their institution if they do not understand the range of applications that can be delivered by virtual means and how these applications are delivered, and in broad terms how the technology works.

10   What are your predictions for the next 10 years of the development of
   (a)   ATMs?
   (b)   EFTPoS?
   (c)   Remote banking?
   (d)   Smart cards?

Again, I'd rather confine my predictions to up to the new century.

As I've suggested, there's bound to be a national ATM network, and the *range* of functionality ATMs deliver is likely to be much wider. There are also too many ATMs in the UK at present; many towns have about a dozen in about a quarter of mile of the high street [as does the author's home town of Canterbury]. Most ATMs are under-utilized. Obviously, where there is a national network, the number of ATMs in clusters in town centres can be reduced. We need more ATMs in supermarkets and railway stations, too.

EFTPoS will, I am sure, make great headway. The education process and general willingness of many customers to rely on this payment method has taken longer than many bankers expected, but this payment method is now making real progress. I also expect EFTPoS-delivered 'Cashback' to become more popular; this is an extremely useful and completely under-utilized facility, which illustrates perfectly the nature of the virtualization process.

There is also abundant scope for EFTPoS cards to become loyalty cards, with customer benefits won through an incentive scheme capable of being stored on the card. This, however, requires a crossover from EFTPoS to smart cards, as you need a microprocessor in the card to accumulate benefits.

Incidentally, banks must move fast to dominate the loyalty card business. At present retailers are, generally, issuing their own cards without the banks' involvement. Banks should seek to gain mileage out of their card processing skills and facilities and make sure they share in the loyalty card business.

I would also expect homebanking and smart cards to reach maturity; with increasing standardization of service and the movement towards just one network for each for the whole country. There is still a substantial educational task to be carried out: in particular, schools and colleges need remote banking terminals to be installed so that pupils can become familiar with this kind of banking.

It is also essential that a nationwide smart card standard is introduced sooner rather than later: the idea of smart card schemes competing with one another – such as Mondex competing with Visa's stated aim of creating its own cashless card system – is absurd.

John Hardy

1   How do you define the word 'virtual' in terms of its application to financial services?

I do not think there is currently a universal definition of 'virtual' in relation to financial services, but in general, I would suggest it is commonly applied to service delivery mechanisms which are both *remote* – in the sense that contact is made via some telecommunications media – and *automated* – in the sense that the delivery is controlled by computer or by some associated software.

2   Do you regard the move towards virtual financial services as being led by public demand, institutions' commercial motivations or technological progress?

I think the move towards virtual financial services is currently led largely by technology and partially by experimental applications of technology by financial institutions for possibly ill-defined commercial motivations.

3   What do you think consumers really think of electronic banking facilities?

I suspect there are really only two groups of customers: those who are really enthusiastic about electronic banking services and those who are essentially unconvinced or, perhaps, do not care. For most people, banking requirements are simple: these people probably don't really need electronic banking other than ATMs and EFTPoS.

4   How virtual can a bank get?

I am not yet convinced that a bank can become 100 per cent virtual, although I am sure some will develop in this direction over time. In my view it is a moot point whether it is really in a bank's interests to become entirely virtual: they may ultimately lose out on important possibilities for winning market share that would arise from retaining some face-to-face contact with customers.

5   How can banks outperform new non-banking entrants in the virtual world?

I think the answer is that they probably cannot do so; but of course any non-banking entrant which sets up a virtual bank becomes, by definition, a bank itself. I do think that some of the 'fringe' financial institutions such as major software houses and so on, may be able to offer services that are unfettered with the baggage of traditional banking. This will probably be a big initial advantage for them.

6   How can banks outperform other banks in the virtual world?

I suspect that successful banks in the virtual world will be those with a philosophy of marketing to a unit of one: in other words the size of the group marketed to will – from the point of view of how the institution views its target marketing area conceptually – be diminished to just the one customer. As a result, customers will be enabled to take their pick of what is on offer so that almost every banking package becomes unique. But institutions can only offer packages which are unique in this way if their products are extremely flexible and they themselves adopt a corporate culture where they genuinely want to react to customers' demands rapidly. We can reasonably expect that a proportion of customers will gladly pay for individual attention and choice.

7   What major structural and organizational changes do you expect to see within the retail banking sector during the next few years?

Fewer but essentially larger players, but with each mega-player effectively split into more and more and smaller and smaller operating units, each with separate tasks and targets. Outsourcing will increase significantly. Many more institutions than at present will develop their activities across national boundaries: boundaries which will become less important, anyway.

8   What role, if any, will bricks-and-mortar branches be playing in the year 2008?

They will be more limited in their role than they are now but they will still be relatively important. I think we will probably see the emergence of shared branches, and of financial supermarkets operated by third parties on behalf of institutions.

9   How do the senior management skills required within virtual banks differ from those required within traditional banks?

Greater strategic vision, higher speed of response to problems and faster formulation of successful solutions, a more entrepreneurial attitude and an understanding of the need for an institution to have greater flexibility across all the spheres of its operation.

10   What are your predictions for the next 10 years of the development of
   (a) ATMs?
   (b) EFTPoS?
   (c) Remote banking?
   (d) Smart cards?

   (a) ATMs: continued growth, more functionality delivered, much greater connectivity and virtually universal sharing at a national level, widespread international sharing.
   (b) EFTPoS: almost universal in advanced countries: standard payment method for all except low-value items.
   (c) Remote banking: this will be widely used, with the Internet playing a key role as delivery network for remote banking services.
   (d) Smart cards: these will have largely replaced magnetic stripe cards in the interests of greater security. Electronic purses [i.e. cashless cards] will be widely used, but I expect cash to have retained its importance. Smart cards are likely to be multi-functional, with the issuer being in many cases separate from the service provider.

Onwards to tomorrow

The virtual banking revolution rolls on. Ingenious, determined, and backed by money and a passion for competitive edge, the banks and other financial institutions which are making the revolution happen have created a banking industry where, ironically perhaps, a consequence of using more and more technology has been to make the very human needs of customers paramount. Ultimately, whether a bank succeeds or fails within the virtual banking revolution, and whether it lives to tell the tale, depends on how effectively the bank responds to these needs.

But if there is one point which I have tried to emphasize in this book, it is that the virtual banking revolution is much more than simply a localized phenomenon within the banking industry. It affects us all, and the new types of tools and delivery systems which the revolution is furnishing for us are giving us a level of control over the money-related aspects of our lives that is absolutely unprecedented in history.

Index